KNOWLEDGE MANAGEMENT
TEXT & CASES

Bholanath Dutta
B. Rose Kavitha
B. Shivraj

I.K. International Publishing House Pvt. Ltd.

NEW DELHI   •   BANGALORE

Published by

I.K. International Publishing House Pvt. Ltd.
S-25, Green Park Extension
Uphaar Cinema Market
New Delhi–110 016 (India)
E-mail: info@ikinternational.com
Website: www.ikbooks.com

ISBN: 978-93-81141-78-6

Published by Krishan Makhijani for I.K. International Publishing House Pvt. Ltd., S-25, Green Park Extension, Uphaar Cinema Market, New Delhi–110 016 and Printed by Rekha Printers Pvt. Ltd., Okhla Industrial Area, Phase II, New Delhi–110 020.

Dedicated to our Parents, Family and Kids

PREFACE

The concept of knowledge management (KM) is twenty years old. Yet it is one of the hottest topics today in both the industrial world and information research world. In our daily life, we deal with huge amount of data and information. Data and information is not knowledge until we know how to dig the value out of it. KM has morphed into many paths of management and IT. This is the reason why we need knowledge management.

Today's business environment is characterised by continuous, often radical change. Such a volatile climate demands a new attitude and approach within organisations—actions must be anticipatory, adaptive and based on a faster cycle of knowledge creation.

We are now living in a knowledge economy where the principal economic resource businesses have to offer their customers knowledge. While most businesses can now claim to be knowledge businesses, it is only the 'knowledge assets' that contribute to the nation's wealth.

Knowledge management has been recognised as an essential component of a proactively managed organisation. If a country or an organisation seeks to attain competitive advantage, they have to deal with 'knowledge assets'. The key concepts include converting data, organisational insight, experience and expertise into reusable and useful knowledge that is distributed and shared with the people who need it. Knowledge management addresses business challenges and enhances customer responsiveness by creating and delivering innovative products or services; managing or enhancing relationships with existing and new customers, partners and suppliers; and administering or improving more efficient and effective work practices and processes. Effective solutions are aligned with the organisation's business strategy and result in enhanced individual and organisational performance.

Because of this ever growing importance of managing knowledge, knowledge management as a subject, has got a place in management education, technical education and even people from corporate exploring this complex area.

After reading the chapters in this book, the students should be able to:

- Understand knowledge management from historical, economical, technical and cultural perspectives, and
- Develop a working vocabulary in the field of KM. Thus, the book has been designed and developed to meet the demand of management students and corporate executives. This book covers the syllabus of all Indian universities.

We feel great pleasure in expressing our profound gratitude to Dr. KC Sabita Ramamurthy, President, CMR Jananadhara Trust (CMRJT); Shri KC Ramamurthy (Retd. IPS), Chairman, CMRJT; Shri Jayadeep (CEO-CMRJT); Ms. Tristha Ramamurthy, Vice-President, CMRJT; Dr. KVS Anand Babu, Principal, CMRIT; Dr. L Sudarshan Reddy, Vice-Principal, CMRIT; Dr. Col. (Retd.) Mukesh

Kumar V, Director, PG Studies, CMRIT; Prof. K Ravi, Director, Career Guidance & Placement Bureau, CMRIT; Prof. Sundar Raj Vijaynagar; Prof. MB Lobo and all our esteemed colleagues in CMRIT for their incessant guidance, stimulation and encouragement in our academic endeavour.

We request the readers to send their feedback/queries/suggestions to bhola_dutta@yahoo.com/ arkavithain@yahoo.com.

Happy Reading.

Prof. Bholanath Dutta
Dr. B. Rose Kavitha
Dr. B. Shivraj

CONTENTS

KM system—quality assurance—training users—managing change—post system evaluation—a new model for KM system life cycle—case.

AUTHORS

BHOLANATH DUTTA

Management teacher, consultant, trainer and academic leader having more than two decades of experience as varied as industry, academic, teaching, administration, research and consultancy. He is presently working with the CMR Institute of Technology, Bangalore. He is the Founder & Convener of Management Teachers Consortium, Global (www.mtcglobal. org).

He is an accredited management teacher by the All India Management Association. He is an accredited trainer cum motivator for developing entrepreneurship in college campus by Visvesvaraya Technological University and a certified soft-skill trainer by Infosys. He is a consultant in management education and offers his services to many institutions and faculty members. He is a corporate trainer too and has conducted training for companies like Shoppers, Stop, Raheja Group, Syntex Marketing, etc. He is the recipient of "Best Professor— 2009", by 24/7, a leading US based MNC and "Arch of Excellence in Education—2009", a national level award. He has received 19 awards and appreciations. He is in the advisory board of Global Touch, ISB&T, Saicom Consulting, Singapore and many other organisations.

He has authored 17 books in the area of marketing, entrepreneurship and general management. His books have been recommended by many Indian Universities like JNTU, GTU, XIME-B, Osmania University and many autonomous B-schools. He has over 100 publications to his credit including research papers, articles, conference proceedings and chapters in edited books. His participation in national & international seminars, conferences, invited lectures, workshops, etc. exceeds 100. He has presented over 30 papers in various international and national conferences.

He is the Founder and Chief Editor of a national level research journal— "*Jnanatapsa*" and departmental e-bulletin "*Optimus*". He has chaired many sessions in national and international conferences. He is in the advisory board and editorial board of many reputed national and international journals.

B. SHIVRAJ

He is the Dean, Department of Management Studies, Manasagangothari, Mysore University and his area of specialisation is finance. He has published various research articles and books in the area of financial management. He has rich experience of over three, decades in the field of management education.

B. ROSE KAVITHA

Dr. B. Rose Kavitha a (Ph.D.) from Karnatak University, Dharwad, is presently associated with the CMR Institute of Technology as Professor and Coordinator Soft Skills. She is actively involved in conducting Management Development Programmes and in establishing a Training Institute to coordinate with all the HR Heads. She has graduated in MBA specialising in HR and has done her M.Sc. in (Industrial Psychology) and also continued to acquire diplomas in Human Resource Development and Software Management.

She comes with nearly 11 years of professional experience in handling subjects like Human Resource Management, Organisational Behaviour, Organisational Culture, Change & Development and Learning Organisations & Leadership. She has played the role of Student Developer and Counsellor in all the institutions that she has worked for.

Her academic and training experience includes her service for various Indian and international institutions such as:

- Alliance Française, France and Indian Institute of Management, Bangalore. She is a Visiting Faculty and Trainer in various management institutes like Oxford Engineering College, SRN, Adarsh College, Nehru Group of Institutions, to name a few.

As a *member of NIPM* she has contributed 32 articles in various magazines and research journals and has co-authored 4 books on Organisational Behaviour and Knowledge Management. *She has presented research papers and has served as chairperson for both national and international seminars and also received two best paper awards from IIM Kozhikode, and Sivasivani Institute of Management, Hyderabad respectively.* She is currently associated with the CMR Institute of Technology as Professor, Dept. of Management Studies.

She is an honorary member of McGraw-Hill Publications, involving reviewing a few of their OB related publications. She conducts Personality Development Training Programmes for officers in Hindustan Aeronautics Limited, Integrated Property Management (Pvt.) Ltd., Airtel and a few other public sector undertakings. Some of the topics handled by her an are self-awareness, assertiveness, attitude and personality, negotiating skills, stress management and conflict handling.

CHAPTER 1

Introduction

OBJECTIVE

At the end of this lesson, you would be able to understand:

- The concept of Knowledge Management.
- Definition & importance of Knowledge Management.
- History of KM.
- Importance of people, process and technology in Knowledge Management.
- Managing the Knowledge.
- Basic Knowledge Management Models.
- Drivers and Benefits of Knowledge Management.

INTRODUCTION

> *The essence of knowledge is, having it, to apply it; not having it,*
> *to confess your ignorance.*
>
> —Confucius

In today's competitive business environment Knowledge Management (KM) plays a pivotal role in tackling the challenging situations that arise due to various uncertain events. At the moment KM is emerging as the most important function of Human Resource Department (HRD) in every organisation. From HR perspective the definition of KM is the process by which the organisation generates wealth from its intellectual or knowledge-based assets. HRD has a key responsibility in strengthening and nurturing KM through cultural change initiatives, learning initiatives and employees' competency development. KM helps in organising visible knowledge sharing events and by establishing all necessary monitoring systems.

KM is about survival in today's competitive business world. At the moment KM is emerging as the most important function of HRD in every organisation. HR department has a crucial role to play in involving each individual in KM movement as a key competency because talent management and KM are closely interrelated. Talent management focuses on individual level like recruitment, selection, induction/ training, individual skills and competencies development and career planning but 'knowledge management' focuses on collective level as how to influence the collective knowledge of the enterprise through mentoring, collaborative teamwork and knowledge sharing. To strengthen KM activities in an organisation the HR department needs to introduce a system of rewards and recognition.

Knowledge (experience-based know-how) is a key resource in any organisation. The more you know, the better you perform. Knowledge Management is about systematically and routinely

1

making use of the knowledge in the organisation, and applying it to key activities; tapping into 'what you collectively know' to help deliver your goals, objectives and mission. It aims towards never making the same mistake twice, and making every decision in the light of the full knowledge base of the organisation. This lesson will make you understand about the overview, evolution and drivers of knowledge management.

Can knowledge be managed? The words management and knowledge at first sight appear uneasy bedfellows. Knowledge is largely cognitive and highly personal, while management involves organisational processes. Many knowledge workers do not like to be managed in the traditional sense. However, knowledge is increasingly recognised as a crucial organisational resource that gives market leverage.

Momentum of Knowledge Management

The last few years have seen a rapidly growing interest in the topic of knowledge management. 'Leveraging Knowledge for Sustainable Advantage' was the title of one of the first conferences (in 1995) that brought knowledge management onto the management agenda. From 1997 a surge of books, magazines and websites have come onto the scene. Today, most large organisations have some form of knowledge management initiative. Many companies have created knowledge teams and appointed CKOs (Chief Knowledge Officers). Knowledge is firmly on the strategic agenda.

Why Now?

Knowledge management is about pragmatic and thoughtful application as it is not the *theoretical definition* but deals with *real life execution* and focuses on the greatest opportunities and challenges lying ahead. Any 'definition', therefore, must be understood within the specific context of expected performance outcomes and value propositions that answer the question 'why' about the study and relevance of KM.

The level of interest has been building for several years. Many innovative companies have long appreciated the value of knowledge to enhance their products and customer service. Our analysis indicates several reasons why the level of interest has grown dramatically during the recent years:

Globalisation and competition—Many organisations rely on knowledge to create their strategic advantage. With the available knowledge widely dispersed and fragmented, organisations often waste valuable time and resources in 'reinventing the wheel' or failing to access the highest quality knowledge and expertise that is available.

Knowledge can command a premium price in the market—Applied know-how can enhance the value (and hence the price) of products and services. Examples are the 'smart drill' that teaches how to extract more oil from an oilfield, and the hotel chain that knows your personal preferences so that it can give you a more personalised service.

Restructuring and downsizing—If one can capture the knowledge of experienced employees or organisations one can avoid making bigger mistakes during restructuring or downsizing and one doesn't have to pay again for intellectual capital.

Sharing of best practices—Companies save millions a year by taking the knowledge from their best performers and applying the same in similar situations elsewhere.

Successful innovation—Companies applying knowledge management methods have found that through knowledge networking they can create new products and services faster and better.

These and other benefits, such as improved customer service, faster problem solving and more rapid adaptation to market changes, have resulted from an explicit focus on corporate knowledge as a strategic resource.

CLASSIC DATA TO KNOWLEDGE HIERARCHY

Understanding KM requires that understanding of knowledge and the knowing process and how that differs from information and information management. It is important to understand the meaning of data and information, as the interchange of the words data and information is widespread.

Data

The word data derives from Latin 'datum' meaning "that which is given". It is the collection of facts, statistics used for reference or analysis. It contains numbers, characters, symbols, images, etc., which can be processed by a computer. data must be interpreted, by a human or machine, to derive meaning and "data is a representation of information".

Information

Information is the knowledge derived from study, experience (by the senses), or instruction. It is the communication of intelligence. Information is any kind of knowledge about things, facts, concepts, etc., in some context, that is exchangeable amongst people. Information is nothing but interpreted data.

For example, researchers who conduct market research survey might ask members of the public to complete questionnaires about a product or a service. These completed questionnaires are data; they are processed and analysed in order to prepare a report on the survey. This resulting report is information.

Knowledge

Knowledge is what we know. Think of this as the map of the world we build inside our brains. Like a physical map, it helps us know *where* things are—but it contains more than that. It also contains our beliefs and expectations. "If I do this, I will probably get that." Crucially, the brain links all these things together into a giant network of ideas, memories, predictions, beliefs, etc.

It is upon this "map" that we base our decisions, not the real world itself. Our brains constantly update this map from the signals coming through our eyes, ears, nose, mouth and skin.

You can't currently store knowledge in anything other than a brain, because a brain connects it all together. Everything is interconnected in the brain. Computers are not artificial brains. They don't understand what they are processing, and can't make independent decisions based upon what you tell them. There are two sources that the brain uses to build this knowledge—information and data.

Knowledge resides in the user's subjective context of action based on that information. It is the potential for action that has an immediate link to performance. It is the theoretical and practical understanding of a subject. Knowledge is something that is known in a particular field or in total like facts and information. Knowledge is, fundamentally, the application of data and information It answers "how" questions.

> *Be curious always, for knowledge will not acquire you; you must acquire it.*
> —Sudie Back

According to Russell Ackoff, a systems theorist and professor of organisational change, the content of the human mind can be classified into five categories:

1. **Data**: It is represented in symbols.
2. **Information**: Data that is processed to be useful; provides answers to "who", "what", "where", and "when" questions.
3. **Knowledge**: The term knowledge means the expertise, skills acquired by a person through experience or education. In the learning organisations knowledge is generated through internal execution, experimentation, problem solving teams and R & D departments.
4. **Understanding**: It is the appreciation of "why".
5. **Wisdom**: It is evaluated understanding.

Ackoff indicates that the first four categories relate to the past; they deal with what has been or what is known. Only the fifth category, wisdom, deals with the future because it incorporates vision and design. With wisdom, people can create the future rather than just grasp the present and past. But achieving wisdom isn't easy; people must move successively through the other categories.

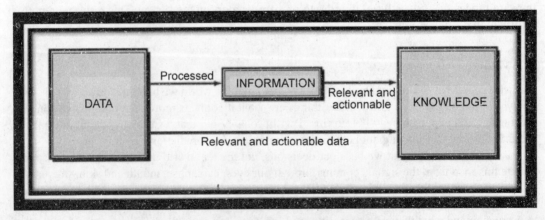

Fig. 1.1   Data, Information and Knowledge

WHAT IS KNOWLEDGE MANAGEMENT?

Knowledge management is the explicit and systematic management of vital knowledge and its associated processes of creating, gathering, organising, diffusing, using and exploiting. It requires turning personal knowledge into corporate knowledge which can be widely shared throughout an organisation and appropriately applied.

KM is basically a managed system for ensuring that the right knowledge reaches the right people at the right time to help them make the right decisions. There are generally two broad thrusts in applying knowledge management:

1. Sharing existing knowledge in a better way: The first is making implicit knowledge more explicit and putting in place mechanisms to move it more rapidly to where it is needed. But what is the difference between implicit and explicit knowledge. Let us try to understand a few differences among what is tacit knowledge, implicit knowledge and explicit knowledge.

The second form of knowledge is tacit knowledge that is ingrained at a subconscious level and therefore difficult to explain to others. An machinist may be extremely skilled at operating a particular machine, for example, but be unable to instruct an apprentice on exactly how to duplicate his expertise. Most knowledge involving pattern recognition skills fall under the category of tacit knowledge.

For example, a seasoned radiologist can generally look at a typical radiographic film of a patient's chest and instantly decide if the film is normal or abnormal. However, eliciting the process that the expert diagnostician used to make her determination is virtually impossible.

When forced to teach residents and students how to read radiographic studies, radiologists use a systematic approach, looking at bones first, then soft tissues, and so on, so that the learner has a place to start in the learning process. However, the system most radiologists teach isn't the system that they use. Similarly, pathologists, like master chess players, use one system and teach another.

Implicit knowledge, like tacit knowledge, is typically controlled by experts. However, unlike tacit knowledge, implicit knowledge can be extracted from the expert—through a process termed knowledge engineering.

For example, an expert at assigning risk to insurance prospects might use the risk heuristics discussed earlier, assigning risk as a function of age and marital status. Once a new employee is given the same heuristics, either in the form of a set of rules or drawn as a decision tree, he or she can make a risk assignment with the same level of accuracy as the expert, who may have developed the heuristic through years of experience.

The third form of knowledge, explicit knowledge, can easily be conveyed from someone proficient at a task to someone else through written or verbal communication. The recipe for a cake, the steps involved in bolting a car door to the main chassis on an assembly line, and the list of ingredients required for a chemical process are all explicit knowledge. Unlike tacit and implicit knowledge, explicit knowledge can often be found in a book or operating manual.

2. Innovation: This is the second thrust area in the application of knowledge management, making the transition from ideas to commercialization more effective.

Knowledge management programmes typically have one or more of the following activities:

■ Appointment of a knowledge leader—to promote the agenda, develop a framework.
■ Creation of knowledge teams—people from all disciplines to develop the methods and skills.

- Development of knowledge bases—best practices, expertise directories, market intelligence, etc.
- Enterprise intranet portal—a 'one-stop-shop' that gives access to explicit knowledge as well as connections to experts.
- Knowledge centres—focal points for knowledge skills and facilitating knowledge flow.
- Knowledge sharing mechanisms—such as facilitated events that encourage greater sharing of knowledge than would normally take place.
- Intellectual asset management—methods to identify and account for intellectual capital.

DEFINITION

Knowledge management can be discussed in general as the ability to create, communicate, and apply the knowledge to achieve organisational (business) goals. From the HR perspective the definition of KM is the process by which the organisation generates wealth from its intellectual or knowledge-based assets (Butowitz and Ruth, 2000). It explains that 'people' must be the key resource of KM (Civic, 2000; Gooijer, 2000; Soliman and Spooner, 2000). According to Garavan, 2000 and Armstrong, 2000—building knowledge base and learning organisation is the routine task of HRD. KM is to understand things through the practice of 'know-how', i.e., through the gathering of facts, rules and different procedures. KM is to be found differently in different places and it is a systematic leveraging of information and expertise. In the US, KM process application is more aggressive in Information Technology sector than other sectors. In Europe the KM process is managing intellectual capital in all knowledge organisations and in Japan it is used for developing knowledge workers.

Unfortunately, there's no universal definition of knowledge management (KM), just as there's no agreement as to what constitutes knowledge in the first place. For this reason, it's best to think of KM in the broadest context. Succinctly put, KM is the process through which organisations generate value from their intellectual and knowledge-based assets. Most often, generating value from such assets involves codifying what employees, partners and customers know, and sharing that information among employees, departments and even with other companies in an effort to devise best practices.

"KM [Knowledge Management] involves blending a company's internal and external information and turning it into actionable knowledge via a technology platform."—Susan DiMattia and Norman Oder in Library Journal, September 15, 1997.

"Knowledge Management (KM) is an effort to increase useful knowledge within the organisation. Ways to do this include encouraging communication, offering opportunities to learn, and promoting the sharing of appropriate knowledge artifacts."—Claire McInerney (2002). Knowledge management and the dynamic nature of knowledge. JASIST, 53 (2).

Knowledge is a fluent mix of structured experience, values, relevant information and intuition of experts, which provide the structure for evaluation and incorporation of the new experience and information. At the beginning its source and application is only in the thoughts of those who possess knowledge. In companies knowledge is often reflected not only in the documents or data banks, but also in organisational routines, processes, practices and norms.—(Davenport & Prusak, 1996).

Knowledge management is a process of knowledge creation, capturing and application through its documentation and codification, storage and dissemination through data banks and communication channels with the purpose of increasing the organisational effectiveness (Bassi, 1997).

"The creation and subsequent management of an environment, which encourages knowledge to be created, shared, learnt, enhanced, organised and utilised for the benefit of the organisation and its customers."-Abell and Oxbro–(2001).

"Knowledge management is a process that emphasises generating, capturing and sharing information know-how and integrating these into business practices and decision making for greater organisational benefit." Maggie Haines, NHS Acting Director of KM.

"The capabilities by which communities within an organisation capture the knowledge that is critical to them, constantly improve it, and make it available in the most effective manner to those people who need it, so that they can exploit it creatively to add value as a normal part of their work." BSI's *A Guide to Good Practice in KM.*

"Knowledge is power, which is why people who had it in the past often tried to make a secret of it. In post-capitalism, power comes from transmitting information to make it productive, not from hiding it!" Peter Drucker.

Some of the corporate definitions are:

"Knowledge management involves efficiently connecting those who know with those who need to know and converting personal knowledge into organisational knowledge." Yankee Group.

"Knowledge management is not about data, but about getting the right information to the right people at the right time for them to impact the bottom line."—IBM.

"The capability of an organisation to create new knowledge, disseminate it throughout the organisation and embody it in products, services and systems."—Nonaka & Takeuchi, 1995.

"Knowledge management is a relatively young corporate discipline and a new approach to the identification, harnessing and exploitation of collective organisational information, talents, expertise and know-how."—Office of the envoy, 2002.

"Knowledge management is the explicit and systematic management of vital knowledge and its associated processes of creating, gathering, organising, diffusing, using and exploiting. It requires turning personal knowledge into corporate knowledge that can be widely shared throughout an organisation and appropriately applied."—David J Skyrme, 1997.

HISTORY OF KNOWLEDGE MANAGEMENT

The recorded history of knowledge dates back to Plato and Aristotle, but its modern day understanding is credited to scholars like Daniel Bell (1973), Michael Polanyi (1958, 1974), Alvin Toffler (1980), and the Japanese guru, Ikujiro Nonaka (1995). Other writers like Sveiby (1997) and Stewart (2000) promoted the concept of knowledge as the core asset of an organisation.

> *Knowledge comes through practice.*
> —Celtic proverb

As the Celtic proverb describes, the learned scholars, Polyani and Nonaka have identified two kinds of knowledge: ***Tacit knowledge and explicit knowledge.*** Tacit knowledge is highly experiential and is found in the heads of employees, customers and vendors; explicit knowledge can be found in books, documents, data banks, corporate policy manuals and the likes. The learning process involves the intersection of both kinds of knowledge and the resulting knowledge transformation process.

In the 1960s, Drucker coined the terms "knowledge work" and "knowledge worker" when he was discussing the role of knowledge in an organisation. In the early 1970s, researchers at MIT and Stanford were analysing ways in which companies produced, used and diffused knowledge. The idea of knowledge being a corporate asset had caught up only in the 1980s when companies truly began to value knowledge. During the 1990s, the onset of the internet, the information superhighway, allowed KM to take off.

Knowledge management as a conscious discipline would appear to be somewhere between five and 15 years old. It evolved from the thinking of academics and pioneers such as Peter Drucker in the 1970s, Karl-Erik Sveiby in the late 1980s, and Nonaka and Takeuchi in the 1990s. During that time, economic, social and technological changes were transforming the way that companies worked. Globalization emerged and brought new opportunities and increased competition. Companies responded by downsizing, merging, acquiring, reengineering and outsourcing. Many streamlined their workforce and boosted their productivity and profits by using advances in computer and network technology. However, their successes in doing so came with a price. Many companies lost their knowledge as they grew smaller. And many lost company knowledge as they grew bigger–they no longer "knew what they knew".

By the early 1990s a growing body of academics and consultants were talking about knowledge management as "the" new business practice, and it began to appear in more and more business journals and on conference agendas. By the mid-1990s, it became widely acknowledged that the competitive advantage of some of the world's leading companies was being carved out from those companies' knowledge assets such as competencies, customer relationships and innovations. Managing knowledge, therefore, suddenly became a mainstream business objective as other companies sought to follow the market leaders.

Many of these companies took the approach of implementing "knowledge management solutions", focusing almost entirely on knowledge management technologies. However, they met with limited success and so questions began to be asked about whether knowledge management wasn't simply another fad that looked great on paper, but in reality did not deliver. In fact, for a while, it looked as if knowledge management was destined to be confined to the "management fad graveyard". However, on closer inspection, companies realised that it wasn't the concept of knowledge management that was the problem as such, but rather the way that they had gone about approaching it. Reasons for their limited success included:

- The focus was on technology rather than the business and its people.
- There was too much hype—with consultants and technology vendors cashing in on the latest management fad.
- Companies spent too much money (usually on "sexy" technologies) with little or no return on their investments.
- Most knowledge management literature was very conceptual and lacking in practical advice, which led to frustration at the inability to translate the theory into practice—"it all makes so much sense but why isn't it working?"
- Underestimating scope and knowledge complexity during the planning stage.

- Knowledge management was not tied into business processes and ways of working.
- It was seen as another laborious overhead activity or yet another new initiative.
- A lack of incentives—employees quite rightly asked the "what's in it for me?" question.
- There was not any sufficient senior executive to understand and execute the level of KM in practice.

Fortunately companies are now recognising these early mistakes and are beginning to take a different approach to knowledge management—one in which the emphasis is more on people, behaviours and ways of working, than on technology. Of course there are still some skeptics who believe that knowledge management is just a fad. But according to a number of company surveys, it would seem that they are in a minority. A more popular view is that knowledge management may not remain as a distinct discipline, but will rather become embedded in the way organisations work. This can be compared to Total Quality Management which was the "in thing" in the 1980s; nobody talks about "TQM" any more, but many of its principles and practices are an integral part of how most organisations operate. It looks likely that this could also be the future for knowledge management.

SCOPE AND SIGNIFICANCE OF KNOWLEDGE MANAGEMENT

A new word for the consumer in today's market, 'prosumer', refers to the consumer who is no longer in the passive market where goods are offered at the exact face value. Prosumers are more educated consumers, and they demand more. They provide feedback to manufacturers regarding the design of products and services from a consumer perspective. This has initiated new and radical changes in the business world. Even with recent technology developments such as networking, e-mail and the web businesses.

KM has already demonstrated a number of benefits and has offered justification for further implementation. The internet facilitated its development and growth via fast and timely sharing of knowledge. By sharing knowledge, an organisation creates exponential benefits people learn from it. This makes business processes faster and more effective and empowers employees in a unique way. For example, Microsoft's hotmail service advanced the wide use of e-mail that allowed users to exchange information through any web browser. Today's web-based interface is the norm for most internet service providers.

KM has had a positive impact on business processes. The goal is to capture the tacit knowledge required by a business process and encourages knowledge workers to share and communicate knowledge with peers. With such knowledge, it is easier to determine which processes are more effective or less effective than others. The main constraint in KM, however, is initially capturing it. However, if an organisation can succeed in capturing and dispersing knowledge, the benefits are endless. A company can leverage and more fully utilize intellectual assets. It can also position itself in responding quickly to customers, creating new markets, rapidly developing new products and dominating emergent technologies.

Another benefit of KM is the intangible return on knowledge sharing rather than knowledge hoarding. Too often, employees in one part of a business start from the 'scratch' on a project because the knowledge needed is somewhere else but not known to them.

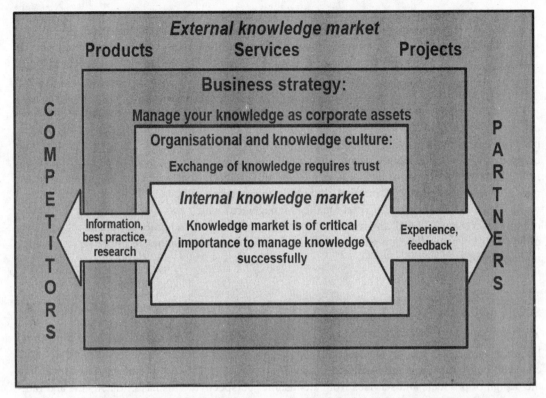

Fig. 1.2 Knowledge Management in the Organisational Strategy

As a result of KM, systems have been developed to gather, organise, refine and distribute knowledge throughout the business. In this study of Smart Business, Botkin (1999) suggests six top attributes of knowledge products and services.

- *Learn:* The more you use them, the smarter they get and the smarter you get too.
- *Improve with use:* These products and services are enhanced rather than depleted when used, and they grow instead of being used up.
- *Interactive:* There is two-way communication between you and them.
- *Remember*: They record and recall past actions to develop a profile.
- *Customize:* They offer unique configuration to your individual specifications in real time at no additional cost.

KM has changed the business environment and introduced new competitive imperatives. Among them are:

- Reacting instantly to new business opportunities, which led to decentralized decision making (and competency) at the front lines, where the action is. With that came the desire to build mutual trust between knowledge workers and management and to cooperate in handling time-sensitive tasks.

- Building better sensitivity to 'brain drain'. It has been said that 'expertise gravitates toward the highest bidder'. More and more companies realise the importance of managing and preserving expertise turnover. For the human resource department, the key question is 'how does the firm replace expertise when it retires, resigns, or simply leaves?'
- Ensuring successful partnering and core competencies with suppliers, vendors, customers and other constituents. Today's technology has enabled companies to re-engineer ways to do business. Getting partners up to your speed requires more than fast technology. Knowledge workers and others within the company should ensure that cooperation and coordination of work are practiced for the good of the firm.

PEOPLE, PROCESS & TECHNOLOGY

Knowledge management involves people, technology, and processes in overlapping parts. These areas have developed perspectives on the working of individual and systematic knowledge. The goal for an organisation is to view all its processes as knowledge processes. This includes knowledge creation, dissemination, upgradation, and application towards organisational survival. Today's knowledge organisation has a renewed responsibility to hire knowledgeable employees and specialists to manage knowledge as an intangible asset in the same way that one calls on an investor to manage a financial portfolio. A firm seeks to add value by identifying, applying and integrating knowledge in unprecedented ways; much like an investor adds value by unique combination of stocks and bonds.

One of the three pillars of knowledge management is people and this component is given the least importance when compared to process and technology. This wide gap can be attributed to many factors of which the first and foremost would be lack of vision in using knowledge management for the

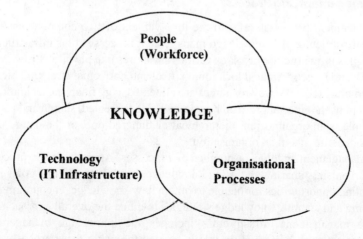

Fig. 1.3 Key Knowledge Components

benefit of the organisation vis-à-vis people and process. People's apprehension of knowledge management is somewhat skewed by overdeveloped technology at one hand and their evolved beliefs and practices taught to them since their early childhood, as we know that knowledge management, from the perspective of people, is nothing more than sharing knowledge.

Knowledge in the organisation is present mainly in two forms as tacit and explicit. Tacit knowledge is kept in the heads of the people at all levels of the organisational hierarchy and hard to obtain. This is due to flaws in our overall system of educating people. We taught them not to share their work with others and rewarded them for it while punishing them for contrary behaviour in schools. So we have to change our strategy for people's incentive and reeducate them. We have to provide this sense of security that knowledge sharing is for the benefit of people and in turn for the organisation.

Earlier technology was thought to be the engine of knowledge management. Those who relied on this notion have faced bitter outcomes by the implementation of knowledge management technology. Technology is definitely a tool to achieve knowledge management but this in itself does not justify the reason to have knowledge management practices in the first place. People who participate in knowledge management discipline include decision makers, knowledge workers and workers at the operation level. At strategic level, decision makers have to make sure that knowledge management goals are in tune with the business goals. Most decision makers have the fallacy that they do not take people into consideration at a strategic level. 'HR practices' are not the only ones to harness the capacity of the knowledge creating resource vis-à-vis people.

Of the three, operational workers are worst in understanding this phenomenon. People at the operational level are too busy to share knowledge and do not have a clue for the significance of this process. Moreover, they are also scared of rumours that knowledge management practices are being introduced to replace people with technology. One reason of their reluctance to participate in this productive process is their belief that knowledge management starts and ends with technology. With this concept at the operational level organisations get marginal benefit in it, although strategically they may be sound.

Knowledge Management and Process

Knowledge management processes refer to the involvement of two components – organisational processes plus infrastructure and knowledge management processes plus infrastructure. Organisational processes plus infrastructure involves various structures like physical structure, e.g., building in which we work and its geographical location, vertical and horizontal structure, hierarchical structure and other structures like the way resources are allocated, e.g., finances, technology, equipment, etc. These layers play an important role on how knowledge is created, shared and used in an organisation. An example is an organisation, hierarchical or flattered one, or the nature of relationships between various departments in an organisation.

Knowledge management involves a number of processes. Apart from the processes like finding, acquiring, organising, sharing and using knowledge, it needs to meet its goals like sharing the knowledge, creating opportunities for people to obtain new knowledge, encouraging people to give priority to learning and creating knowledge strategies to guide the overall approach.

A knowledge management infrastructure includes the knowledge management processes, and also the organisational infrastructure that is created to enable these processes—the essential

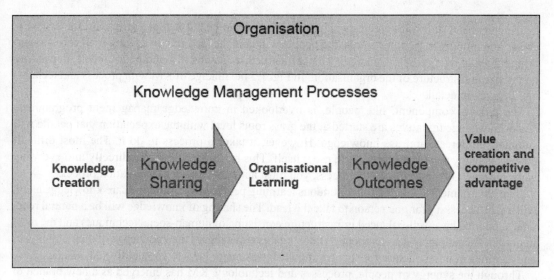

Fig. 1.4 Knowledge Management Processes

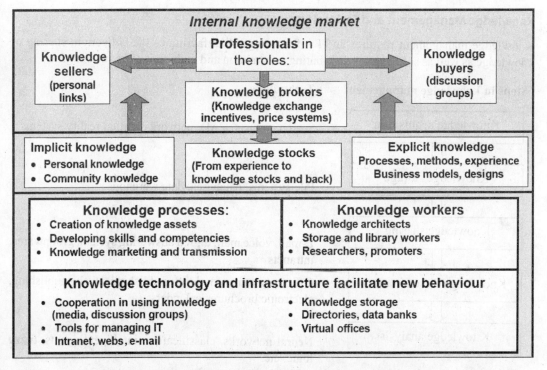

Fig. 1.5 Flow of Process, People Knowledge and Technology

management and staff roles and responsibilities that need to be put in place to support the new processes and initiatives. In other words, the people will take the lead role in driving it all forward and bringing about the necessary changes. This infrastructure may have a number of levels, depending on the size and structure of the organisation. In Fig. 1.5 the linkage of KM with process and technology is given in detail.

The process component, like people, is overlooked in knowledge management programmes. Many knowledge initiatives are started at the grass roots level with the expectation that people will automatically create and use knowledge. However, it takes a process to do it. The most difficult process in many ways is the process to use it itself. This has to be engineered directly into everyday work process. On top of the work process, you must actually engineer the creation process.

If an environment is created for continuous learning, people will willingly share knowledge and it will not be necessary for one person to take the lead. The sharing of knowledge will be a natural reaction, supported by a well-balanced infrastructure consisting of human-social techniques and the most important technological developments. Many organisations regard the knowledge of their employees and an efficient infrastructure for sharing knowledge as major keys to competitive advantage.

Through the synergy of people, processes and technology, KM has emerged as a new branch of management for achieving breakthrough in business performance. The goal of KM is continuous learning, unlearning and adapting to sustainable business performance. Scholars have put it this way: "the focus of KM is 'doing the right thing' instead of 'doing things right'.

Knowledge Management and Technology

Knowledge management requires an IT infrastructure that facilitates the collection, sharing of knowledge as well as software for distributing information and making it more meaningful.

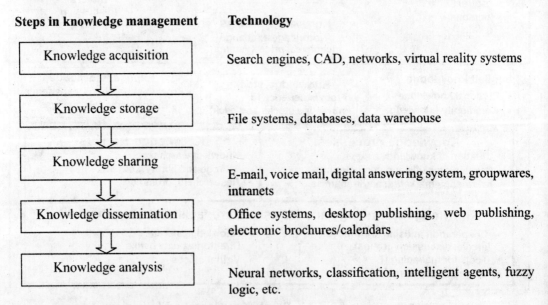

Steps in knowledge management   **Technology**

Knowledge acquisition — Search engines, CAD, networks, virtual reality systems

Knowledge storage — File systems, databases, data warehouse

Knowledge sharing — E-mail, voice mail, digital answering system, groupwares, intranets

Knowledge dissemination — Office systems, desktop publishing, web publishing, electronic brochures/calendars

Knowledge analysis — Neural networks, classification, intelligent agents, fuzzy logic, etc.

Fig. 1.6 IT Infrastructure to Facilitate Knowledge Management

TECHNIQUES OF KNOWLEDGE MANAGEMENT

Expression management, text management, hypertext management, database management are various techniques involved in knowledge management.

Expression management

Expression management is valuable for helping decision makers with ad hoc calculations that arise in the course of decision making. The main objects of interest with this technique are expressions, variables, functions and macros. Methods for processing them include the following:

- Defining existence of variables, macros, functions
- Store/load, list, view, change, delete them
- Specify expression in terms of them plus literals and operators

Text management

Text management gives decision makers the ability to work with electronic documents. These are not restricted to representing any particular kind of knowledge. However, such representations are processed simply as documents, without concern for the type of knowledge held.

Objects of interest: Documents representing any form of knowledge, textual passages, boxes, control indicators. Methods for processing them can relate to document as whole, lines of text, words.

Hypertext management

This allows knowledge to be organised into an interconnected network of documents called a hyper document. The decision maker can follow markers or a map to navigate through the network to access those documents that seem relevant to the decision at hand. The main objects of interest include: hyper document—documents with embedded markers. The methods for processing them are by specifying documents, specifying links by a matching pair of markers, navigation among documents by choosing desired markers.

Database management

Database management gives a comparatively structured way for organising knowledge and has historically been used primarily for descriptive knowledge. When such a database management system is implemented, it will contain software known as a database control system and the knowledge system will hold one or more databases. Using the relational approach to database management, each database is composed of one or more tables. Each table has a structure defined in terms of fields and a content organised into records. With a query facility, decision makers can extract desired data from a database on the spur of the moment. The main objects of interest include databases, tables, data dictionary, distinction between table structure and content. Methods for processing them are table processing, operations on structure.

CAN YOU MANAGE KNOWLEDGE?

Some people argue that knowledge can't be managed – that it is a personal human attribute, which is too elusive to manage. Certainly knowledge can't be controlled, but capturing and sharing knowledge can be encouraged and facilitated, and the environment within which knowledge flourishes can certainly be managed. Managing knowledge involves creating the:

Right Conditions; you need a culture of trust, openness, sharing and learning.

Right Means; you need to have a systematic approach, tools, and processes for exchanging knowledge, and the,

Right Actions; where people instinctively seek, share, and apply experience, best practice, know-how and new ideas.

Intellectual Capital

The structure of global economy has shifted from industrial age to information age where the importance of intangibles or intellectual capital is highlighted. In the knowledge economy, intellectual capital is central to the value creation process (Ashton, 2005).There is no precise definition for intellectual capital.

In traditional management of the early 20th century that dealt with the optimum utilisation of labour, parts, and other physical resources, capital was considered limited to factories, machines, and other human-made inputs into the production process. In the modern corporation with a KM initiative, the concept of capital is extended to include ephemeral intellectual capital and its impact on individual and organisational behaviour. Although intellectual capital can be combined into one concept, from a KM perspective, it's equally useful to consider the constituent components individually.

The three major components of intellectual capital are:

1. **Human capital:** The knowledge, skills, and competencies of the people in the organisation. Human capital is owned by the employees and managers that possess it. Without a KM system in place, when employees and managers leave the company, they take their skills, competencies, and knowledge with them.
2. **Customer capital**: The value of the organisation's relationships with its customers, including customer loyalty, distribution channels, brands, licensing, and franchises. Because customers often form bonds with a salesperson or customer representative, customer capital is typically jointly owned by the employee and the employer. The proportion of customer capital held by employees and employers depends on the relative contribution of customer loyalty to customer capital.
3. **Structural capital:** The processes, structures, information systems, and intellectual properties that are independent of the employees and managers who created them. Intellectual properties are sometimes considered a separate, fourth component of intellectual capital.

The study of intellectual capital has become an important accounting issue in the corporate, as this capital would improve the informational relevance of financial statements in making economic decisions.

Intellectual Capital Components

Human
Attitude
Competencies
Education
Knowledge
Skills

Customer
Brand
Company name
Customer
Distribution channels
Franchise agreements
Licence agreements
Loyalty

Structural
Copyright
Corporate culture
Design rights
Financial relations
Information technology
Management processes
Service marks
Trade secrets
Trademarks

Fig. 1.7 Components of Intellectual Capital

Intellectual capital and the knowledge repository can have a dramatic impact on any organisation. However, it will only be funded and supported if management recognises the value of their employee's knowledge and it will only work with appropriate incentives and an honest orientation on how it will be used.

Information technology plays an effective facilitating role towards managing intellectual capital. In the knowledge based organisations, intellectual capital is addressed as Chief Knowledge Officers (CKOs) and Chief Learning Officers (CLOs). For the most part, the CKO's responsibilities are distillations of activities already addressed by senior management, but in an unfocused, often informal way.

For example, typical CKO responsibilities include:

■ **Defining KM policy.** Establishing employee policy regarding the documentation of work processes is one of the several tasks that may be championed sporadically by the senior management.

However, the CKO is in a position to focus on the documentation process in detail and on an ongoing basis.

- *Evangelizing Knowledge Management.* Motivating employees to accept knowledge management by illustrating how it will benefit the company and the overall process of asset management.
- *Coordinating education.* A KM initiative involves education, assigning individual responsibility and a point person in each working group who is responsible for assuring compliance with the KM project and for updating information.
- *Safeguarding information.* As an information gatekeeper, the CKO is often in a position to determine access to information and the granularity of information to make available on a need-to-know basis.
- *Employee-management liaison.* In many companies, one of the CKO's chief roles is to act as liaison between employees and management. By performing a function that solicits employee input, the CKO can often better encourage employees to go along with the KM project.
- *Technologist.* The CKO must be familiar with the available software and information tools to implement knowledge management in an organisation. Although the CKO doesn't necessarily need to be from the information technology world, he or she has to understand the tools in sufficient depth to estimate the overhead associated with their use.

One of the most significant issues regarding the CKO position is whether it warrants full- or part-time focus. In most cases, because the tasks of the CKO are simply amplified and focused versions of those performed by general management, there is usually a critical organisation size below which a full-time CKO isn't needed. In addition, someone has to be constantly in charge of collecting, organising, maintaining, archiving and distributing information. Normally, this function isn't performed by the CKO but by knowledge integrators, who are also responsible for actively seeking information to add to the knowledge store.

Because of the variability in what can be expected of the CKO, the requirements for the position are necessarily broad. Although there is no formal CKO certification and no university tracks

Copyright Grantland Enterprises

M405

www.greatcartoons.com

leading to a degree in CKO, most successful CKOs share some general traits. As Mary illustrated in her dealings with managers and employees at Medical Multimedia Company, regardless of the position or title, managing a KM initiative requires exceptional interpersonal communications skills, knowledge of best practices in the industry, fluency in information technology, ability to speak the language of employees and management, and management experience.

> *True knowledge exists in knowing that you know nothing. And in knowing that you*
> *know nothing, that makes you the smartest of all.*
>
> —Socrates

KNOWLEDGE MANAGEMENT SYSTEM

Knowledge Management System (KM System) refers to a (generally IT based) system for managing knowledge in organisations, supporting creation, capture, storage and dissemination of information. It can comprise a part (neither necessary nor sufficient) of a knowledge management initiative.

Knowledge Management Systems (KMSs) refer to the use of modern information technologies (e.g., the internet, intranets, extranets, Lotus Notes, software filters, agents, data warehouses) to systematise, enhance, and expedite intra- and inter-firm knowledge management (Alavi and Leidner, 1999).

The idea of a KM system is to enable employees to have ready access to the organisation's documentation of facts, sources of information, and solutions. For example, a typical claim justifying the creation of a KM system might run something like this: an engineer could know the metallurgical composition of an alloy that reduces sound in gear systems. Sharing this information organisation with the entire can lead to more effective engine design and it could also lead to ideas for new or improved equipment.

A KM system could be any of the following:

- Document based, i.e., any technology that permits creation/management/sharing of formatted documents such as Lotus Notes, web, distributed databases, etc.
- Ontology/Taxonomy based: these are similar to document technologies in the sense that a system of terminologies (i.e., ontology) are used to summarise the document, e.g., author, subject, organisation, etc. as in DAML & other XML based ontologies.
- Based on AI technologies which use a customised representation scheme to represent the problem domain.
- Provide network maps of the organisation showing the flow of communication between entities and individuals.
- Increasingly social computing tools are being deployed to provide a more organic approach to creation of a KM system.

KMS deal with information (although Knowledge Management as a discipline may extend beyond the information centric aspect of any system) so they are a class of information system and may build on, or utilise other information sources. Distinguishing features of a KMS can include:

Purpose: A KMS will have an explicit Knowledge Management objective of some type such as collaboration, sharing good practice or the likes.

Context: One perspective on KMS would see knowledge as information that is meaningfully organised, accumulated and embedded in a context of creation and application.

Processes: KMS are developed to support and enhance knowledge-intensive processes, tasks or projects, for e.g., creation, construction, identification, capturing, acquisition, selection, valuation, organisation, linking, structuring, formalisation, visualisation, transfer, distribution, retention, maintenance, refinement, revision, evolution, accessing, retrieval and last but not least the application of knowledge, also called the knowledge life cycle.

Participants: Users can play the roles of active, involved participants in knowledge networks and communities fostered by KMS, although this is not necessarily the case. KMS designs are held to reflect that knowledge is developed collectively and that the "distribution" of knowledge leads to its continuous change, reconstruction and application in different contexts, by different participants with differing backgrounds and experiences.

Instruments: KMS support KM instruments, e.g., the capture, creation and sharing of the codifiable aspects of experience, the creation of corporate knowledge directories, taxonomies or ontologies, expertise locators, skill management systems, collaborative filtering and handling of interests used to connect people, the creation and fostering of communities or knowledge networks.

A KMS offers integrated services to deploy KM instruments for networks of participants, i.e., active knowledge workers, in knowledge-intensive business processes along the entire knowledge life cycle. KMS can be used for a wide range of cooperative, collaborative, adhocracy and hierarchy communities, virtual organisations, societies and other virtual networks, to manage media contents; activities, interactions and work flow purposes; projects; works, networks, departments, privileges, roles, participants and other active users in order to extract and generate new knowledge and to enhance, leverage and transfer in new outcomes of knowledge, providing new services using new formats and interfaces and different communication channels.

The term KMS can be associated with Open Source Software, Open Standards, Open Protocols and Open Knowledge licences, initiatives and policies.

The goal of Knowledge Management for an organisation is to be aware of individual and collective knowledge so that it may make the most effective use of the knowledge it has (Bennet and Bennet, 2003). Historically, MIS has focused on capturing, storing, managing, and reporting explicit knowledge. Organisations now recognise the need to integrate both explicit and tacit knowledge in formal information systems.

KMSs are intended to help an organisation cope with turnover, rapid change, and downsizing by making the expertise of the organisation's human capital widely accessible. They are being built partly because of increased pressure to maintain a well informed, productive workforce. Moreover, they are built to help large organisations provide a consistent level of customer service.

A functioning Knowledge Management System follows six steps in a cycle. To have a better understanding let us have a look at the knowledge life cycle in Fig 1.8.

The reason the system is cyclical is because knowledge is dynamically refined over time. Knowledge in a good KM system is never finished because, over time, the environment changes, and the knowledge must be updated to reflect the changes. The cycle works as follows:

1. *Create knowledge.* Knowledge is created as people determine new ways of doing things or develop know-how. Sometimes external knowledge is brought in.

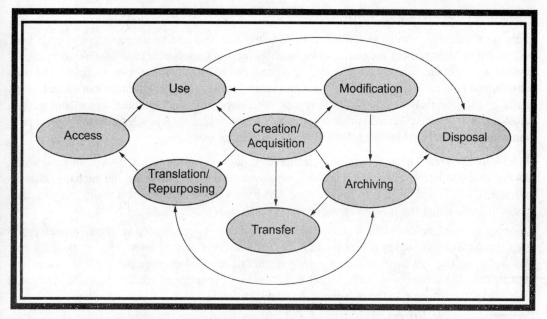

Fig. 1.8 Knowledge Life Cycle (*Source:* Bergeron B, 2003).

2. *Capture knowledge.* New knowledge must be identified as valuable and be represented in a reasonable way.

3. *Refine knowledge.* New knowledge must be placed in context so that it is actionable. This is where human insights (tacit qualities) must be captured along with explicit facts.

4. *Store knowledge.* Useful knowledge must then be stored in a reasonable format in a knowledge repository so that others in the organisation can access it.

5. *Manage knowledge.* Like a library, the knowledge must be kept current. It must be reviewed to verify that it is relevant and accurate.

6. *Disseminate knowledge.* Knowledge must be made available in a useful format to anyone in the organisation who needs it, anywhere and anytime.

WHAT DOES KNOWLEDGE MANAGEMENT MAKE POSSIBLE?

The value of Knowledge Management is delivered in three areas:

Better and faster decisions: By tapping into the experience of the organisation, you can avoid pitfalls, reapply proven solutions, and make the right decision the first time.

Greater empowerment: By enabling people to access and use the knowledge of their peers, you empower them to take accountability for their own performance.

Faster learning: Cutting the personal and organisational learning curve in everything new that you do.

Knowledge Management will increase effectiveness in the short term, and at the same time provide an inventory of experience and expertise for the future, allowing a flexible, fast-paced approach to your key activities.

DRIVERS OF KNOWLEDGE MANAGEMENT

There are a number of claims as to the "drivers", or motivations, leading organisations to undertake a Knowledge Management programme. Popular business objectives include gaining competitive advantage within the industry and increasing organisational effectiveness with improved or faster learning and new knowledge creation. As Knowledge Management programmes can often lead to greater innovation, better customer experiences, consistency in good practices, knowledge access across a global organisation, and other organisational benefits, many Knowledge Management programmes will usually set some of these as end objectives as well.

Technology Drivers: The proliferation of technology, data communications, networking and wireless transmission has revolutionized the way employees store, communicate and exchange data at high speed. The World Wide Web has changed KM from a fad to an e-business reality. Anyone can access information at any time and from anywhere.

Process Drivers: One of the most critical assets of KM drivers is designed to improve work processes. Implied in this area is the elimination of duplicate mistakes by learning from the past and by transferring the best experiential knowledge from one location or project in the firm to another. Starting from the scratch with each project makes no sense in terms of efficiency, productivity and value-added contribution to the company's bottom line.

Personnel-Specific Drivers: This area of KM drivers focuses on the need to create cross-functional teams of knowledge workers to serve anywhere in the organisation and minimise personnel turnover as a threat to collective knowledge. More and more of what was once viewed as independent firms are now closely coupled. Products and services are jointly handled from diverse disciplinary areas where creative cooperation is essential for innovation. Brainstorming, competitive response, and proactive positioning all require collaboration and coordination of various tasks within and among corporations.

Knowledge-related Drivers: Several KM drivers relate to the very concept of knowledge sharing and knowledge transfer within the firm. They include revisiting overlooked employee knowledge, making critical knowledge available at the time it is needed, and finding a mechanism to expedite available knowledge for immediate use.

Financial Drivers: As an asset, knowledge defies economic theory, where assets are subject to diminishing returns over the long run. Knowledge assets increase in value as more and more people use them. With this in mind, knowledge follows the law of increasing returns – the more the knowledge is used, the more value it provides. KM provides a worthwhile opportunity to integrate knowledge in a way that enriches the quality of decision making throughout the organisation.

Some typical considerations driving a Knowledge Management programme include:

- Making available increased knowledge content in the development and provision of products and services.
- Achieving shorter new product development cycles.
- Facilitating and managing organisational innovation and learning.
- Leveraging the expertise of people across the organisation.
- Increasing network connectivity between employees and external groups with the objective of improving information flow.

- Managing the proliferation of data and information in complex business environments and allowing employees to access appropriate information sources.
- Managing intellectual capital and intellectual assets in the workforce (such as the expertise and know-how possessed by key individuals) as individuals retire and new workers are hired.

KNOWLEDGE MANAGEMENT VERSUS PROCESS REENGINEERING

Business consultants and software information system vendors often bundle a KM initiative with other "flavours of the month," from process reengineering and empowerment to various forms of teams. However, although Knowledge Management may be a component of other management initiatives, it's often best addressed as a distinct entity. For example, although many vendors include a KM component in most process reengineering efforts, implementing both simultaneously is at best a waste of time and resources.

A KM initiative typically involves documenting and sharing information about what is, whereas process reengineering is about designing what should be. Knowledge Management is best applied in times of stable processes and as a follow-on to a reengineering effort, not as a parallel process.

This means that KM activities should be avoided during and immediately following process reengineering and major hiring or downsizing activities, whether they are related to the reengineering effort or not. Many KM initiatives fail because Knowledge Management is performed to parallel a reengineering initiative.

Consider, for example an employee by name called Sheeba. Now Sheeba has experience with Medical Multimedia, in which she first deals with process reengineering and then with Knowledge Management. One has to list down the competencies of Sheeba's profile and then only the processes surrounding the handling of multimedia needs to be optimised and this is how the KM initiative begin. Since a company in the midst of a reengineering effort is influx, best practices have yet to be crystallized, and it's a waste of time and resources to document what will likely change in a matter of weeks or months.

Process reengineering is concerned with benchmarking and best practices, implementing alternative business models, and process optimisation. The goal is to increase corporate competitiveness

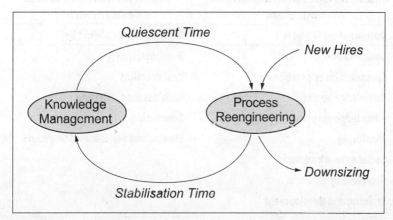

Fig. 1.9 Difference between Knowledge Management and Process Reengineering

by eliminating non value-added steps, copying the methods of successful companies, and reducing unnecessary employees through intelligent downsizing.

Knowledge Management, in contrast, is about documenting and sharing what is there through activities such as:

- *Knowledge audits.* Determining exactly what intellectual capital exists in the company at a given point in time. Knowledge audits can take the form of informal interviews, such as illustrated by Mary's activities in the Medical Multimedia, self-reporting formal paper-based surveys, or through group meetings with management and employees.
- *Collaboration.* Formal task- or project-oriented groups designed to facilitate information sharing. Formal collaboration normally involves the participation of employees who normally would not work together in the course of their regular work. Table 1.1 gives us in detail differences between the characteristics of KM and that of Process Reengineering.
- *Communities of practice.* Employees who share tasks, projects, interests, and goals, normally within a specific work area. For example, the programmers and artists in Medical Multimedia formed two communities of practice, defined largely by their common work function. Communities of practice are generally self-forming, dynamic entities.
- *Knowledge mapping.* A process of identifying who knows what, how the information is stored in the organisation, where it's stored, and how the stores of information are interrelated.
- *Mentoring.* Experts sharing heuristics, values, and techniques with employees new to processes within the company.
  Mentoring, like the formation of communities of practice, can be fostered by the corporation but not dictated.
- *Social network analysis.* The process of identifying who interacts with whom and how information is communicated from one individual or group to another.

Table 1.1   Differences between the Characteristics of KM to that of Process Reengineering

Characteristics of Knowledge Management	Characteristics of Process Reengineering
Documenting "What Is"	Defining "What Should Be"
Collaboration	Benchmarking
Communities of practice	Best practices
Knowledge audits	Business model change
Knowledge mapping	Downsizing
Mentoring	Eliminating nonvalue adding steps
Social network analysis	
Storytelling	
Training and development	

- *Storytelling.* Otherwise known as the case-based method of teaching, storytelling is a way of communicating corporate values and other implicit forms of knowledge.
- *Training and development.* The traditional method of dispersing explicit knowledge. However, in Knowledge Management, training and development normally involves internal experts from different disciplines, as opposed to professional trainers.

It's important to note that these activities aren't limited to KM initiatives, and rarely are all techniques used in the same initiative and at the same time.

IMPLICATIONS FOR KNOWLEDGE MANAGEMENT

The knowledge developer has a number of challenges in choosing knowledge capture tools. First, the technique that best taps the knowledge of the domain expert must be determined. Certain techniques are ideal for single experts and others are mores suitable for multiple experts. Second, advance planning and preparation for knowledge capture can best be carried out through using the most efficient tools, thereby making the best use of the expert's time and resources.

The managerial aspects of tools selection have to do with the organisation's commitment to providing proper training and support for the knowledge developer. The knowledge developer should be an effective manager of time. Selecting the right knowledge capture techniques means saving time on ensuring reliable representations of knowledge.

The knowledge developer must also be able to communicate with experts, regardless of their background or expertise. Communication breakdown could spell disaster for any project, large or small.

There is so much of imbalance between supply and demand that the advance of new technology undergoes many changes. In knowledge-based organisations the focus is on replacing bureaucracy with values and visions. The future companies are looking out for voluntary followership of its members. Ikujiro Nonaka, the management writer, elaborates the Japanese view that "A company is not a machine but a living organism, and, much like an individual it can have a collective sense of identity and fundamental purpose".

Finally, the knowledge developer's success depends on cultivating good relations with management in general. In other words, a knowledge developer must be aware of the organisations' politics, its grapevine and what steps are necessary to get systems accepted. The support of a champion could make the entire knowledge process easier.

Management support also includes continued commitment to fund the project. Lack of proper financial support can lead to a low-quality product, an incomplete system, or dissatisfied users. In the final analysis, management must see the KM system project as an investment from beginning to end and gauge its support according to the gain it hopes to realise.

Knowledge awareness benefits entire organisations. With today's emphasis on sustainable competitive advantage, added value, and improved productivity, a firm's management needs to create, innovate, monitor and protect its knowledge inventory. More specifically, a KM environment means a focus on generating new knowledge, transferring existing knowledge; embedding knowledge in products, services and processes; developing an environment for facilitating knowledge growth; and accessing valuable knowledge from inside and outside the firm. When this happens, it is beyond survival. In fact, it is beyond intranets and databases the technology that supports KM.

Several ideas should be considered for how a company should perform in order to create and maintain sustainable competitive advantage. First, there should be more emphasis on tapping, sharing and preserving tacit knowledge and total knowledge base of the company. A company's knowledge base includes explicit and tacit knowledge. Second, company should focus on innovation and processes that convert innovation to new products and services. Knowledge sharing and an emphasis on total knowledge base promote innovation.

In practice, Knowledge Management often encompasses identifying and mapping intellectual assets within the organisation, sharing of best practices, making vast amounts of corporate information accessible, generating new knowledge for competitive advantage within the organisation, and technology that enables all of the above—including groupware and intranets.

Finally, it is important to consider a renewed focus on organisational learning systems and systematic thinking throughout the organisation. This is a realistic expectation, because knowledge is closely related to learning, which is the outcome of regular and continuous interactive learning. Systems thinking reflects on understanding how the various parts of the company work. This includes learning behavioural patterns in the system and culture or system environment in which employees and administrators operate. In other words, systematic thinking is expected to support innovation and continuous improvement processes social competence, and interactions, as well as the total knowledge base.

BENEFITS OF KM TO ORGANISATION

Having identified what KM is, it is important to prove why KM is so vital in today's digital economy. As a summary KM can offer the following:

- KM can offer competitive advantage.
- May help to reduce cost and increase organisational efficiency.
- Enables organisations to be flexible enough to react and adapt to changing business and customer requirements.
- Enhancement of innovation and creativity.
- Ensuring sustainable excellence.
- Improves "working on the go" by implementing knowledge repositories.
- Increases employee productivity, and makes management decisions more efficient.

The list can grow longer still. Certainly in the information driven society of today, an organisation cannot ignore KM. Of course not all organisations have the resources and capabilities to build KM systems, but that does not necessarily mean that corporations should close their eyes to the benefits of KM.

SUMMING UP

Unfortunately, there's no universal definition of Knowledge Management (KM), just as there's no agreement as to what constitutes knowledge in the first place. Knowledge Management involves people, technology, and processes in overlapping parts. These areas have developed perspectives on the working of individual and systematic knowledge. The goal of an organisation is to view all its processes as knowledge processes. This includes knowledge creation, dissemination, upgradation, and application towards organisational survival.

Knowledge Management Processes refer to involvement of two components – Organisational Processes plus infrastructure and Knowledge Management Processes plus infrastructure. Knowledge Management requires an IT infrastructure that facilitates the collection, sharing of knowledge as well as software for distributing information and making it more meaningful. Database Management gives a comparatively structured way for organising knowledge and has historically been used primarily for descriptive knowledge.

Some people argue that knowledge can't be managed - that it is a personal human attribute, which is too elusive to manage. Certainly knowledge can't be controlled, but capturing and sharing knowledge can be encouraged and facilitated.

CASE

Acquisition Spree Leaves Marconi in Need of Knowledge Management

When Marconi went on a shopping spree and acquired 10 telecommunications companies over a three-year period, it faced a serious challenge: How could the $3 billion manufacturer of telecommunications equipment ensure that its technical support agents knew enough about the newly acquired technology to provide quick and accurate answers to customers on the phone? And how could Marconi bring new agents up to speed on all the company's products?

Marconi's technical support agents have 500 engineers scattered in 14 call centres around the globe and field approximately 10,000 questions every month about the company's products. Before the acquisitions, agents had relied on Tactics Online, an extranet where they and customers could search for frequently asked questions and text documents. As new agents and products joined the company's ranks, Marconi wanted to supplement the website with a more comprehensive knowledge management system. As engineers from the newly acquired companies came on board, however, they were hesitant to share their knowledge about the products they had been supporting. "They felt that their knowledge was a security blanket that helped guarantee their jobs," says Dave Breit, director of technology and R&D for managed services in Warrendale, Pa. "With all of the acquisitions, it was essential that we all avoid hoarding knowledge and share it instead."

At the same time, Marconi wanted to streamline its customer service organisation by making more of its product and systems information available directly to customers and shortening the length of customer calls. "We wanted to leverage the Web for customer self-service versus increasing the number of agents," Breit says. "We also wanted to provide our frontline engineers [who interact directly with customers] with more information more quickly so that they could resolve more calls faster."

Building on a KM Foundation

When Marconi began evaluating Knowledge Management technologies in the spring of 1998, the concept of sharing knowledge among agents was nothing new. Agents were already accustomed to working in teams of three or four people, gathering in war room fashion to solve customers' technical issues. And a year earlier, Marconi had started basing a percentage of agents' quarterly bonuses on the amount of knowledge they submitted to Tactics Online as well as their involvement with mentoring and training other agents. "Each agent was expected to teach two training classes and write 10 FAQs to earn their full bonus," says Breit. "When we brought new companies on-line, the new agents received the same bonus plan. This approach allowed us to build a very open knowledge-sharing environment."

To augment Tactics Online, Marconi chose software from ServiceWare Technologies, in part because its technology would integrate easily with the company's Remedy CRM System, which agents use to log incoming calls from customers and track other customer interactions. In addition, says Breit, Marconi wanted its agents to populate its existing Oracle database of product information.

Breit's division spent six months implementing the new system and training agents. The system dubbed KnowledgeBase is linked to the company's CRM System and is powered by the Oracle database. The integrated view of Marconi's customers and products provides agents with a comprehensive history of interactions. Technical support agents can, for example, put markers in the database and immediately pick up at the point where the customer last spoke to another agent.

On the Front Line

Tactics Online complements the new system. "The data stored in KnowledgeBase are specific troubleshooting tips and hints on our various product lines," says Zehra Demiral, manager of Knowledge Management Systems. "Tactics Online, on the other hand, is more of a doorway for customers to come into our customer support organisation. From there, customers can access KnowledgeBase or their service requests or our online training manuals."

Technical support agents now rely on KnowledgeBase for the latest solutions to customers' product and systems problems. Level 1 agents answer all incoming calls, solve customers' problems when possible, record the calls in the company's CRM System and transfer the more difficult calls up the line to Level 2 agents. Level 2 agents, meanwhile, are the heart of the organisation, composing about 70% of the technical support organisation. They handle the more difficult calls and troubleshoot and diagnose equipment and network problems. "They're the majority of our knowledge users and contributors," says Breit. "They write up a synopsis of the call and feed it into KnowledgeBase [on an ongoing basis] so that other agents can refer to the solution later."

After Level 2 agents submit their knowledge "raw" to a holding queue, Level 3 agents confirm the accuracy of the information, make any necessary changes and then submitting the document to Demiral. (Level 3 agents also act as consultants, helping Level 2 agents solve problems and serving as intermediaries between the agents and the company's engineering departments.) The entire process of updating the KnowledgeBase System with a new solution typically takes between three days and two weeks.

Changing Roles

As Breit anticipated, implementing KnowledgeBase has changed the agents' roles. Level 1 agents, for example, now do more in-depth troubleshooting because they have more information available at their fingertips. In fact, they solve twice as many calls themselves (50% instead of 25%) in a shorter time (10 minutes versus 30 minutes). Since Level 1 agents can handle more calls, this group has doubled in size during the past two years.

The transition wasn't quite as painless, however, for the Level 2 and Level 3 agents. Indeed, their roles changed significantly. "Rather than simply submitting HTML pages to Tactics Online, they were now asked to analyze the problems in a very procedural way and create diagnostic 'trees," says Breit. "That's a more analytical way to think through a problem. Most of these guys had thought in terms of 'what is the fastest way to solve a problem' rather than 'what is the most efficient way to solve a problem.'"

With hundreds of people submitting solutions, Marconi tended to get a lot of wheel reinvention. "There can be five or six ways to solve the [same] problem, but there's one way that's most efficient," Breit says. To unearth and disseminate the most efficient solutions, agents were required to flow chart each of their solutions for the first three months following KnowledgeBase's launch. "It's amazing how many [agents] were unconscious of their own methodologies," says Breit. "It was somewhat painful, but they eventually felt they benefited because they understood how they solve problems."

As a result, agents now create technical solutions for customers in the most efficient and logical way possible instead of simply offering a "quick and dirty" solution. Think of the difference between simply being told what keys to strike on your PC and being taught how your software works and the logic behind executing a certain sequence of keystrokes. Once you actually understand how the product works, you can use the software more effectively and resolve more problems yourself.

Agents also had to change the way they presented the solutions to customers. "We wanted to provide a collaboration tool for employees and a library source for our customers," says Demiral. "Engineers wanted to provide a lot of detailed information yet we needed a degree of simplicity for customers. Most of the time, the immediate focus is on what a great collaboration tool this is and how it overcomes geographical distance among agents. Then I have to remind [agents] that this is a tool that we want customers to use and that they'll have to organise, write and present the content with customers in mind."

Making It Work

Demiral spent a lot of time working with the Level 3 agents to make their solutions less complex and streamline the review process. "We had to go through two iterations of how to organise and present the content," Demiral says. "Customers tend to think in terms of the product and then the problem. But engineers often think about the problem first and then the product."

The result: Customers often wouldn't fully understand the solution. At the same time, Marconi had to work at easing Level 3 agents' concerns that making them responsible for reviewing solution content would suddenly turn them into technical writers.

Marconi confronted cultural issues as well. "Business needs are different in different parts of the world," says Demiral. "What may be normal business practice for Americans may not be common elsewhere." In Europe, for example, the value of the KnowledgeBase system was not readily accepted. But once employees there saw that customers could use the system to solve some of their own problems, they got on board. Such an experience has been incorporated into how Marconi approaches KM. "We sometimes have to introduce the idea of knowledge management over time, validate it, and then move forward," Demiral says.

To ensure that agents continue contributing new knowledge to KnowledgeBase, Marconi uses rewards. Besides bonuses, knowledge contributors receive recognition during meetings and in a newsletter. "Rewards help feed this culture," Breit says. "Peer pressure also plays a role. Everyone wants to contribute because it's the right thing to do. You also have to make sure that the system works well and that employees use it long enough to see it work. It has to be embedded in training and fully integrated into daily operations so that it just becomes part of how you do business."

Source: The above case is developed and designed *Louise Fickel.*

KEYWORDS

Knowledge Management: It is the process through which organisations generate value from their intellectual and knowledge based assets. Most often, generating value from such assets involves codifying what employees, partners and customers know, and sharing that information among employees, departments and even with other companies in an effort to devise best practices.

Expression Management: Expression Management is valuable for helping decision makers with ad hoc calculations that arise in the course of decision making. The main objects of interest with this technique are expressions, variables, functions, and macros.

Text Management: Text Management gives decision makers the ability to work with electronic documents. These are not restricted to representing any particular kind of knowledge. However, such representations are processed simply as documents, without concern for the type of knowledge held.

Hypertext Management: This allows knowledge to be organised into an interconnected network of documents called a hyper document. The decision maker can follow markers or a map to navigate through the network to access those documents that seem relevant to the decision at hand. The main objects of interest include: hyper document documents with embedded markers. The methods for processing them is by specifying documents, specifying links by a matching pair of markers, navigation among documents by choosing desired markers.

QUESTIONS FOR DISCUSSION
Part-A

1. Define KM.
2. Explain history of KM.
3. Explain the scope of KM? Describe briefly the drivers of KM.
4. Write a note on KM as a management discipline that seeks to enhance knowledge processing.
5. Bring out the practical distinction between knowledge and information.
6. Why managing knowledge is so difficult? Explain.
7. What are the advantages of KM?
8. Learn about the Knowledge Life Cycle as a target of KM interventions.
9. Write small notes on: (i) Expression Management (ii) Database Management (iii) Text Management (iv) Hypertext Management.
10. Explain the concept of Knowledge Management System.
11. What is the difference between KM and Process Reengineering?
12. Frame a sample Knowledge Management Life Cycle for your Institute.

INDIVIDUAL ASSIGNMENT

How would you define the concept of Knowledge Management? State with reasons whether is it fair to say that there is considerable confusion surrounding Knowledge Management and its application in organisations.

EXERCISES

1. Investigate and research the literature for new measures of success (metrics) for Knowledge Management and intellectual capital. Prepare a report on your findings.
2. Describe how to ride a motorbike, drive a van, or make a peanut butter and jelly sandwich. Now have someone else try to do it based solely on your explanation. How can you best convert this knowledge from tacit to explicit?
3. Consider why Knowledge Management Systems would be so important to modern organisation than conventional firms.
4. On the basis of understanding each of the key elements of a Knowledge Management infrastructure explain how you, as a team, can contribute the same KM infrastructure elements to any hospital.
5. Make a list of all the Knowledge Management methods you use during your day (work and personal). Which are the most effective? Which are the least effective? What kind of work or activities does each Knowledge Management method enable?

GROUP ASSIGNMENTS

1. Compare and contrast the capabilities and features of electronic document management with those of collaborative computing and knowledge management systems. Each team represents one type of system. Present the ways in which these capabilities and features can create improvements in an organisation.
2. Search the internet for Knowledge Management products and systems and create categories for them. Assign one vendor to each team. Describe the categories you created and justify them.

INTERNET EXERCISES

1. Read the article by A. Genusa titled "Rx for Learning," available at *cio.com* (February 1, 2001), which describes Tufts University Medical School's experience with Knowledge Management. Determine how these concepts and such a system could be implemented and used at your college. Explain how each aspect would work, or if not, explain why not.
2. Search the internet to identify sites dealing with knowledge management. Start with *google.com, kmworld.com,* and *km-forum.org.* How many did you find? Categorise the sites based on whether they are academic, consulting firms, vendors, and so on. Sample one of each and describe the main focus of the site.

SUGGESTED READINGS

Alberthal, Les. Remarks to the Financial Executives Institute, Dallas. TX, October 23, 1995.

Awad, M. Elias & Ghaziri Hassan *Knowledge Management*, Pearson Education, 2005.

Davidson, Mike, *The Transformation of Management*, Butterworth-Heinemann, 1996.

Frappaoli, Carl. *Knowledge Management*, Wiley, 2006.

Nonaka, Ikujiro, The Knowledge-Creating Company, *Harvard Business Review*, November–December, p. 313, 1991.

Senge, Peter, *The Fifth Discipline: The Art & Practice of the Learning Organisation*, Doubleday-Currency, 1990.

Tiwana, Amrit, The knowledge Management Toolkit, Pearson Education, 2005.

WEBSITES

http://www.slideshare.net/nickmilton/
http://www.unc.edu/~sunnyliu/inls258/Introduction_to_Knowledge_Management.html
http://www.crito.uci.edu
http://www.ischool.washington.edu
http://www.ndu.edu
http://iakm.kent.edu
www.km.org
www.wikepedia.km

CHAPTER 2

Knowledge Organisation

OBJECTIVE

This chapter has two parts, Part-A deals with Knowledge Organisation and Part-B deals with Learning Organisation.

At the end of this lesson, you would be able to understand:

From Part-A

- The concept of Knowledge Organisation.
- What comprises an ideal Knowledge Organisation?
- The various sources of knowledge.
- Nature and Scope of Knowledge Organisation.
- Different functions of Knowledge Organisation.

From Part-B

- Difference between Organisational Learning and Learning Organsation.
- Learning Organisation and Its Characteristics.
- The Role of a Manager in Learning Organisation.
- Innovation, Creativity and Learning Organisation.

INTRODUCTION

Knowledge fills a large brain; it merely inflates a small one.

—Sydney J. Harris

A Knowledge Organisation is a management idea, describing an organisation in which people use systems and processes to generate, transform, manage, use, and transfer knowledge-based products and services to achieve organisational goals. A knowledge organisation also links past, present, and future by capturing and preserving knowledge in the past, sharing and mobilizing knowledge today, and learning and adapting to sustain itself in the future.

The term "knowledge organisation" or "organisation of knowledge" may designate a field of study related to Library and Information Science (LIS) or a kind of organisation (belonging to management studies).

Knowledge Organisation (KO) as related to LIS is about activities such as document description, indexing and classification performed in libraries, databases, archives, etc. These activities are done by librarians, archivists, subject specialists as well as by computer algorithms. KO as a field of study is concerned with the nature and quality of such Knowledge Organising Processes (KOP) as well as the Knowledge Organising Systems (KOS) used to organise documents, document representations and concepts.

There exist different historical and theoretical approaches to theories about organising knowledge, which are related to different views of knowledge, cognition, language, and social organisation. Each of these approaches tends to answer the question: "What is Knowledge Organisation?" differently. Library Information Service professionals have often concentrated on applying new technology and standards, and may not have seen their work as involving interpretation and analysis of meaning. That is why, library classification has been criticised for a lack of substantive intellectual content.

Traditional human-based activities are increasingly challenged by computer-based retrieval techniques. It is appropriate to investigate the relative contributions of different approaches; the current challenges make it imperative to reconsider this understanding. The leading journal in this field is *Knowledge Organisation* published by the International Society for Knowledge Organisation (ISKO).

Knowledge organisations can be viewed from a number of perspectives: their general nature, networks, behaviour, human dimensions, communications, intelligence, functions, and services. This lesson will help you to understand the different aspects of Knowledge Organisation.

IDEAL KNOWLEDGE ORGANISATION

Society, community, family are all conserving institutions. They try to maintain stability, and to prevent, or at least to slow down, change. But the organisation of the post-capitalist society of organisations is a destabilizer. Because its function is to put knowledge to work – on tools, processes, and products; on work; on knowledge itself – it must be organised for constant change.
—Peter F. Drucker

The ideal Knowledge Organisation is one where people exchange knowledge across the functional areas of the business by using technology and established processes. People exchange ideas and knowledge for policy formulation and strategy. Knowledge is also internalised and adopted within the culture of the organisation. All knowledge workers are in an environment where they can freely exchange and produce knowledge assets by using various technologies. This process influences the company as a whole in a positive way.

A Knowledge Organisation is a management idea, describing an organisation in which people use systems and processes to generate, transform, manage, use, and transfer knowledge-based products and services to achieve organisational goals. A Knowledge Organisation also links past, present, and future by capturing and preserving knowledge in the past, sharing and mobilising knowledge today, and learning and adapting to sustain itself in the future.

SOURCE OF KNOWLEDGE

Knowledge is the prime need of the hour.
— Mary McLeod Bethune

A Knowledge Organisation derives knowledge from several sources:

Customer Knowledge: Their needs, who to contact, customer buying power, etc.

Product Knowledge: The products in the market place, who is buying them, what prices they are selling at, and how much money is spent on such products.

Financial Knowledge: Capital resources, where to acquire capital and at what cost, and its integration in financial practices.

Personnel Practices Knowledge: The expertise available, the quality service they provide, and how to go about finding experts, especially in customer service.

Roadblocks in the adoption of Knowledge Management solutions

There have been many roadblocks in the adoption of formal knowledge management activities. In general, managing knowledge has been perceived as an unmanageable kind of problem—an implicitly human, individual activity—that was intractable with traditional management methods and technology.

We tend to treat the activities of knowledge work as necessary but ill-defined costs of human resources, and we treat the explicit manifestations of knowledge work as forms of publishing—as byproducts of "real" work.

As a result, the metrics associated with knowledge resources—and our ability to manage those resources in meaningful ways—have not become a part of business infrastructure.

But it isn't necessary to throw up one's hands in despair. We do know a lot about how people learn. We know more and more about how organisations develop and use knowledge. The body of literature about managing intellectual capital is growing. We have new insights and solutions from a variety of domains and disciplines that can be applied to making knowledge work manageable and measurable. And computer technology — itself a cause of the problem — can provide new tools to make it all work.

We do have to accept that the nature of business itself has changed, in at least two important ways rather than another "paradigm shift":

I. Knowledge work is fundamentally different in character from physical labour.
II. The knowledge worker is almost completely immersed in a computing environment. This new reality dramatically alters the methods by which we must manage, learn, represent knowledge, interact, solve problems, and act.

One can't solve the problems of Information Age business or gain a competitive advantage simply by throwing more information and people at the problems. And one can't solve knowledge-based problems with approaches borrowed from the product-oriented, print-based economy. Those solutions are reactive and inappropriate.

Applying technology blindly to knowledge-related business problems is a mistake too, but the computerised business environment provides opportunities and new methods for representing "knowledge" and leveraging its value. It's not an issue of finding the right computer interface — although that would help, too. We simply have not defined in a rigorous, clear, widely accepted way the fundamental characteristics of "knowledge" in the computing environment. (See "Cooperative development of a classification of Knowledge Management functions.")

NATURE OF KNOWLEDGE ORGANISATION

Drucker (1974) may have been the first to describe knowledge workers and knowledge work. Savage (1990) observed that the nature of an organisation based on knowledge rather than industrial society notions of land, labour, or capital was not well understood. Mcgee and Prusak (1993) noted that core competencies are not what an organisation owns, but rather what it knows.

Knowledge Organisations have a network dimension. Davis (1977) states that networks would not replace hierarchies, but that the two would coexist within a broader organisational concept. Similarly, Amidon (1997) points out those traditional industrial-era hierarchies are neither flexible nor fluid enough to mobilize an organisation's intellectual capacity and that much less constrained networked organisational forms are needed for modern decision making. Tapscott (1998) notes that there is an underlying logic and order to the emerging digital organisational form. It is networked, involves multiple enterprises, is based on core competencies, and knowledge is actively created, exchanged, and used.

There is also a behavioural approach. Bartlett (1999) indicates that organisational structure is just a skeleton. Knowledge organisations also have a physiology in the form of the flow of information and knowledge, as life blood. They also have a psychology represented by people's values and how they act as individuals and collectively.

Knowledge is created and used by people. Strassman (1985) described the transformation of work in the electronic age from the standpoint of education and training for managers and employees, human aspects of the working environment, and issues of morale, motivation, privacy, and displacements. Bartlett (1999) indicates that empowerment is not possible in an autocratic organisation, where networks cannot be sustained in fixed hierarchical structure, and that learning is not possible in an environment constrained by rigid policies and procedures. Davenport (1997) used an information ecology approach, in which he explored the use and abuse of information in the context of infighting, resource hoarding, and political battles as well as appropriate management in such a context.

Simard (2000) states that knowledge is inextricably linked to organisational mandates. Some providers strive for objectivity, others selectively disseminate information and knowledge, while still others use information to further their agenda. Users must understand that information is not innocent, and that all information is not created equal.

Knowledge Organisations also have collective intelligence. Liautaut (2001) points out that in the knowledge economy, being an intelligent business is not only a prerequisite to winning, but even to compete in the first place. In a fluid, fast-paced knowledge market, companies that can find and exploit the slightest advantage for faster, better decision making will dominate. He also indicates that the greater the exchange of data and information across an organisation, the more intelligent it will be.

FUNCTIONS OF KNOWLEDGE ORGANISATION

Simard et al. (2007) described five functions of a knowledge-service organisation:

- Generate content.
- Transform content into useful products and services.
- Preserve and manage content to enable organisational use and external transfer.
- Use content to achieve organisational goals.
- Transfer content externally, in the form of products and services.

ORGANISATIONAL KNOWLEDGE MANAGEMENT—THE NEED

> *We don't know a millionth of one per cent about anything.*
> —Thomas A. Edison

1. Traditional capital-intensive companies are in the process of becoming knowledge intensive. Knowledge is rapidly displacing capital, monetary prowess, natural resources and labour as the basic economic resources. Knowledge infuses quality into any company's product and service offerings and brings about unprecedented ways to accelerating product life cycles and service time to market.
2. Unstable markets necessitate reshaping of product and project lines in the disastrous position of being with the wrong product, at the wrong time, and in the wrong place.
3. Only the knowledgeable will survive. The survival of the fittest organisation becomes an outmoded thought in the knowledge-based economy. The ability to survive and thrive comes only from the organisation's ability to create, acquire, process, maintain and retain old and new knowledge in the face of complexity, uncertainty and rapid change.
4. Knowledge is the key driver for decision support and enables effective decision by making knowledge about past projects, initiatives, failures, successes and efforts readily available and accessible.
5. KM requires a strong culture of sharing that information systems do not inherently support.
6. Tacit knowledge is mobile. When an employee leaves an organisation, the knowledge, skills, competencies, understanding and insight that the employee possessed also leaves the organisation. KM can save an organisation from losing critical capabilities.

ORGANISATIONAL KNOWLEDGE MANAGEMENT DRIVERS

> *Knowledge is like a garden: if it is not cultivated, it cannot be harvested.*
> —African Proverb

Organising Knowledge

The knowledge economy brings with it significant changes in terms of how we manage and store knowledge, some of which may pose a form of threat to the status quo. That is not a new problem — people have been struggling to classify and understand knowledge for centuries. The ancient Greeks had concerned themselves about the nature of human knowledge. That concern is called epistemology, and is the branch of philosophy that studies the nature of knowledge, its presuppositions and foundations, and its extent and validity.

Aristotle saw that knowledge reflected the organisation of the world, which brings us directly to the Royal Library of Alexandria, said to have been seeded by one of Aristotle's students, Demetrius Phalereus. The Library was meant to hold every possible book on every possible subject, effectively to know everything on earth. To ensure no work escaped its grasp, Ptolemy III of Egypt decreed that any book or scroll brought into the city was to be surrendered and then copied by official scribes for the library; only then would the original (but sometimes the copy) be returned to its owner. But even the library's half a million volumes were too much for any one person to make sense of, and the librarians devised a cataloguing system where they listed works they deemed of particular importance, appending a brief description to the title.

Fast forward to 1876, when the Dewey Decimal System was published by Melvil Dewey. Dewey's system is a way to organise knowledge for libraries uniformly, clustering books by topic. In Dewey's system, a book could only be placed in one category, regardless of whether it actually belonged to five or even 10 categories. In fact, that has been the case since early man began piling and sorting rocks outside the cave.

The advent of information technology, on the other hand, has changed the rules and created an ability to place knowledge in multiple categories. More significantly, it allows knowledge workers to control the work environment, specifically referencing the placement and organisation of information. Similar to how knowledge workers own the means of production as compared to factory workers, they also exert far more control over the work environment.

While in the factory, the owner dictates the organisation of work, where things are placed, at what time things are done, participants in the knowledge economy may often experience just the opposite. Many knowledge workers are free to organise their work environment (meaning both computer and office) in the manner that best suits their work habits; in many cases, work will be performed at a time convenient for the knowledge worker, rather than in accordance with a fixed shift schedule. That alone explains why companies need to provide knowledge workers with flexible, collaborative business environments that facilitate knowledge work rather than hinder it.

An example: The world of knowledge workers is divided into browsers and searchers. Browsers move through taxonomies looking for information; searchers use the search bar. 50% of information is found through browsing, and 50% through searching. What is interesting is that this does not mean that half of the world prefers one method over the other, but that knowledge workers choose the appropriate method based on their needs.

Before proceeding to understand the framework and the infrastructural requirements for implementing a KM system within any organisation, it is essential to understand the key drivers that are applicable to any business enterprise.

In the earlier decades technology was the key for an organisation to ensure sustenance of its competitive advantage over its rivals. A cash rich organisation could easily outscore its rivals because of its ability to procure and deploy the advanced technological platforms available. The rapid growth in technology, especially in the field of semiconductor technologies and microelectronics, witnesses the design and development of microprocessors with massive computing powers and its availability at a cheaper cost. This resulted in the negation of the advantages held by huge enterprises and the subsequent quest of innovative methodologies to harness and sustain their competitive advantage.

The primary driver behind the implementation of a KM solution is to improve profits and expand revenue streams, while other secondary drivers include employee retention and increased customer satisfaction. However, while profit is the major driver behind KM implementation, one of the major hindrances in the success of any KM implementation or solution is a lack of understanding to information and knowledge sharing.

ORGANISATIONAL KNOWLEDGE MANAGEMENT APPROACHES

There are quite a few approaches for implementing knowledge in organisations.They are:

Repository Model Approach: This is one of the most common approaches to KM employed by organisations. The key focus of this approach is on document management and the reuse of explicit forms of knowledge.

Communities of Practice Approach: This approach facilitates the transfer of knowledge by experts within affinity groups through dialogue and interpersonal discussions.

Continuous Learning Approach: This approach facilitates the application of the knowledge acquired by individuals in problem solving as well as enhanced decision making.

Business Intelligence Approach: This approach involves the creation of enterprise wide repositories and the extraction of valuable information and knowledge through the mining of these repositories.

Innovation: This involves placing an emphasis on R&D, marketing and knowledge acquirement for new products and services.

Quality Control: The goal is improvement of quality by means of quality control systems.

Strategic Competency Development: This includes the control and extension of the core competence, emphasis on key knowledge and competitive advantages.

Networking: The major objective is to foster knowledge sharing, through intensifying collaboration agreements and alliance between entities internal as well as external to an organisation.

Knowledge Technology: Emphasis on the transfer of knowledge, made explicit in knowledge systems.

Human Resource Management: Emphasis on self-governing teams, cooperation, motivation and stimulation of leadership to aid people within organisations to adjust and change.

Learning Organisation: This involves stimulation of organisational learning and management of change.

Information and Communication Technologies: Emphasis on the contribution of information and communication technology to the coordination, communication and sharing of knowledge.

Organisational: This approach places due emphasis on organisational development to implement KM.

Intellectual Capital: This approach is characterised by placing emphasis on representing knowledge for the benefit of valuation.

Customer Focus: The organisational focus is on developing products and services tailored to meet customer requirements.

LEARNING ORGANISATION

Learning organisation is not a new concept as the traces of this concept could be found in eastern philosophies. Today, we live in a world of mounting expectations as both shareholders and employees are expecting more from organisations. Demand for immediate fulfilment of needs and wants has never been so intense. How to survive in this environment? Change is the only process that can lead us to survive along with continuous learning.

The crisis of today is due to human beings' unwillingness to change and belong to the future. In future the progress of organisations depends all the more on their people. Organisations have to unlock the potential of their people. Top managements can no longer afford to set agendas and expect people to march on to fulfil them. They have to accept them as partners. To motivate the people, first they have to understand them. People have to be seen as creatures who are here to realise their potential selves.

In the last 200 years there has been tremendous progress in the outside environment (I refer to the instruments we use, the complexity of activities we involve in). But as individuals, we remained the same. Our mental makeup remained the same. We are still driven by the same old motives: power, hunger, sex, and belongingness. When the environment around us is changing, we also have to change our mental habits to align with it (I assume that motives are a reflection of habits). For example, command and control style was appropriate in the 1950s and 1960s. Today, the same style is no longer relevant. Knowledge economy needs teamwork. A leader of knowledge economy, unlike one of the past, has to share his power. If we do not change with the times and environment, we will naturally be overwhelmed by the environment.

Organisational learning is the capacity or processes within an organisation to maintain or improve performance based on experience. Learning is a system-level phenomenon because it stays within the organisation, even if individuals change. Learning is as much a task as the production and delivery of goods and services. While companies do not usually regard learning as a function of production, research on successful firms indicates that three learning-related factors are important for the success:

- Well developed core competencies that serve as launch points for new products and services.
- An attitude that supports continuous improvement in the business value added chain.
- The ability to fundamentally renew or revitalise business functions based on need.

According to Peter Senge 'the organisations where individuals continually expand their capacity to create the desired results' are defined as Learning Organisations.

The Learning Organisation differs in certain dimensions from the traditional organisation. These dimensions are identified as Five Basic Diciplines and there is a sixth discipline which we will discuss in the later chapters.

The basic disciplines are:

1. Personal Mastery
2. Mental Mosels
3. Building Shared Vision
4. Team Learning
5. Systems Thinking.

Introduction to Systems Thinking

People, when initially introduced to structures, also referred to as archetypes; often find them a bit overwhelming. They really aren't at all difficult once you get used to them. The following is an introduction to structures and how to read the stories associated with the diagrams.

The basic idea of structure(s) is to point out the influence one thing has on another. That is, how do things influence other things to change?

If I have two things, thing 1 and thing 2, there are only two ways thing1 can influence thing 2.

Fig. 2.1   Add Relationship

As indicated in Figure 2.1, thing 1 can add to thing 2, as indicated by a "+" sign, thus increasing thing 2.

Fig. 2.2   Subtract Relationship

The alternative is that thing 1 can subtract from thing 2, as indicated by the "-" sign in Figure 2.2, thus decreasing thing 2.

Let's also consider a couple of specific examples.

Fig. 2.3   Sales Increase Revenue

Figure 2.3 indicates that sales add to revenue. Even if sales decrease it will still add to revenue, just not quite as rapidly as before. On the other hand, if sales increase it will add even more readily to revenue.

Fig. 2.4   Product Sales and Inventory

Figure 2.4 indicates that product sales subtract from finished goods inventory. If product sales increase it will subtract even more from finished goods inventory. On the other hand, if product sales decrease it will still subtract from finished goods inventory, just not quite so much.

Within systems diagrams there are often items that are held constant within the context of what is being considered. These items will have neither a "+" nor a "-" attached to them.

resources   Finished goods inventory   productivity

Fig. 2.5 Constant Contribution

Figure 2.5 indicates that resources interact with productivity in such a way as to add to the finished goods inventory. The indication is that resources are a constant within the structure being considered so it neither adds to nor subtracts from, it just is. You might think of a constant as a catalyst for the result. If productivity increases it will interact with resources and add even more to finished goods inventory. If productivity decreases it will still interact with resources to add to finished goods inventory, just not so readily.

Now that we've covered connections, let's cover connections that complete to form loops. There are only two types of loops, reinforcing and balancing.

Reinforcing Loop

A reinforcing loop is one in which the interactions are such that each action adds to the other. Any situation where action produces a result which promotes more of the same action is representative of a reinforcing loop.

Figure 2.6 indicates what happens in a typical savings account. The principal in the savings account interacts with the interest rate and adds to the interest. Note that the interest rate is considered to be a constant in this example. Interest then adds to the principal. This reinforcing action happens every so many months depending on the period over which the institution computes the interest. The snowball rolling downhill is your signal that the loop is a reinforcing loop. The small graph to the right of principal indicates that the growth of principal is exponential.

Typical examples of reinforcing loops are population growth and decline, uncontrolled nuclear reactions, snowballs rolling downhill, runs on banks, wall street market crashes, etc.

Balancing Loop

A balancing loop is one in which action attempts to bring two things to agreement. Any situation where one attempts to solve a problem or achieve a goal or objective is representative of a balancing loop.

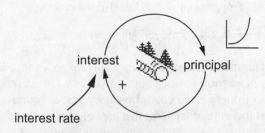

interest   principal
+
interest rate

Fig. 2.6 Reinforcing Loop

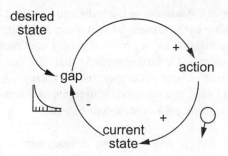

Fig. 2.7   Balancing Loop

Figure 2.7 provides the basic form of the balancing loop. The desired state interacts with the current state to produce a gap. The gap adds to the action and the action adds to the current state. The current state then subtracts from the gap. The small clock to the right of the arc between action and current state indicates some time delay that it takes for the action to change the current state. As the current state gets closer to the desired state the gap gets smaller and smaller so it adds less and less to the action, which is adding to the current state. Once the action has moved the current state to a point where it equals the desired state, the gap is zero and there's no more addition to the action, so there is no more action. The balance in the centre of the loop is your indication that the loop is a balancing loop.

Typical examples of balancing loops are driving from location A to location B, developing a skill, building something, fixing a problem, etc.

Initially you might consider it difficult to figure out one loop from the other, yet it's simply a matter of counting. All you need to do is count the number of minus signs around the loop. If there is an even number, or zero, minus signs then it is a reinforcing loop. If there is an odd number of minus sign then it's a balancing loop.

These two loops can combine in numerous ways resulting in typical situation characteristics we recognise in our daily lives. The Way of Systems matches situation descriptions to common combinations of reinforcing and balancing loops which have very distinct characteristics.

ORGANISATIONAL LEARNING vs LEARNING ORGANISATION

Before moving with the difference between Organsiational Learning and Learning Organisation, let us understand some of the lessons in learning. Organisations have engaged in a massive restructuring due to the unprecedented pressures of rapid change.Therefore, the managers in these organsiations have realised that:

1. Their competitiveness depends on their ability to learn.
2. And this learning must be organisation-wide.
3. Both individuals and teams have to take the responsibility of learning.
4. Both the external and internal knowledge have to be pooled together to forecast the future changes.
5. The managers learning must focus on present and future learning and not on the past.

There is a difference between organisational Learning and Learning Organisation. Argyris (1977) defines Organisational Learning as the process of "detection and correction of errors" while Senge (1990) defines Learning Organisation as "a group of people continually enhancing their capacity to create what they want to create". He further remarks that "the rate at which organisations learn may become the only sustainable source of competitive advantage". Ang & Joseph (1996) contrast Organisational Learning and Learning Organisation in terms of process versus structure.

The Organisational Learning Process has identifiable stages:

Knowledge Acquisition: This stage deals with the development or creation of skills, insights, relationships.

Knowledge Sharing: This stage involves the dissemination of learning throughout the organisation.

Knowledge Utilization: This stage provides the integration of learning so that it is broadly available and can be generalised to suit new situations.

Core Activities of a Learning Organisation

Learning Organisations focus on systematic problem solving with the proper deployment of tolls, viz:

- Brainstorming tools, dynamic thinking tools, structural thinking tools, computer based tools.
- Systematic experimentation.
- Employee-friendly performance management and compensation schemes.
- Rewarding of good performance and positive behaviour after evaluation.
- Employment of people who can execute the organisation's quality philosophy.

Senge perceives learning as a lifelong programme of study, what he describes as discipline. He goes on to explain that discipline according to him is not 'enforced order' or a means of punishment, but is a body of theory and techniques that must be put together into practice. A discipline is a developmental path for acquiring certain skills or competencies. As with any discipline, anyone can develop proficiency through practice.

The biggest asset of learning organisations is their commitment to learn from every aspect of their experience. The focus of the management, as also of the employees, is to create an environment that encourages experimentation, fosters open communication, and promotes sharing of knowledge. Employees themselves are responsible for gathering, examining and using this knowledge that further reinforces the learning process. Constructive dissent is encouraged so that shared mental models are constantly subjected to scrutiny and examination. In learning organisations, customers become a part of a learning relationship.

But, how does one embark on a journey towards building a learning organisation? The following aspects could go a long way:

Support from top management: A learning organisation required unflinching support from the top management.

Unlearning: For those who would like to make their organisation a learning organisation, the journey must begin with unlearning our past experiences and be ready to accept new ways of thinking.

Flexible Boundaries: They must have flexible and permeable boundaries and absorb good ideas.

Experimentation: The organisation must allow experimentation and encourage risk-taking.

Proper Reward System: All this needs to be backed up by proper reward systems and appropriate human resource practices.

Smart Information System: A smart information system is necessary to ensure the availability of information at points where it is needed.

An understanding and recognition of the learning characteristics prevalent in an organisation can help managers to focus on the agenda that needs to be followed for building and adopting a learning behaviour.

LEARNING ORGANISATION

Generating new perspectives is the only feasible option open to a management when the future is unknown. Organisations cannot really see any coherent picture of its long-term future because of the disturbance in the business environment. How then can organisation survive in this volatile environment? The only answer is change as change makes experience outdated. Today's change is complex, fast and uncertain. Accordingly the organisations must move towards the process of learning to cope with change and when an organisation starts learning, it also starts providing training for its employees and thus becomes a learning organisation.

A Learning Organisation is viewed as a holistic system that integrates problem-solving, providing internal knowledge, leading to innovation, seeking external information and providing opportunity for experimentation.

A Learning Organisation is an organisation that learns and encourages learning among its people in an effort to create a more knowledgeable and flexible workforce capable of adapting to cultural changes.

Some definitions:

- "The Learning Organisation is an organisation which facilitates the learning of all its members and continuously transforms itself" (Pedler et al., 1989).
- "Organisations where people continually expand their capacity to create the results they truly desire, where new and expansive patterns of thinking are nurtured, where collective aspiration is set free, and where people are continually learning to learn together" (Peter Senge, 1990).
- According to Sandra Kerka (1995) most conceptualisations of the Learning Organisations seem to work on the assumption that 'learning is valuable, continuous, and most effective when shared and that every experience is an opportunity to learn'.

CHARACTERISTICS OF A LEARNING ORGANISATION

In the words of (Kerka, 1995)

- Are adaptive to the external environment.
- Continually enhance their capability to change and adaptation.
- Develop collective as well as individual learning.
- Embrace creative tension as a source of energy and renewal.

- Foster inquiry and dialogue, making it safe for people to share openly and take risks.
- Link individual performance with organisational performance.
- Provide continuous learning opportunities.
- Use the results of learning to achieve better results.
- Use learning to reach their goals.

Overlooking the above points, the author's observation and research identifies four types of factors:

Learning Culture: An organisational climate that nurtures learning. There is a strong similarity with those characteristics associated with innovation.

Processes: Processes that encourage interaction across boundaries. These are infrastructure, development and management processes, as opposed to business operational processes.

Tools and Techniques: Methods that aid individual and group learning, such as creativity and problem solving techniques.

Skills and Motivation: To learn and adapt.

The basic rationale for Learning Organisations is that in situations of rapid change only those organisations that are flexible, adaptive and productive will excel. For this to happen, it is argued that organisations need to 'discover how to tap people's commitment and capacity to learn at all levels' (Peter Senge, 1990) and that "the pressure of change in the external environments of organisations has to be high such that they need to learn more consciously, more systematically, and more quickly than they did in the past. (Pearn, 1997) He also feels that organisations must learn not only in order to survive but also to thrive in a world of ever increasing change.

The key ingredient of the Learning Organisation is in how organisations process their experiences and how they learn from their experiences rather than being bound by their past experiences.

According to Sandra Kerka (1995) most conceptualisations of the Learning Organisations seem to work on the assumption that 'learning is valuable, continuous, and most effective when shared and that every experience is an opportunity to learn' (Kerka 1995). The following characteristics appear in some form in the more popular conceptions. Learning Organisations:

- Provide continuous learning opportunities.
- Use learning to reach their goals.
- Link individual performance with organisational performance.
- Foster inquiry and dialogue, making it safe for people to share openly and take risks.
- Embrace creative tension as a source of energy and renewal.
- Are continuously aware of and interact with their environment. (Kerka 1995)

As Kerka (1995) goes onto comment, the five disciplines that Peter Senge goes on to identify (personal mastery, mental models, shared vision, team learning and systems thinking) are the keys to achieving this sort of organisation. Here, rather than focus too strongly on the five disciplines one may want to comment briefly on his use of systemic thinking and his interest in 'dialogue'. These two elements in many respects mark out his contribution.

Systems Theory and the Learning Organisation

Systemic thinking is the conceptual cornerstone ('The Fifth Discipline') of Peter Senge's approach. It is the discipline that integrates the others, fusing them into a coherent body of theory and practice (1990: 12). System theory's ability to comprehend and address the whole, and to examine the interrelationship between the parts provides, for Peter Senge, both the incentive and the means to integrate the disciplines. Three things need to be noticed here. First, systems theory looks to connections and to the whole. In this respect it allows people to look beyond the immediate context and to appreciate the impact of their actions upon others.

To this extent it holds the possibility of achieving a more holistic understanding. Second, while the building blocks of systems theory are relatively simple, they can build into a rather more sophisticated model than are current in many organisations. Senge argues that one of the key problems with much that is written about, and done in the name of management, is that rather simplistic frameworks are applied to what are complex systems. When we add these two points together it is possible to move beyond a focus on the parts, to begin to see the whole, and to appreciate organisation as a dynamic process.

Thus, the argument runs, a better appreciation of systems will lead to more appropriate action. Third, systemic thinking, according to Senge, allows us to realise the significance of feedback mechanisms in organisations. He (Senge, 1990) concludes that the systems viewpoint is generally oriented towards the long-term view. That's why delays and feedback loops are so important. In the short term, you can often ignore them; they're inconsequential. They only come back to haunt you in the long term.

Dialogue and the Learning Organisation

Peter Senge also places an emphasis on dialogue in organisations—especially with regard to the discipline of team learning. Dialogue (or conversation) as Gadamer has argued is is a process of two people understanding each other. As such, it is inherently risky and involves questioning our beliefs and assumptions.

Thus, it is a characteristic of every true conversation that each opens himself to the other person, truly accepts his point of view as worthy of consideration and gets inside the other to such an extent that he understands not a particular individual, but what (Gadamer 1979) he says. The thing that has to be grasped is the objective rightness or otherwise of his opinion, so that they can agree with each other on a subject.

The concern is not to 'win the argument', but to advance understanding and human well being. Agreement cannot be imposed, but rests on common conviction (Habermas 1984). As a social relationship it entails certain virtues and emotions.

It is easy to see why proponents of the Learning Organisation would place a strong emphasis upon dialogue. As Peter Senge has argued, for example, team learning entails the capacity of members of a team to suspend assumptions and enter into a genuine "thinking together". Dialogue is also necessary to other disciplines, e.g., building a shared vision and developing mental models. However, there are significant risks in dialogue to the organisation. One factor in the appeal of Senge's view of dialogue (which was based upon the work of David Bohm and associates) was the promise that it could increase and enrich corporate activity. It could do this, in part, through the exploration and questioning of 'inherent, predetermined purposes and goals'. There is a clear parallel here with Argyris and Schön's work on double-loop learning, but interestingly one of Bohm's associates has subsequently suggested that their view was too optimistic: 'dialogue is very subversive'.

Some Problems and Issues

In our discussion of Senge and the Learning Organisation, we point to some particular problems associated with his conceptualisation. These include a failure to fully appreciate and incorporate the imperatives that animate modern organisations; the relative sophistication of the thinking he requires of managers and questions around his treatment of organisational politics. It is certainly difficult to find real-life examples of Learning Organisations (Kerka 1995). There has also been a lack of critical analysis of the theoretical framework.

It is concluded that it is not possible to transform a bureaucratic organisation by learning initiatives alone. But there is a belief that by referring to the notion of the Learning Organisation it was possible to make change less threatening and more acceptable to participants. 'However, individual and collective learning which has undoubtedly taken place has not really been connected to organisational change and transformation'. Part of the issue, they suggest, is to do with the concept of the Learning Organisation itself. They argue the following points.

The concept of the learning organisation:

Focuses mainly on the cultural dimension, and does not adequately take into account the other dimensions of an organisation. To transform an organisation it is necessary to attend to structures and the organisation of work as well as the culture and processes. 'Focusing exclusively on training activities in order to foster learning favouring this purely on cultural bias'.

Favours individual and collective learning processes at all levels of the organisation, but does not connect them properly to the organisation's strategic objectives. Popular models of organisational learning assume such a link. It is, therefore, imperative, 'that the link between individual and collective learning and the organisation's strategic objectives is made'. This shortcoming, Finger and Brand argue, makes a case for some form of measurement of organisational learning—so that it is possible to assess the extent to which such learning contributes or does not contribute towards strategic objectives that remain rather vague. The exact functions of Organisational Learning need to be more clearly defined.

In our view, Organisational Learning is just a means to achieve strategic objectives. But creating a Learning Organisation is also a goal, since the ability, permanently and collectively, to learn is a necessary precondition for thriving in the new context. Therefore, the capacity of an organisation to learn, that is, to function like a Learning Organisation, needs to be made more concrete and institutionalized, so that the management of such learning can be made more effective.

Finally, Finger and Brand conclude, that there is a need to develop 'a true management system of an organisation's evolving learning capacity'. This, they suggest, can be achieved by defining indicators of learning (individual and team and organisational) and by connecting them to other indicators.

It could be argued that the notion of the Learning Organisation provides managers and others with a picture of how things could be within an organisation. Along the way, writers like Peter

Senge introduce a number of interesting dimensions that could be personally developmental, and that could increase organisational effectiveness—especially where the enterprise is firmly rooted in the 'knowledge economy. However, as we have seen, there are a number of shortcomings to the model–it is theoretically underpowered and there is some question as to whether the vision can be realised within the sort of dynamics that exist within and between organisations in a globalised capitalist economy. It might well be that 'the concept is being oversold as a near-universal remedy for a wide variety of organisational problems' (Kuchinke, 1995 quoted in Kerka, 1995).

In one of the more interesting developments there has been an attempt to take the already substantial literature on trust in organisations (Edmondson and Moingeon 1999) and to link it to developments in thinking around social capital (especially via the work of political theorists like Robert Putnam).

We could also link this with discussions within informal education and lifelong learning concerning the educative power of organisations and groups (and hence the link to Organisational Learning). Here the argument is that social capital makes an organisation more than a collection of individuals. (Social capital can be seen as consisting of 'the stock of active connections among people: the trust, mutual understanding, and shared values and behaviours that bind the members of human networks and communities and make cooperative action possible', Cohen and Prusak, 2001. Social capital draws people into groups.

This kind of connection supports collaboration, commitment, ready access to knowledge and talent, and coherent organisational behaviour. This description of social capital suggests appropriate organisational investments—namely, giving people space and time to connect, demonstrating trust, effectively communicating aims and beliefs, and offering equitable opportunities and rewards that invite genuine participation, not mere presence. Cohen and Prusak 2001. In this formulation one can see many of the themes that run through the approach to the Learning Organisation that writers like Watkins and Marsick (1993) take. The significant thing about the use of the notion of social capital is the extent to which it then becomes possible to tap into some interesting research methodologies and some helpful theoretical frameworks.

LEARNING ORGANISATION CONCEPTS

The major Learning Organisational concepts focus on "Continuous Improvement", "Culture" and "Innovation and Creativity".

The concept of Organisational Learning evolved from the individual learning process, but Organisational Learning is not simply collective individual learning processes, but it engages interaction between:

- Individuals in the organisation.
- Interaction between organisations as an entity.
- Interaction between the organisation and its environment.

Table 2.1   A Review of the Concept of Organisational Learning, 2002

	Focus	The concept of Learning Organisation	Practices
1.	Continuous Improvement	"A learning organisation should consciously and intentionally devote to the facilitation of individual learning in order to continuously transform the entire organisation and its context" (Pedler et al. 1991)	The adoption of Total Quality Management practices
2.	Culture	"A learning organisation should be viewed as a metaphor rather than a distinct type of structure, whose employees learn conscious communal processes for continually generating, retaining and leveraging individual and collective learning to improve performance of the organisational system in ways important to all stakeholders and by monitoring and improving performance" (Drew & Smith, 1995)	Creation and maintenance of learning culture: adapting to cultural change, collaborative team working, employee empowerment and involvement, etc.
3.	Innovation and Creativity	Organisation learning is the process by which the organisation constantly questions existing product, process and system, identify strategic position, apply various modes of learning, and achieve sustained competitive advantage	Facilitation of learning and knowledge creation; focus on creative quality and value innovation

ACTIVITIES AND SKILLS NEEDED BY LEARNING ORGANISATION

Dr. Garvin includes the following in the activities of a Learning Organisation:

- **Systematic problem solving:** Thinking with systems theory; insisting on data rather than assumptions; using statistical tools.

- **Experimentation with new approaches:** Ensure steady flow of new ideas; incentives for risk taking; demonstration projects.

- **Learning from their own experiences and past history:** Recognition of the value of productive failure instead of unproductive success.

- **Learning from the experiences and best practices of others:** Enthusiastic borrowing.

- **Transferring knowledge quickly and efficiently throughout the organisation:** Reports, tours, personnel rotation programmes, training programmes.

Learning Organisations need to be skilled at the following five main activities (Gravin, 1993):

1. Systematic problem solving

Systematic Problem Solving is done in Learning Organisations by brain storming, interviewing and surveying.

The Learning Organisation is the foundation that will facilitate continuous innovation and improvement that will produce a World-class Organic Enterprise. Applying and expanding one's wisdom in the enterprise's ecosystem, while being nimble and flexible, will enable a firm to gain industry-independent global recognition for its leadership, excellence, and the principles that guide it. Then, that corporation will be synonymous with worldclass. The following diagram represents how the organisations can or may move to world-class organisations.

2. Experimentation with new approaches

This activity involves systematic search for new knowledge, through the use of scientific method. Generally, it is motivated by opportunity and expanding horizons and it involves stages of knowledge from superficial to deeper understanding, from knowing how to knowing why, in terms of underlying cause–and–effect relationships. It also involves interpreting exceptions, adaptations and events that are uncertain.

3. Learning from own experience and past history

Employees require a mindset that enables companies to recognise the value of productive failure as contrasted with unproductive success. This is because companies review their success and failures, assess them logically and systematically and record them in a form that is easily accessible to them.

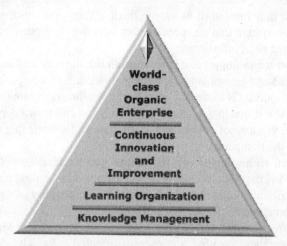

Fig. 2.8 Diagram representing the Growth of Learning Organisations

4. Learning from the experiences and best practices of others

Learning from the experiences and best practices of others involves 'benchmarking'. Benchmarking refers to adopting an in-depth investigation and learning from the best industry practices and making a comparative study to where their organisation is at present.

This involves discovering, understanding, analysing and adopting such best practices. Learning Organsiations have the thirst to learn from both the external and internal environment like their customers, suppliers, competitors and business partners.

5. Transferring of knowledge

Knowledge has a greater impact when it is shared throughout the organisation. Henceforth, transferring knowledge throughout the organisation can happen quickly and efficiently through teaching the behaviour needed and creating opportunities for actively experiencing things.

THE ROLE OF THE MANAGER IN THE LEARNING ORGANISATION

Before understanding the role of manager in learning organisation, one must be clear with understandings of certain myths revolving around different tasks of knowledge leaders.

Yogesh Malhotra, founder, chairman and CKO of the @Brint Institute in Fort Lauderdale, Fla., and @Brint LLC, a website devoted to Knowledge Management (www.brint.com), has identified some myths that surround the murky confluence of information technology and Knowledge Management.

MYTH: Knowledge Management technologies deliver the right information to the right person at the right time. Information Systems in the old industrial model mirror the notion that businesses will change incrementally in an inherently stable market, and executives can foresee change by examining the past. "The basic premise is that you can predict…how and what you'll need to do and that IS can simplify this and do it efficiently," he says. The new business model of the Information Age, however, is marked by fundamental, not incremental, change. Businesses can't plan long-term; instead, they must shift to a more flexible "anticipation-of-surprise" model. Thus, it's impossible to build a system that can predict even who the right person at the right time is, let alone what constitutes the right information.

MYTH: Information technologies can store human intelligence and experience. Information is context-sensitive. The same assemblage of data can evoke different responses from different people. The reason this is important is that many information textbooks say that while people come and go, their experience can be stored in databases. But unless you can scan a person's mind and store it directly into a database, you cannot put bits into a database and assume that somebody else can get back the experience of the first person.

MYTH: Information technologies can distribute human intelligence. Again, this assumes that companies can predict the right information to distribute and the right people to distribute it to. And bypassing the distribution issue by compiling a central repository of data for people to access doesn't solve the problem either. "The fact of information in a database doesn't ensure that people will see or use the information," Malhotra says. "Most of our Knowledge Management technology concentrates on efficiency and creating a consensus-oriented view. The data therein is rational, static and without context." "And such systems", he adds, "do not account for renewal of existing knowledge and creation of new knowledge".

So when you next hear that KM is an IT-based activity, capitalise the *I* and lower case the *t*.

Senge (1990) argues that the role of the manager in the Learning Organisation is that of a designer, teacher, and steward who can build a shared vision and is responsible for learning. The manager is responsible for building organisations where people are continually expanding their capabilities to shape their future.

Leading a Learning Organisation - An Introduction

A manager or a leader's role in a Learning Organisation is different from that of a decision maker. In a Learning Organisation a leader is a designer, a teacher, and a steward. The skills required for these roles are an ability to bring shared vision to the surface and challenge existing mental models, and an ability to foster systematic ways of thinking in the organisation. Leaders in Learning Organisations have to make sure that their people expand their capacities and shape their futures. In other words, they are responsible for the learning of their people and their organisation.

According to Peter Senge, leadership in a Learning Organisation is based on the principle of creative tension. Creative tension occurs when the leader sees clearly where the organisation should be, and understands clearly where the organisation is currently. The gap between where the organisation should be and where it is generates creative tension. As Peter Senge says, there are two ways of resolving creative tension. First, raise the current reality towards vision and second, lower vision towards reality. Organisations which learn to work with creative tension know how to channel the energy created by that tension to move reality towards their visions.

Leader as a Designer

An organisation with poor design will be an ineffective organisation, even if it is led by a great leader. Organisation design is concerned with designing governing ideas of purpose, vision, and core values by which people will live. The first task of leadership is designing governing ideas to be followed by policies, strategies, and structures that can translate guiding ideas into business decisions. The appropriateness of policies, strategies, and structures to a large extent depends upon effective learning processes. Thus, the manager or a leader's third task in a Learning Organisation is to create such processes.

Leader as a Teacher

A leader's main responsibility is to define reality. He should help his people get accurate, insightful, and empowering views of current reality. Thus, the leader assumes the role of a teacher. According to Peter Senge, teaching role in a learning organisation can be developed by giving attention to people's mental models and with the help of systems thinking. A leader, as a teacher, has to bring people's mental models of important issues to surface. This is important because, a mental picture of how the world works (people hold this mental picture), influences how people perceive various problems and opportunities. It also influences how the courses of action are identified and how people make their choices.

A leader's job is not over with revealing the hidden assumptions. People mistake reality for events. They see the pressures they have to bear, the crises they must react to, and the limitations they must accept as reality. But these are just obvious and temporary conditions. There are some underlying causes that cause these problems. A leader, as a teacher, shows what is beyond these obvious events. There can be a pattern behind these events. And there can be basic problem behind this pattern. A leader has to make his people restructure their views of reality. By addressing the problems behind pattern of events (here crises, and pressures), a leader can help his people create a new future.

Explanations that explain events promote a reactive stance to change. Pattern of behaviour explanations attempt to identify long-term trends and measure their implications. These explanations help organisations over a period of time to adapt to changing circumstances. Structural explanations are the most beneficial. They try to provide explanations on underlying causes of behaviour. With these explanations they offer a hope that patterns of behaviour can be changed to organisation's advantage. Today's leaders mostly concentrate on events and to a lesser extent on patterns of behaviour. Under their leadership, organisations also largely do the same (concentrate more on events and to a certain extent on patterns of behaviour).

This is the reason why most of the organisations are reactive and a few are generative. Leaders in learning organisations try to understand reality at all the three levels but concentrate more on systematic structure. They also encourage their people to do the same. As a result, Learning Organisations are better prepared for the future.

Leader as a Steward

A leader in a Learning Organisation is considered a learned person or intellectual capital leading the team. The terms intangibles, intellectual capital, and knowledge assets are popular in research and frequently used interchangeably. Many researchers, however, observe that there is no consensus on a precise definition of these terms (Beattie and Thomson, 2007; Marr et al., 2004). This notion is backed by Lev (2001) who claims that the terms "are widely used—intangibles in the accounting literature, knowledge assets by economists, and intellectual capital in the management and legal literature—but they refer essentially to the same thing: a non-physical claim to future benefits."

Regarding the role of leader as steward, Peter Senge says, "This is the subtlest role of leadership. Unlike the roles of designer and teacher, it is almost solely a matter of attitude. It is an attitude critical to learning organisations." Peter Senge says that while people have realised that stewardship is an aspect of leadership, its source is not properly understood. He feels that Robert Greenleaf's seminal book, Servant Leadership, provides some explanation on stewardship. In this book, Greenleaf says, "The servant leader is servant first... It begins with the natural feeling that one wants to serve, to serve first. This conscious choice brings one to aspire to lead. That person is sharply different from one who is leader first, perhaps because of the need to assuage an unusual power drive or to acquire material possessions."

As a steward, a leader can operate at two levels. First, stewardship for people and second, stewardship for the larger mission that underlies the organisation. At the first level, the leader understands the impact his leadership can have on his people. He understands that people can suffer economically, emotionally, and spiritually under incompetent leadership. People working in a Learning Organisation are going to be more influenced by their leader due to their commitment and sense of ownership. A leader who understands all this develops a sense of responsibility.

At the second level, leaders of Learning Organisations have a sense of personal purpose and commitment towards achieving their organisation's larger mission. As Peter Senge says, they unleash energies of their people by appealing to their natural impulse to learn. They do this by engaging their people in endeavour they consider worthy of their fullest commitment. Lawrence Miller [4] puts it beautifully, "Achieving return on equity does not, as a goal, mobilise the most noble forces of our soul." Leaders involved in building Learning Organisations feel part of a higher purpose that extends beyond their organisation. They attempt to transform the way businesses operate with the conviction to create organisations that are more productive; that can achieve higher levels of organisational successes; and that provide personal satisfaction.

Lessons for Business & Technology Executives

So what can executives do to realign their focus from the old world of 'information management' to the new paradigm of 'knowledge management' discussed here? A condensed checklist of implementation measures for business and technology managers is given in Table 2.2.

DIFFERENT VIEWS IN MOVING TOWARDS LEARNING ORGANISATION

Brook Manville, Director of Knowledge Management at McKinsey, views the implementation of these issues in terms of the shift from the traditional emphasis on transaction processing, integrated logistics and workflows to systems that support competencies for communication building, people networks, and on-the-job learning. He distinguishes between the three *architectures* needed for enabling such competencies:

- a new *information architecture* that includes new languages, categories, and metaphors for identifying and accounting for skills and competencies.
- a new *technical architecture* that is more social, transparent, open, flexible, and shows respect for individual users.
- a new *application architecture* oriented towards problem solving and representation, rather than output and transactions.

Manville observes that technology will continue to yield disappointing results until IS managers and business executives realise that IT must provide a way to form communities, not simply provide communications.

In the final analysis, managers need to develop a greater appreciation for their intangible human assets captive in the minds and experiences of their knowledge workers, because without these assets, the companies are simply not equipped with a vision to foresee or to imagine the future while being faced with a fog of unknowingness. As noted by Strassmann, elevating computerisation to the level of a magic bullet may lead to the diminishing of what matters the most in any enterprise: educated, committed, and imaginative individuals working for organisations that place greater emphasis on people than on technologies.

Table 2.2 Implementation Measures for Facilitating Knowledge Management

■ Instead of the traditional emphasis on controlling people and their behaviours by setting up predefined goals and procedures, they would need to view the organisation as a human community capable of providing diverse meanings to information outputs generated by the technological systems.
■ De-emphasize the adherence to the company view of 'how things are done here' and 'best practices' so that such ways and practices are continuously assessed from multiple perspectives for their alignment with the dynamically changing external environment.
■ Invest in multiple and diverse interpretations to enable constructive conflict mode of inquiry and, thus, lessen oversimplification of issues or premature decision closure.
■ Encourage greater proactive involvement of human imagination and creativity to facilitate greater internal diversity to match the variety and complexity of the wicked environment.
■ Give more explicit recognition to tacit knowledge and related human aspects, such as ideals, values, or emotions, for developing a richer conceptualisation of Knowledge Management.
■ Implement new, flexible technologies and systems that support and enable communities of practice, informal and semi-informal networks of internal employees and external individuals based on shared concerns and interests.
■ Make the organisational information base accessible to organisation members who are closer to the action while simultaneously ensuring that they have the skills and authority to execute decisive responses to changing conditions.

A Toolbox for Knowledge Management Initiatives

Any information on Knowledge Management would not be complete without providing leads for continuous self-learning on issues discussed in the article. Here is a short checklist of books, magazines and websites that business and technology managers can utilize to get up to speed on the 'new' paradigm of Knowledge Management.

SUMMING UP

The term 'Knowledge Organisation' was first used by Peter Drucker. A Knowledge Organisation is a management idea, describing an organisation in which people use systems and processes to generate, transform, manage, use, and transfer knowledge-based products and services to achieve organisational goals.

The ideal knowledge organisation is one where people exchange knowledge across the functional areas of the business by using technology and established processes.

Table 2.3   A Toolbox for Knowledge Management Initiatives

Illustrative Books on the New Paradigm of Knowledge Management
■ De Geus, Arie. *The Living Company*, Boston, MA, Harvard Business School Press, 1997.
■ Leonard-Barton, Dorothy. *Wellsprings of Knowledge: Building and Sustaining the Sources of Innovation*, Boston, MA, Harvard Business School Press, 1995.
■ Nonaka, Ikujiro & Hirotaka Takeuchi. *The Knowledge-Creating Company*, Oxford University Press, New York, NY, 1995.
■ Stewart, Thomas A. *Intellectual Capital: The New Wealth of Organisations,* Currency/Doubleday, New York, NY, 1997.
■ Sveiby, Karl Erik. *The New Organisational Wealth: Managing and Measuring Knowledge-Based Assets,* Berrett-Koehler, San Francisco, CA, 1997.
Illustrative Periodical Publications on the New Paradigm
■ *Fortune*: Knowledge Management column by Tom Stewart
■ *CIO*: Knowledge Management column by Tom Davenport
■ *Wall Street Journal*: Friday Front Lines column by Tom Petzinger
■ *Harvard Business Review*: Special Issue on: Knowledge Management, Jul-Aug 1997
■ *Long Range Planning*: Special Issue on Intellectual Capital, June 1997
■ *Forbes ASAP*: Special Issue on Intellectual Capital, April 7, 1997
■ *Knowledge Inc.:* Monthly Executive Newsletter on IT and Knowledge Strategy
Illustrative Websites and Online Discussion Forums
■ WWW Virtual Library on Knowledge Management at http://km.brint.com/
■ Knowledge Management Think Tank Online Forum at http://km.brint.com/

There are various sources of knowledge in an organisation, namely, customer knowledge, product knowledge, financial knowledge, personal practices knowledge, etc.

Learning Organisations are those that have in place systems, mechanisms and processes, that are used to continually enhance their capabilities and of those who work with it or for it, to achieve sustainable objectives - for themselves and the communities in which they participate.

The important points to note about this definition are that Learning Organisations:

■ Are adaptive to their external environment
■ Continually enhance their capability to change/adapt
■ Develop collective as well as individual learning

■ Use the results of learning to achieve better results

CASE
ABN AMRO BANK
An Introduction

Netherlands' former two largest banks Algemene Bank Nederland (ABN) and Amsterdam-Rotterdam Bank (AMRO) merged to form ABN AMRO Bank in 1991. ABN AMRO is an international bank with roots stretching back to 1824. ABN AMRO ranks eighth in Europe and 13th in the world based on total assets. ABN AMRO is Holland's leading bank operating over 800 offices in Holland together with 2,600 worldwide offices in 75 different countries with over 110,000 employees.

Concept 1: Continuous Improvement
A Learning Organisation

The ongoing success of ABN AMRO is attributed to its commitment towards employee learning and personal development; learning is a major priority for the organisation. Being a dynamic and a fast growing organisation, there is the need for staff flexibility, staff mobility and staff adaptation to new technologies, practices, situations and challenges.

In order to support the personal development and career development of employees, ABN AMRO offer continuous learning programmes such as:

■ **Job-related training**
   • Induction programmes to help new employees integrate into the new work environment
   • In-house training seminars
   • In-house training programmes
   • External courses
   • Coaching/mentoring programmes
   • Short-term assignments in overseas offices
■ **Management programmes**
■ **Leadership programmes**
   • E-Learning
   • Products and Professional skills training
■ **Development Programmes**
   • Structural talent management & succession planning
   • Management and leadership programmes
   • Full range of training for new and diversified products
   • Internal mobility programme to encourage horizontal moves across business units for more challenging roles and opportunities.

Learning is an investment and an ongoing process in ABN AMRO adding value both to the organisation and to its employees.

E-learning

E-learning is a training channel which is effectively utilised by ABN AMRO. "We need to make training accessible to people when and where they need it…Our multimedia training is available in every city where we have people…We're very close to implementing intranet-based systems to bring training to people's desks" said Judi Davenport, Director of Training *(Aggressive training key to ABN AMRO acquisition success, Undated).*

E-learning is an innovative learning solution and is the only way forward for a global Learning Organisation such as ABN AMRO where staff is deployed worldwide.

Continuous improvement is achievable through the continued upgrading of the organisational Total Quality Management practices as an ongoing learning experience. TQM can be achieved by having a knowledgeable workforce that continuously strives for self-improvement and through personal development for the benefit of both the organisation and its employees.

Concept 2: Culture
Managing Cultural Change through Learning

One of ABN AMRO's major strategies is the acquisition of financial institutions such as the LaSalle National Bank and the Cragin Federal Bank in the USA. ABN AMRO is an active Learning Organisation and has an aggressive programme aimed to change the traditional banking culture to meet today's challenges.

"We're going through so much change," says Director of Training, Judi Davenport "that I think everybody realises we need to help people through that change…as people need new skills and knowledge, we need to be there to give it to them and not let that happen by chance" *(Aggressive training key to ABN AMRO acquisition success, Undated).*

As part of the acquisition and restructuring process, ABN AMRO ensures that during the transition of the merger of the new staff with the old staff no one will be left behind. All staff will be given equal opportunities and will be given all the necessary training to enhance their skills and personal development in an effort to adapt effortlessly to the new culture and environment. This will ensure a smooth transition which ultimately will benefit the organisation, its employees and its customers.

Change Community

ABN AMRO set up a community programme referred to as 'The Change Community' with the purpose "to live, plant and support action at ABN AMRO towards more meaningful and inspiring work/life." The community meets at regular intervals to engage in dialogue and reflection regarding issues of importance to the organisation and society such as diversity, work-life balance, bringing individual values to work and sustainable development. Together, members exchange ideas and dilemmas with the intent to support the integration of sustainable development in the organisation.

This is another channel that ABN AMRO utilises in addressing its Learning Organisation objectives. *(ABN AMRO Change Community, Undated)*

An Opportunity for Growth

ABN AMRO is always striving to reach new heights by exploring new ways for business growth and business development.

ABN AMRO has begun a new learning experience in its history. ABN AMRO, in cooperation with its new consortium partners, Fortis, The Royal Bank of Scotland and Sandanter, have joined their experiences to integrate and grow their businesses to their full potential. The combination of the consortium businesses together with that of ABN AMRO should result in an enhanced market presence, strengthened products and growth prospects. This should also deliver benefits to customers who will gain from the increased scale and efficiency of the businesses.

"Change is underway and we are in good shape to forge ahead..." said Mark Fisher, Chairman of ABN AMRO Managing Board.

This is an outstanding opportunity for ABN AMRO, bringing a new challenging learning experience to the organisation. Sharing experiences with the consortium partners once again brings new knowledge and enhances the organisational culture.

ABN AMRO is clearly creating and maintaining its learning culture through the adaptation of cultural changes, through collaborative teamwork and through employee empowerment by focusing on employee involvement as a work/life experience.

Concept 3
Innovation & Creativity

Innovation and Creativity is a main pillar in any Learning Organisation. Innovation and Creativity will contribute towards potential increased efficiency in an organisation provided that its employees learn quickly how to adapt themselves to new technologies and innovations in an effort to position the organisation with a competitive edge.

Social and Environmental Innovative Sustainability
A core strategy at ABN AMRO

Sustained social and environmental causes form an integral part of ABN AMRO social responsibility business strategy.

The bank strives to include a concern for social and environmental issues in its decision making and encourages other businesses to create benefit in society. Through its lending practices, the bank seeks out and supports business activities that support social or environmental causes. The innovativeness of this sustainability mindset has led to numerous activities that are creating a shift in the impact of ABN AMRO on both the environment and society.

"Because banks are a part of society, we want our activities to reflect the needs and problems of that society," says ABN AMRO manager Lucian Toia.

ABN AMRO involves employees to practice and promote exceptional philanthropy. In 2004, over 15,000 employees were involved in various initiatives around the world such as the Akatu project in Brazil which is a programme that builds environmental awareness.

Through this initiative ABN AMRO as a Learning Organisation is helping employees enhance their knowledge and skills in areas which are not related to their line of business, brining new opportunities for personal development.

(Sustainability—A core strategy at ABN AMRO, 2006)

Worldwide Common Office Environment (COE) Deployment Project

ABN AMRO's COE Wholesale Client Services business brought innovation and new practices for over 3000 Traders in the organisation with the objective of streamlining common standards across its global business. This project impacted 10 different countries, UK, US, the Netherlands, France, Germany, Hong Kong, Singapore, Australia, Japan and New Zealand, which are key to the ABN AMRO's business.

The challenge was to provide the user training with minimal impact on business operations and without taking the user away from their desks for long periods of time.

This task was entrusted to ILX Group which is a specialist provider of customised training and implementation solutions and services with considerable experience in the financial sector.

ILX deployed a simple and unobtrusive global solution whereby users can self train with a practical hands-on approach from their own PC through graphical step-by-step guides and simple exercises.

This was a new learning experience for the organisation taking advantage of innovative technology as a Learning Organisation process.

(International Learning Xchange, Undated)

High-tech Training Platform—Pathlore Learning Management Solution

ABN AMRO has partnered with Pathlore to deploy a learning management solution in its organisation. This solution enables employees to analyse their training needs and to receive feedback on how to improve their performance. This solution also automates many of the employee development activities handled by a bank's training department such as the registration of employees for training and the launching of courses. This gives the bank's training team an opportunity to concentrate more on the evaluation of the effectiveness of its programmes and to create new and strategic training initiatives rather than wasting its resources on administrative tasks.

"The Pathlore learning management solution also handles the 'commodity activities' associated with getting people into training - things like logistics and registrations." added Pathlore CEO Steve Thomas. *(Pathlore for high-tech training platform, 2004)*

Again this solution engages the organisation in innovation, creativity and continuous development as a Learning Organisation.

ABN AMRO Bank Introduces Service Innovations

"Focus 2005" is a 5-year long-term plan with the objective of redesigning the organisation for more effective customer service in an era where technological developments such as the internet are rapidly altering service requirements.

"With this initiative and our investment in information and communications technology, ABN AMRO Bank is further developing the successful formula of the integrated multi-channel concept," says Managing Board member Mr. Rijkman Groenink, who heads the new European Division.

The bank is investing considerably in Information Communication Technology, giving the organisation a competitive edge.

(ABN AMRO Bank Introduces Service Innovations, 2005)

ABN AMRO Implement Compliant Business Processes and Create a Flexible User Experience

ABN AMRO took the decision to change ABN AMRO Trust working practices in order to create a more agile enterprise by improving its customer service. The goal was to enable employees performing multiple tasks through a single interface together with a common customer information database. This required an integrated approach to its technology, strategy and business processes, yet again bringing innovation and new learning challenges to the organisation.

ABN AMRO opted for an IT solution named edgeConnect to reach its objectives through which it was able to standardise its processes across each jurisdiction, providing each user with a consistent way of working, regardless of location, business function or business role. This solution ensures that the proper ABN AMRO's KYC procedures (Know-Your-Customer checks) are followed throughout the organisation. Furthermore, this technology provides advice to employees on whether a potential client should be accepted or rejected, thus enhancing the decision-making process.

"We could introduce more products to the existing client base with the same staff levels because we could share information across ABN AMRO Trust as a single entity, thereby removing duplication of tasks," says Tony de Bree, former project manager, ABN AMRO Trust.

(ABN AMRO Implement Compliant Business Processes and Create a Flexible User Experience, 2005)

Innovation and creativity is a pillar in a Learning Organisation and it is clear that ABN AMRO is second to none. Through innovative IT solutions ABN AMRO is facilitating learning and knowledge creation throughout the organisation.

Through the deployment of innovative solutions, ABN AMRO focuses on quality, creativity and value innovation. The deployment of new service innovations also streamlines common standards across its business in an effort to fulfil global and legal obligations.

Considerations

It is evident that ABN AMRO is a dynamic Learning Organisation which is always in search of new opportunities for business growth. Living in an ever evolving environment, organisations need to be proactive to anticipate change, to develop new ideas and to manage resources with care. ABN AMRO recognises that its survival depends on continuous development and innovation and creativity which can only be achieved through a never ending learning experience. ABN AMRO is committed and engaged in this Learning Organisation process and from the research carried out we can conclude that ABN AMRO is:

- Building its organisation fit for human beings
- Creating a capacity for self-transformation
- Developing an entrepreneurial spirit
- Encouraging autonomy
- Encouraging innovation
- Ensuring employee morale and satisfaction

- Facilitating change and adaptation
- Harnessing creative energy
- Increasing responsibility at all levels in the organisation
- Making work more enjoyable and productive
- Mobilising every ounce of intelligence in the workforce
- Producing more with less
- Stimulating continuous improvement
- Striving for survival
- Switching on the brains of all employees
- Striving for a competitive edge
- Using human talents to the full.

The above processes are all the characteristics of a Learning Organisation.

The main pillars of a Learning Organisation, i.e., "Continuous Improvement", "Culture" & "Innovation and Creativity" are a living monument in ABN AMRO Bank, which contributes towards the organisation's success, survival and potential future growth.

KEYWORDS

Knowledge Organisation: An organisation in which people use systems and processes to generate, transform, manage, use and transfer knowledge-based products and services to achieve organisational goals.

Ideal Knowledge Organisation: The ideal knowledge organisation is one where people exchange knowledge across the functional areas of the business by using technology and established processes.

Learning Organisation: Organisations whose members commonly and continuously acquire, learn share, store, distribute and use knowledge for their effective, collective action are definable as Learning Organisations.

INDIVIDUAL ASSIGNMENT

Name a knowledge organisation from corporate and explain the various practices adopted by it to imbibe knowledge.

EXERCISE

You just returned from your vacations. It was your first day back at work. As usual your e-mail is full with many messages. Check carefully through them and try to handle them in the best possible way. Check the best ways to handle those tasks/questions; emphasize on the knowledge management aspect. IMPORTANT: You do not actually have to DO the tasks, but I would like to discuss a bit on how for each of those mails you react would handle, prioritise them, make sure the knowledge does not get lost, etc. Carefully read through all the mails, react on each of them. Explain to me your thoughts and planned actions. Your suggested solutions should be based on your thoughts and the practical of the newly applicaton acquired KM understanding and NOT on a correct/wrong basis. This sure is not an easy assignment BUT it is a real life assignment!

Source: http://www.slideshare.net/lritzel/knowledge-management-simple-exercise.

GROUP ASSIGNMENT

J. D. Edwards (*jdedwards.com*) developed a Knowledge Management intranet initiative called the Knowledge Garden. Access both the J. D. Edwards and Microsoft websites and investigate its current capabilities (class or from work), examine some typical decisions in the related project. How would you extract the knowledge you need? Can you use that knowledge in practice? Why or why not?

INTERNET EXERCISE

Why Do Meetings Start Late?
A workshop exercise to introduce systems thinking

Everyone can identify with meetings that start late. To introduce formal systems thinking we often ask a group the question, "why do meetings start late?" and map their responses on flip chart paper using "word and arrow" diagrams. As their thinking progresses, we show how the diagram evolves to include more and more complexity and feedback loops. At some point, we might shift to using a software to represent the emerging model.

Why-Do-Meetings-Start-Late.pdf illustrates this progression from a series of hand-drawn flip charts to a series of more formal diagrams (made in Microsoft Excel using the Draw Toolbar).
This series of diagrams shows the development of a system diagram, not a "finished" model. (Even in the last diagram there is a "thought cloud" that raises a question about the completeness of the model.)
For a group that is learning about systems thinking, it is intended to show that it's "OK" (indeed, necessary) to start out small, sloppy, and poorly thoughtout, and then make changes, rethink the elements, rearrange the appearance, and so on.

QUESTIONS FOR DISCUSSION

Part-A

1. What do you understand by Knowledge Organisation?
2. How you can create a Knowledge Organisation. Explain briefly.
3. Write a brief note on Knowledge Organisation.
4. What is an ideal Knowledge Organisation? Explain in your own words.
5. Name a few sources of knowledge in an organisation and explain each of them in detail.
6. What are the functions of a Knowledge Organisation?

Part-B

1. What is a Learning Organisation?
2. What is the difference between Organisational Learning and Learning Organisation?
3. What are the three phases of learning?
4. What do you understand by 'skills needed to build Knowledge Organisations'?
5. Name a company that you have recognised as a Learning Organisation and bring its characteristics relating to learning practices.

SUGGESTED READINGS

Bartlett, Christopher A., The Knowledge-Based Organisation, in *The Knowledge Advantage* (Ruggles), 1999.

Bergeron, Bryan, *Essentials of Knowledge Management*, Wiley, 2003.

Boughzala, Imed, *Trends in Enterprise Knowledge Management*, 2008.

Frappaoli, Carl, *Knowledge Management*, Wiley, 2006.

Savage, Charles M., *5th Generation Management*, Digital Press.

WEBSITES

ABN AMRO website (Undated). *ABN AMRO Learning Organisation* URL: http://www.abnamro.com.hk/HK/Careers/Learning-O/index.htm [28th April, 2008]

ABN AMRO website (Undated). *ABN AMRO Official website* URL: http://www.abnamro.com [28th April, 2008]

ABN AMRO website (Undated). *An Opportunity for Growth* URL: http://www.future.abnamro.com/en/home.cfm [28th April, 2008]

Case Western Reserve University (2006). *Sustainability: A Core Strategy at ABN AMRO* URL: http://worldbenefit.cwru.edu/innovation/bankInnovationView.cfm?idArchive=467 [29th April, 2008]

AEGEE Europe (1998). *Learning Organisations and Organisational Learning* URL: http://www.karl.aegee.org/aeg-sci.NSF/7560fdaee30cc69bc1256368004b00e3/5132587ef21bba63c12565b100814542?OpenDocument [3rd May, 2008]

Centre for Management Research (2003). *ICMR Case Studies and Management Resources* URL: http://www.icmrindia.org/free%20resources/casestudies/ERM%20at%20ABN%20AMRO.htm [28th April, 2008]

Creative Match (2005). *ABN AMRO Implement Compliant Business Processes and Create a Flexible User Experience* URL: http://www.creativematch.co.uk/viewnews/?91435 [29th April, 2008]

Find Articles (2005). *ABN AMRO Bank Introduces Service Innovations in the Netherlands* URL: http://findarticles.com/p/articles/mi_m0EIN/is_2000_Jan_18/ai_58612625 [29th April, 2008]

IBM (2003). *ABN AMRO banks on world-class HR with IBM Business Consulting Services and PeopleSoft* URL: http://www-935.ibm.com/services/us/gbs/bus/pdf/bccee01014-abn-amro-banks-on-world-class-hr.pdf [29th April, 2008]

INFED.org (2001). *Peter Senge and The Learning Organisation* URL: http://www.infed.org/thinkers/senge.htm[27th April, 2008]

http://www.speedyadverts.com/SATopics/html/learning_organisation6.html#

CHAPTER 3

Knowledge Worker

OBJECTIVE

At the end of this lesson, you would be able to understand:

- The concept of knowledge worker.
- How to manage the knowledge worker?
- The essential personality attributes of the knowledge worker.
- Relationships between technology and the knowledge worker.
- Idea on knowledge age.
- Various hierarchies of the knowledge worker.
- Differentiate between CIO and CKO.
- Traits and behaviour required for a knowledge leader.
- How to develop a knowledge management team?

INTRODUCTION

> *Knowledge is a collective enterprise.*
> *Without it understanding is impossible.*
> *Ignorance is too often a murderous vulnerability.*
> —Jane Rule

Knowledge worker (also referred to as an intellectual worker or a brain worker) is someone who is employed due to his or her knowledge of a subject matter, rather than his ability to perform manual labour. It includes those in the information technology fields, such as computer programmers, system analysts, technical writers and so forth. The term can also refer to people outside of information technology but who are hired for their knowledge of some subject, such as lawyers, teachers and scientists. This lesson will help you understand the concept and background of the knowledge worker.

BACKGROUND

The term coined by Peter Drucker in 1959, refers to one who works primarily with information or one who develops and uses knowledge in the workplace. Due to the constant industrial growth in North America and globally, there is increasing need for an academically capable workforce. A knowledge worker's benefit to a company could be in the form of developing business intelligence, increasing the value of intellectual capital, gaining insight into customer preferences, or a variety of other important gains in knowledge that aid the business.

DEFINITION

The definition of knowledge worker has proved elusive ever since coined by Peter Drucker half a century ago. Drucker intended the term to describe a successor class to factory workers, but today we can define knowledge workers as participants in the knowledge economy. The knowledge economy suggests an economic environment where information and its manipulation are the commodity and the activity (in contrast to the industrial economy where workers produced a tangible object with raw production materials and physical goods). In reviewing the literature, several views and definitions have been proposed for the knowledge worker. Here is a representative sample:

- A knowledge worker is someone who uses IT in conducting day-to-day business and one that has a direct impact on the efficiency and productivity of the job and the work process (Award 1996).
- A knowledge worker is someone who follows a process requiring knowledge from both internal and external sources to produce a product that is distinguished by its specific information content (Kappes and Thomas 1993).
- Anyone who makes a living out of creating, manipulating, or disseminating knowledge is a knowledge worker (Bennett 2001).
- Individuals who add to a company's products and services by applying their knowledge are knowledge workers (Drucker 2001).
- A knowledge worker is anyone who works for a living at the tasks of developing or using knowledge.
- A knowledge worker knows that can actually be accomplished (Dove 1998).
- A knowledge worker is one who gathers data/information from any source; adds value to the information; and distributes value-added products to others (Kappes and Thomas 1993).
- Knowledge workers are people who use their heads more than their hands to produce value (Horibe 1999).

What is necessary for knowledge workers in the knowledge society?

Today, knowledge workers comprise a plurality of the workforce. While at the beginning of the 20th century, unskilled labour accounted for about 90% of the workforce, today that figure is closer to 20%. As a result, the knowledge workforce has become the linchpin to an organisation's success, as the world morphs into a knowledge economy. The change represents a significant challenge to managers who are accustomed to managing workers in more traditional roles. The minimum cost of tools and technologies that support these workers, estimated to be between $5,000 and $10,000 per employee per year, is growing steadily, yet most companies have failed to recognise the changes they need to make in how they conduct business.

The above question has highlighted a number of characteristics that are relevant to the effective functioning of knowledge workers in the knowledge society. At a fundamental level, the objective is to achieve the synergy of data and information processing capacity of information technologies, and the creative and innovative capacity of their human members. Hence, the knowledge workers need to be facile in the applications of new technologies to their business contexts. Such understanding is necessary so that they can delegate 'programmable' tasks to technologies to concentrate their time and efforts on value-adding activities that demand creativity and innovation. More importantly, they should have the capability of judging if the organisation's 'best practices' are aligned with the dynamics of the business environment. Such knowledge workers are the critical elements of the double loop learning and unlearning cycle that should be designed within the organisational business processes.

Of course, such creativity and inquiry-driven learning may be difficult to achieve within traditional command-and-control paradigm. As mentioned earlier, use of the information and control systems and compliance with predefined goals, objectives and best practices may not necessarily achieve organisational competence.

> *The essence of knowledge is, having it, to apply it; not having it, to confess your ignorance.*
> —Confucius

The knowledge workers would also need to have an overall understanding of the business of their organisation and how their work contexts fit within it. Such understanding is necessary for their active involvement in the organisational unlearning and relearning processes. Only if they understand the implications of changes in their work contexts for the business enterprise, can they be instrumental in synchronising the organisational 'best practices' with the external reality of the business environment.

Given the need for autonomy in learning and decision making, such knowledge workers would also need to be comfortable with self-control and self-learning. In other words, they would need to act in an entrepreneurial mode that involves a higher degree of responsibility and authority as well as capability and intelligence for handling both.

MANAGEMENT OF KNOWLEDGE WORKER

Knowledge workers are believed to produce more when empowered to make the most of their deepest skills; they can often work on many projects at the same time; they know how to allocate their time; and they can multiply the results of their efforts through soft factors such as emotional intelligence and trust. Today, without the knowledge worker, much of the business world would come to a standstill. At the same time, companies haven't yet figured out how to manage the knowledge work force, and the average company with 1000 employees loses over $12 million annually as a result.

Knowledge workers are sometimes referred to as information workers, and sometimes people argue that information workers perform more menial tasks than knowledge workers. But Drucker cited a wide spectrum of knowledge workers, ranging from the file clerk to the X-ray technologist and junior accountant, to the surgeon and engineer. Because a quick glance in the dictionary reveals that "knowledge" is defined as "specific information..." and "information" defined as "knowledge," it is better to say that there is no distinction between knowledge workers and information workers and move on.

Instead of focusing on terminology, corporate managers need to look for ways in which they can view and manage their human resources as a pool of intellectual capital—raw material for the knowledge economy. Knowledge workers spend at least 20% of their time each day searching, and the majority of those searches fail or do not provide complete results. That costs companies thousands of dollars per worker and, more significantly, delays the completion of work. Companies have yet to recognise the high cost of "lag time"— the unproductive time that represents 90% of overall knowledge processes because they provide knowledge workers with outmoded tools. In aggregate, lag time costs the corporate world about $25 billion in 2004; that figure will increase by 15% in 2005.

Organisations designed around the knowledge worker (instead of just machine capital) are thought to integrate the best of hierarchy, self-organisation and networking rather than the worst. Each dictates a different communication and rewards system, and requires activation of knowledge sharing and action learning. A basic pattern rule of human systems is that when you mix them you will get the worst of each unless you contextually and carefully attend to connecting the best.

Activities like planning and scheduling is not possible as there are different comments as:

1. Creativity cannot be scheduled.
2. Too much paperwork has to be updated.
3. People are of the view "good idea for others and not for me, as I am different".
4. There is difficulty stemming from two sources.
   a. The inherent nature of people.
   b. The planning approach.

So who is a knowledge worker?

- A knowledge worker is a person who transforms business and personal experience into knowledge.
- A knowledge worker is found to be innovative, creative and he/she is fully aware of the organisational culture.
- A knowledge worker can be thought of as a product of values, experiences, processes, education, and training.

PERSONALITY/PROFESSIONAL ATTRIBUTES

> *The seed of knowledge withers in the harsh*
> *wasteland of ignorance yet grows strong*
> *in the fertile fields of imagination.*
> —Nantala A. Lavarenlavadora

What comprises the knowledge worker? He/she is considered the intellectual capital of an organisation.

Intellectual Capital

What is Intellectual Capital? It's both organisational knowledge as well as industry knowledge. It's the ability to apply skills to complex situations, it's the cognitive knowledge through training and experience, it's the systematic understanding of cause and effects, it's knowing how the business runs, it's knowing how to avoid the minefields, it's the knowledge of how to find information; who knows it and where to get it. It's been said that the power is not knowing all things yourself but knowing where to find the information. This intellectual capital is an organisational asset along with inventory and accounts receivable. The accounting community will not let it be shown on a company's books but it's sometimes part of the "goodwill" entry when a company is acquired.

Preserving Intellectual Capital

The problem today in many organisations is employee attrition; employees retire, resign, get transferred to another department, or take a job with the competitor. Average employee turnover rate is 14.4% per year, according to the Bureau of National Affairs. These employees have knowledge about their job, the business processes, the data that supports their job, how to make things happen, and what works and what does not. Unfortunately, they have no means–or incentive–to share their knowledge. Their knowledge has not been captured, their knowledge has not been transferred or made available to others, and this knowledge is lost to the organisation. New regulations, including Sarbanes Oxley, require documentation of workflows and procedures. Global organisations have an even more demanding requirement given the differences in language, accents, culture, time zones, and communication problems like phones, videoconferencing, e-mail, conference calls, and the absence of the water cooler discussions.

HR Directors are very concerned with the employee turnover and it is discovered that it costs a company one-third of a new hire's annual salary to replace an employee. HR Directors have, therefore, been given the task to preserve the intellectual capital of their organisation and corporate officers are bound to preserve the assets of the organisation. Intellectual capital is such an asset. The challenge is to capture and leverage the knowledge, to expose it to the rest of the organisation by providing a knowledge base that is easily searched. This intellectual capital that we have identified as the knowledge worker possesses certain attributes and traits. Let us brief the same. A knowledge worker is expected to possess the following personality/professional attributes:

- Understands and adopts the organisational culture.
- Aligns personal/professional growth with corporate vision.
- Possesses the attitude of collaboration/sharing.
- Possesses innovative capacity/creative mind.
- Has got a clear understanding of the business (in which he/she is involved).
- Always willing to learn, and willing to adopt new methodologies.
- Possesses self-control and can learn by himself/herself.
- Willing to accommodate uncertainties.

From the above paragraphs, we have drawn the core competencies required for a knowledge worker. They are:

- Thinking skills
- Innovative teams/teamwork
- Continuous learning
- Innovation/Creativity
- Risk taking/Potential success
- A culture of responsibility towards knowledge
- Decisive action taking

Thinking skills

A knowledge worker is expected to possess strategic thinking skills that shed potential on the work performed or the ideas provided on the job. Strategic thinking means having a vision of how the product can be better, how the company can improve by the value-added contributions of its employees, and how continuous learning contributes to a knowledge worker's career, loyalty to the firm and satisfaction on the job. The organisational behaviour literature cites two ways of thinking: right-brained thinkers, who tend to be intuitive and non-linear in their approach to problem solving, and left-brained thinkers, who are known for logic and decision making, based on facts. For either type of thinker, the point is for the knowledge worker to stretch his or her thinking to achieve worthwhile results.

Continuous Learning

Knowledge work implies innovation through continuous learning on the job, professional seminars, and working in an environment conducive to creativity and advancement. This implies unlearning and relearning to be intone with the fast-changing business. It also means that the learning corporation must provide both the support and the funding for allowing its employees to continue to learn, in the hope that the outcome is better products or better quality service, or both. In one professional's words "learning is about working and working is about learning (Frank 2002).

Innovative teams and teamwork

As competition becomes more intense, the problems facing today's corporation become more complex, requiring innovative teamwork and joint decision making for solutions. Teamwork requires collaboration, cooperation and coordination based on a knowledge-sharing attitude and commitment to knowledge exchange. A prerequisite for successful teamwork is management support and attractive rewards, both intrinsic and extrinsic.

Innovation and Creativity

The spirit behind innovation and creativity is for knowledge workers to expand their vision and dream of a new or a different product or service for the advancement of the firm.

Risk taking and potential success

Innovation and creativity mean risk taking. Maintaining the status quo requires minimum risk, but it also breeds no change for the betterment of knowledge workers or the organisation. Like investing in stocks, the greater the chance of higher return on investment but it could also result in a greater loss. In risk taking you have to be willing to lose as much as you hope to gain. Vision, experience and seasoned knowledge enter the picture in risk taking for the forward-looking firm.

Decisive action taking

With all these factors considered, a decisive action taking means that knowledge workers should be willing to embrace professional discipline, patience and determination. Motivation is a critical factor in keeping the focus on a product or a service for the future. Analysing, choosing among alternatives, testing and the selling of change must come before final adoption.

A culture of responsibility toward knowledge

This core competency means loyalty and commitment to one's manager or leader. Knowledge workers must consistently support their leaders, their peers and the company as a whole. When a problem arises, a knowledge worker is expected to take the problem to a responsible source, discuss or brainstorm it, settle on a 'best solution' outcome, and let it go at that. This route finds no winners.

To sum up, the specific traits of a knowledge worker are:

- primarily identify themselves with their profession rather than their workplace; more sensitive to the kudos and esteem they receive from their peers than what they receive from the management.
- highly mobile and quick in changing jobs.
- driven primarily by the pride of accomplishment.
- have strong beliefs and personalities; they respond much better to being pulled than being pushed.
- informal networking with peers, inside and outside their own company, helps them benchmark their personal efforts and their company's competitiveness.

Expectation from the bottom line knowledge workers

An individual knowledge worker's effectiveness is based on results and credibility, perceived reputation, and network of relationships rather than formal authority, job description, or position in the hierarchy.

Team Knowledge:

> *Integrity without knowledge is weak and useless,*
> *and knowledge without integrity is dangerous and dreadful.*
> —Samuel Johnson

Team knowledge and the socialisation of team knowledge requires the integration of different minds. Knowledge builds off of other knowledge; it is cumulative. One thought or idea is built from preceding thoughts or ideas. The internet and computing technology offers many vehicles for the socialisation of knowledge:

- Groupware and collaborative software
- Wikis
- Portals
- Threaded conversations
- E-mail lists
- Online chats
- Social networking
- Concept maps (C-Maps) and mind maps

Exibit 3.1   Silicon Valley Incorporated

Silicon Valley Incorporated—A Virtual Company

Silicon Valley is often characterised as a community where people really don't work for individual firms—everyone works for a virtual company: Silicon Valley Incorporated. "Skills are both so abundant and in such demand that most people could quickly contribute at several Valley firms." A unique Valley norm is that when you are facing a really tough problem, you may contact anyone who may help, regardless of where they work, even if they work for competitors. "The inducements that companies have historically used to secure loyalty have lost their clout; compensation and benefit party is essential to get people through from the door, but it won't be sufficient to retain them."

Flat and Participative Management Structures

Organisational and management structures in Silicon Valley firms are flat and participative. In the meeting rooms at most Silicon Valley companies, the mix of people, expertise, and ages is striking. More importantly, the degree of candour is tremendous. You don't expect to find such level of frankness in hierarchical companies.

In more direct cultures, such as Intel or Sun Microsystems, you can easily witness an intense argument between a senior executive and an entry-level engineer. Status and seniority aren't based on age or position; they're based on what you know and can deliver.

The Collective Power of Passion

Silicon Valley leaders recognise the value of passion and continually try to evoke, rather than mute, people' passions. Once evoked, the passion is tough to control. It can result in a series of 20-hour workdays, fun and pranks. The passion to go well beyond the extra mile is what drives people to create insanely great products and services.

The spirit and passion of Silicon Valley is best seen at the extremes of the workdays. "Flex time" means that there's no time when people aren't willing to probe and test new opportunities.

Idea Evaluation: "The Five Minute Rule"

Several firms in Silicon Valley have installed a "five minute rule." The rule permits anyone to suggest an idea. Then for the first five minutes after the idea is expressed only positive comments can be made. By the time the idea is talked about for five minutes it has usually spun into an impromptu brainstorm session that cultivates truly great ideas and some form of the discussion is often implemented.

Practicing New Approaches

You cannot lead knowledge workers by telling them what to do. You must treat them with respect and dignity, and provide opportunities that they would not be able to have on their own.
To lead knowledge workers effectively and unlock their true potential, you need to define:

- What knowledge work professionals do?
- How they do it best?
- What drives them to do it?

Meeting specific requirements of knowledge workers

- Consider and treat them as professional partners
- Respect their expertise, support them in its application, and help them extend it further
- Give them influence in decisions that determine where and how their expertise is applied to specific innovation initiatives, as well as how it contributes to the overall business strategy. A better example could be provided from a company which is given below in Exibit 3.1.

TECHNOLOGY AND KNOWLEDGE WORKER

IT plays a pivotal role in the Learning Organisation.
IT supports and speeds up many functions of a knowledge
worker effectively and efficiently.

- The primary activities of knowledge work:
  - Assessment
  - Decision making
  - Monitoring
  - Scheduling
- A knowledge worker can act as a manager, a supervisor, or a clerk who is actively engaged in thinking, information processing, analysing, creating, or recommending procedures based on experience and cumulative knowledge.
- IT plays a key role in the Learning Organisation in the following processes:
  - Knowledge capture
  - Information distribution
  - Information interpretation
- There exists a multitude of equipment and software supporting knowledge worker's tasks. They include:
  - E-mail
  - LAN
  - Intelligent workstations
- Intelligent workstations automate repetitive and tedious tasks. They should perform the following functions:
  - Administrative support functions
  - Personal computing functions
  - Managing intelligent databases

THE KNOWLEDGE AGE

The third wave of human socio-economic development is described by Charles Savage in "Fifth Generation Management." The first wave was the Agricultural Age with wealth defined as ownership of land. Some views of the leaders in IT field are given in Exibit 3.2.

In the second wave, the Industrial Age, wealth was based on ownership of capital, i.e., factories. In the Knowledge Age, wealth is based upon the ownership of knowledge and the ability to use that knowledge to create or improve goods and services. Product improvements include cost, durability, suitability, timeliness of delivery, and security.

Information Literate Knowledge Worker

Information Literate Knowledge Workers are able to conduct a number of activities that are unclear in their benefit to an outsider, but are extremely valuable to the overall success of a business. They have the ability to use the best sources to gain the information they need, which are both accurate and current. Next, with the data on hand they excel at extracting the key information, comprehending it, and then manipulating it to provide the organisation the greatest benefit possible.

Exibit 3.2   View of Knowledge Leaders

Views from leaders-The importance of the knowledge worker is not lost on IT industry leaders. "Today, the knowledge worker who makes a difference is less a knower than a learner and applier," notes Mike Wing, IBM's VP for strategy (ibm.com). "We should be long past congratulating ourselves for the simple epiphany that intellectual capital is better than physical capital. The key now is innovation…Yes, it's important to have a unique, differentiating expertise."

According to Anne M. Mulcahy, Chairman and CEO, Xerox, "In every enterprise, there are workers who are thinking up of better ways to capture, manage and deliver information and knowledge. These knowledge workers hold the key to growth and productivity in today's information-driven business world. Now more than ever, they need solutions and services that streamline the way knowledge flows through the workplace."

"Today's competitive environment requires the ability to comprehend and manage vast amounts of information from multiple sources," said Clare Hart, President and CEO of Factiva. "It's not surprising that the knowledge worker is Basex's Person of the Year, recognising the criticality of this role, and the systems that support it, to the success of the enterprise. As a result, smart companies are employing technologies that enable their employees to make better decisions, faster."

"The move to a knowledge-based economy presents companies that recognise this early on with a tremendous competitive advantage," said Andy Mattes, President and CEO of Siemens Communications.

Jeff Raikes, Microsoft Group VP, Information Worker Business, observed that there "is a global change happening in the way we work—a need to be more responsive and more connected to people and information, and a move away from the desk, the office and traditional hours. In today's environment, information workers have more options on how and when they work, and access to more tools to meet their work needs than ever before.

An example of an Information Literate Knowledge Worker is an analyst given the task of developing a database of companies that fit the target customer profile of the business. The analyst must perform data mining for information by using sources such as websites, print and professional associations. The best sources must be used, and only the pertinent information taken, so that maximum efficiency is achieved. In order to produce an acceptable final product, the analyst must be able to define the information that is accurate and current, against that which is not, so that the database provides the greatest advantage to the organisation. Finally, the analyst must be able to explain the information that has been compiled so that the end-users of the database can employ it effectively.

Technology Literate Knowledge Worker

A Technology Literate Knowledge Worker is educated when it comes to the correct applications of technology. The individual understands what type of technology best suits the company by knowing the technology available and weighing the benefits of each option before making the final decision. The worker is also aware that there must be adequate technological infrastructure in order for the product to work effectively. The worker's most important ability is the knowledge of when to apply technology. If the Technology Literate Knowledge Worker applies technology at the correct time it can make, or save the organisation a significant amount, while using technology when it isn't needed can be costly.

An example of a Technology Literate Worker is a database administrator who is responsible for ensuring that the databases are functioning properly, while attempting to maximize the databases' value to the organisation. The database administrator must incorporate a database management system that is compatible with the company's existing systems and goals. Their primary objective is to maintain a system that is effective and efficient, while keeping it easy to operate. They are also given the task of remaining current with the new technologies available, so that any opportunity to improve the company's technology can be capitalised on immediately.

HIERARCHY OF KNOWLEDGE WORK

Knowledge work ranges from tasks performed by individual knowledge workers to global social networks. This framework spans every class of knowledge work that is being or is likely to be undertaken. There are seven levels or scales of knowledge work.

- Knowledge work (e.g., writing, analysing, advising) is performed by subject matter specialists in all areas of an organisation. Although knowledge work began with the origins of writing and counting, it was first identified as a category of work by Drucker (1973).
- Knowledge functions (e.g., capturing, organising, and providing access to knowledge) are performed by technical staff, to support knowledge processes projects. Knowledge functions date from c. 450 BC, with the library of Alexandria, but their modern roots can be linked to the emergence of information management in the 1970s (Mcgee and Prusak, 1993).
- Knowledge processes (preserving, sharing, and integration) are performed by professional groups, as part of a knowledge management programme. Knowledge processes have evolved in concert with general-purpose technologies, such as the printing press, mail delivery, the telegraph, telephone networks, and the internet (Mumford, 1961).

■ Knowledge management programmes link the generation of knowledge (e.g., from science, synthesis, or learning) with its use (e.g., policy analysis, reporting, programme management) as well as facilitating organisational learning and adaptation in a knowledge organisation. Knowledge management emerged as a discipline in the 1990s (Leonard, 1995).

■ Knowledge organisations transfer outputs (content, products, services, and solutions), in the form of knowledge services, to enable external use. The concept of knowledge organisations emerged in the 1990s (Davenport and Prusak, 1998).

■ Knowledge services support other organisational services, yield sector outcomes, and result in benefits for citizens in the context of knowledge markets. Knowledge services emerged as a subject in the 2000s. (Simard et al., 2007).

■ Social networks enable knowledge organisations to co-produce knowledge outputs by leveraging their internal capacity with massive social networks. Social networking emerged in the 2000s (Tapscott and Williams, 2007).

The hierarchy ranges from the effort of individual specialists, through technical activity, professional projects, and management programmes, to organisational strategy, knowledge markets, and global-scale networking.

This framework is useful for positioning the myriad types of knowledge work relative to each other and within the context of organisations, markets, and global economies. It also provides a useful context for planning, developing, and implementing knowledge management projects as well as positioning organisations to participate in the global network economy.

Maslow and the Knowledge Worker Revolution

One of the best known theories explaining the actions of people is that of Dr. Abraham Maslow *(Motivation and Personality,* Harper and Row, New York, 1954). Dr. Maslow hypothesized that people are motivated by a hierarchy of needs. The hierarchy he described may be drawn as follows:

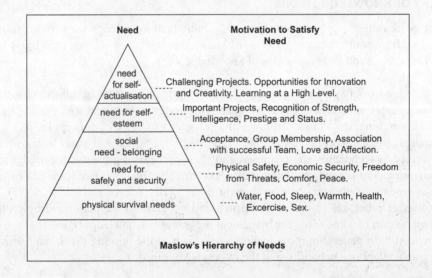

Maslow's Hierarchy of Needs

Why Knowledge Workers happen now but not before?

Despite not being publicised or realised, KW existed long time ago. However, most of the KWs only exist in their later years of career where on job information obtained from experiences the only is sufficient to be turned to knowledge. Furthermore, individuals' characteristics are also important where some individuals might not communicate or make use of their knowledge, therefore being insignificant from normal workers.

Internet has revolutionised the way we work and live. Information is readily available in a very affordable and convenient way. Therefore, the upcoming generation of workers will be divided into two different groups. The first group is the one in which workers will be tempted to the ease of plagiarism and copying of information to complete their work (in which is not KW). The second group is that in which our workers draw information from their findings and will turn it to knowledge to be applied to their work.

Both the groups are quite similar and from a glance you would not be able to differentiate them. However, it will be known once workers are being questioned on their works.

Obstacles towards the New Workforce

The process of information transformation to knowledge can only occur effectively when all information is in one language. Otherwise, translation will introduce overhead to the model.

In the current environment, language is one of the major barriers. Most current 'mass-produced' graduates do not possess a good command over English even though they have graduated in universities or colleges from overseas.

Other obstacles are as below:

1. Not having good presentation or communication skills.
2. Do not have good knowledge of high productivity tools (word processing, presentation or multimedia application, diagramming tools).
3. Information or Knowledge overload–have a way to do mind-mapping.

How to start preparing yourself to be a Knowledge Worker?

The expectations of having the luxury of 9 to 5 jobs should be avoided and one should be more task-oriented / focused.

KNOWLEDGE CAREERS

To accept the global standards and develop continuously corresponds directly to the availability of opportunities like revenue potential, growth and technology advancements. When the KM field is expanding, organisations depend on knowledge workers to identify ideas, generate them and to manage both the tacit and explicit knowledge.

When a company goes global with its first product or service, then comes the opportunity for KM business. KM basically supports the business process through wining customers and retaining business in the value chain and winning back the clients from severe competition.

KM provides opportunities through cohesive and purposeful application of an integrated collection of sound principles and practices than other disciplines.

In the beginning those who transferred knowledge and information were called KM Initiatives. The KM Initiatives include Schools, Libraries and Trainees. According to this the librarians and teachers were classified as knowledge managers. Now the list has expanded to include professions like CKOs, Knowledge Engineers and Knowledge Controllers. The major focus for knowledge professionals is in the following areas:

- Knowledge and Innovation specialists
- Knowledge Management
- Knowledge Cataloguers, Researchers, Librarians and
- Knowledge and Competitive Intelligence Professionals
- Knowledge Facilitators, Trainers and Educators
- Knowledge Strategists
- Knowledge Linked with Technology and Expert Systems

NEW KNOWLEDGE MANAGEMENT ROLES

Traditional roles do not cater to the KM needs of the cross-functional processes where huge amount of knowledge is created, shared and applied. Organisations need to have a visionary role and a CKO is needed to handle these roles. Some organisations form expert centres to generate the body of knowledge. Some of the new roles that are created in knowledge organisations are listed below in the hierarchical order in Exibit 3.3.

DIFFERENCE BETWEEN CHIEF INFORMATION OFFICER (CIO) AND CHIEF KNOWLEDGE OFFICER (CKO)

> *Knowledge is power. Information is power.*
> *The secreting or hoarding of knowledge or information*
> *may be an act of tyranny camouflaged as humility.*
> —Robin Morgan

The following are some of the CIO responsibilities identified in general. The Clinger-Cohen Act of 1996 created the Chief Information Officer position and assigns to the CIO these responsibilities:

1. Provide advice and assistance to senior managers on IT acquisition and management.
2. Develop, maintain, and facilitate implementation of a sound and integrated IT architecture.
3. Promote effective and efficient design and operation of all major IRM processes for the agency, including improvements to work processes.

In addition, this position has primary duties annually, as part of the strategic planning process:

a. to assess requirements for personnel regarding knowledge and skills needed to achieve performance goals that have been established for IRM,
b. to assess the extent to which all managers at the agency meet those requirements,
c. to develop strategies and specific plans for hiring and training,
d. to report to the division head on progress made in improving IRM capability.

Exibit 3.3   Different Knowledge Management Roles

Managerial

1. Chief Learning Officers
2. Chief Knowledge Officers
3. Knowledge Managers
4. Knowledge Initiative Managers
5. Knowledge Management Experts
6. Knowledge Transfer Experts
7. Knowledge Engineers
8. Knowledge Foot Soldiers
9. Knowledge Strategists

Technical

1. Knowledge Analysts
2. Knowledge Mapping Specialists
3. Knowledge Content Creators
4. Knowledge-Base Architects and Administrators

Non-Management

1. Cybrarians
2. Librarians
3. Information Brokers

The Federal CIO Council has defined ten competency areas for the CIO. Although it is simply a list, these areas are commonly illustrated in the form of the 'CIO Wheel' given in Figure 3.1. Some of the other duties identified are as follows:

The CIO has to ensure that the money for acquiring and managing IT work is spent wisely. He has to justify the money spent with reference to the business cases. He has to follow a methodology based on best practices. He has to adhere to certain standards.

He has to identify the business so that IS/IT goals come first. He has to give preference to Information Technology (IT) so that IT work maps to the business mission. IT work must start with user requirements and end with measurable improvement and IT work must lead to business process improvement.

Improve business processes by providing quality information to actors and reducing data entry effort. His priority is to see that data is kept secured.

The CIO has to assure interoperability through the following standards. Maintain a comprehensive IT architecture repository. Study best practices for information resources management and train people in them. Also he needs to plan for the incremental development of IT and offer modular contracts. He also needs to look into the sharing of data processing projects and resources to

Fig. 3.1   CIO Wheel of Competencies

accomplish shared missions. Make a business case for IT work to be done. Identify and manage IT risks. He has to maintain the skills and capabilities to manage information resources. For a better understanding let us look into the job description of Chief Knowledge Officer.

Chief Knowledge Officer Job Description

The role of the Chief Knowledge Officer (CKO) is to maximise the creation, discovery, and dissemination of knowledge in the organisation. The CKO blends cultural, business and technical responsibilities and ensures their co-evolution. The CKO focuses on improving productivity, profitability and customer value, rather than solely on knowledge management (KM) technology. The CKO drives the adoption of knowledge use in the organisation. The CKO usually reports to the CEO or the highest-ranking position in the company.

The performance of a CKO can be tied to his/her progress in many areas, such as increasing revenue, increasing corporate education and learning, and/or establishing and reusing best practices, increasing efficiency, and retaining employees.

The CKO position would comprise, but would not be limited to the following responsibilities:

- Create and sell the knowledge management vision.
- Communicate commitment to KM and strategy for KM to shareholders—articulate how establishing knowledge, as a true corporate asset, will benefit the business.
- Build a customer-centred KM operation and include customers as knowledge partners.
- Design and implement a knowledge-learning culture and a knowledge-learning infrastructure.

■ Align and integrate diverse groups and functions in order to leverage knowledge management strategically across the entire corporation.

■ Provide guidance and policy on processes to "institutionalise" KM practices.

■ Develop strategies to make tacit knowledge explicit—tie together the information in the corporation's databases, historical records, file cabinets, and intranet, as well as employee's information knowledge that has yet to be identified or recorded in a systematic way.

■ Champion development of a KM budget and advocate and dedicate KM resources to ongoing initiatives.

■ Develop the measurements and standards to ensure compliance, to support continuous quantifiable productivity of knowledge efforts and to determine their strategic outcomes.

■ Use technology to support knowledge capture, sharing, and retention.

■ Keep abreast of the organisation's core business and departmental functions policies, procedures and business practices.

■ Understand the benefits that technology can offer, but should also focus as much, if not more, on changing the corporate culture to one that embraces and rewards knowledge sharing.

■ Expertise in several areas, including: training and development, information technology, legal and technical knowledge, and corporate information.

Experience in one or more disciplines such as management consulting, training specialist, technology expert, organisational development (OD), general management, or any one of many other business unit disciplines.

Designing the Knowledge Management Team

In the fifth step on the KM road map, you form the KM team that will design, build, implement, and deploy your company's KM system. To design an effective KM team, you must identify key stakeholders both within and outside your company; identify sources of expertise that are needed to design, build, and deploy the system successfully while balancing the technical and managerial requirements. We examine the issues of correctly sizing the KM team, managing diverse and often divergent stakeholder expectations, and using techniques for identifying critical failure points in such teams.

THE ROLE OF KNOWLEDGE DEVELOPERS

The knowledge developer is the architect of the knowledge system. He must identify the problem domain, spend more time in capturing knowledge and should coordinate the entire report or project.

The main attributes of a knowledge developer are:

1. Good communication skills.
2. Ability to capture knowledge.
3. Ability to work as a team.
4. Tolerance for fear of the unknown.
5. Ability to interact with knowledge workers in the organisation, and
6. His / her thinking process must be conceptual.

SUMMING UP

The term 'Knowledge Worker' coined by Peter Drucker in 1959, means one who works primarily with information or one who develops and uses knowledge in the workplace. Knowledge workers are believed to produce more when empowered to make the most of their deepest skills; they can often work on many projects at the same time; they know how to allocate their time; and they can multiply the results of their efforts through soft factors such as emotional intelligence and trust.

Knowledge work ranges from tasks performed by individual knowledge workers to global social networks. This framework spans every class of knowledge work that is being or is likely to be undertaken.

Few personality traits of knowledge workers are like understanding and adopting the organisational culture, aligning personal/professional growth with corporate vision, possessing the attitude of collaboration/sharing, possessing innovative capacity/creative mind, etc.

CASE

Jon Healey is a member of the editorial board at the *Los Angeles Times*.

On a warm April afternoon outside Detonation Media's headquarters in Mountain View, California, a couple dozen members of the Software Engineers Guild marched in protest, toting signs that likened the company's management to the blood-soaked villains of the video games that had spurred Detonation's growth. Though the programmers were well paid, their deadline-driven, round-the-clock coding marathons made for very brief careers. Of Detonation's 10,000 total employees, nearly half belonged to the SEG and had been working without a contract for three months. Adding to the labour-management tensions were the layoffs that had hit the gaming industry in waves since late 2008, fuelling rumours of potential cutbacks at Detonation.

Most of the programmers, however, remained at their computers. *Couch Ninjas 2,* the new title by star developer Tetsui Wakatanabe, was weeks behind schedule. Though Tetsui hadn't thought much about the contract talks, the discord lurked at the back of his mind. A strike would prevent his team from working on *Couch Ninjas 2,* but it wouldn't stop Detonation from completing the job with non-union programmers—and he was determined to see the project through to completion.

Fighting for the Spoils

Two months later, Carol Lee, Detonation's general counsel and lead negotiator, wandered around the vast show floor of the E3 expo in Los Angeles, thinking about a couple of internal reports she'd recently read. The first asserted that Detonation's revenue from internet games would be negligible for at least the next three years, a conclusion that seemed at odds with the profusion of games offered at the expo this year. The second report provided hard evidence that the sour economy was finally hurting the supposedly recession-proof video game sector. For example, one of Detonation's top rivals, GameCrack Software, had just laid off more than 10% of its workforce.

For the umpteenth time, Carol reviewed the three-year deal that Detonation had proposed to SEG last December. Though the company had offered to boost pay and benefits 5% annually, talks had stalled over Detonation's desire to transition the SEG from revenue sharing to profit sharing and the guild's demand to extend its jurisdiction to games made for the internet as well as those for PCs and consoles.

Carol's Blackberry buzzed. It was Detonation's CEO, Emilio Teti, who suggested starting up negotiations again, but this time taking the pay raise off the table in light of GameCrack's layoffs.

"The raise is the least of our problems," said Carol.

"Tell me about it," said Emilio, pointing out that the company's stock had traded sharply lower that day and that the latest sales figures showed the company down year over year. "But maybe the economy gives us some leverage."

Carol agreed to try to restart the negotiations.

The Soundstage and the Fury

Early in July, Carol stood in a soundstage watching Tetsui redo the motion capture for *Couch Ninjas 2*. Scanning the room, she noticed some of Detonation's most senior programmers gathered along a back wall, caucusing with Dan Hontz, a coder who was on the SEG negotiating committee. The contract stalemate had worsened a rift in the guild between hardliners, who dominated the negotiating committee, and pragmatists like Dan, who were eager to claim the raises that the company had offered late last year. Noting the vehement body language, Carol wondered whether the action at the back of the room might signal an impending coup.

Sure enough, she saw Dan huddling later with Tetsui. Pulling Dan aside, Carol remarked, "You know, the way the market is going, the company's offer is looking less tenable by the day. Are you ready to come back to the table?"

"It's not my call," said Dan, but he conceded that things had dragged on way too long.

New Cast, Same Story

Three days later, both sides met in a conference room of the Crowne Plaza Hotel for the first formal talks since the contract had lapsed. Over the weekend Dan had become the lead negotiator, and he was unnerved that Carol hardly seemed surprised at the change. He hoped she didn't also know about Tetsui's recent ultimatum: that at the drop of a picket sign, he would leave to start his own non-union internet game development shop—and lift out the *Couch Ninjas* team to staff it.

Dan started things off by announcing that SEG members were ready to give up their demand for accelerated revenue sharing. "But we don't want to shift to profit sharing," he said, "and we still want jurisdiction over high-budget games made for the internet."

"Dan, neither of those terms is acceptable," Carol responded. "The downturn is decimating sales! In fact, we're now offering pay increases of 2% in the first year, then 4% and 5% in the second and third years. And no retroactivity."

Dan looked startled. "The members won't accept that, Carol! Detonation needs *Couch Ninjas 2*. That means it needs Tetsui. And he's with us." (He chose not to mention Tetsui's threat.)

The talks ground to a halt once again.

Spoiling for a Fight

The next morning, Carol made her pitch to Emilio about a modified negotiating strategy. "It wouldn't hurt Detonation to give a little ground on internet jurisdiction," she ventured, "as long as we get the compensation provisions right. Plus, I'm confident that SEG will go for a shift from revenue sharing to profit sharing soon."

"Hey, I leave the strategy up to you," said Emilio, "but I think you ought to just declare a last, best, and final offer—no further concessions. The guild's a mess! If we play hardball, they'll have another power struggle and lose more members. And we'll keep paying last year's rates, plus buy time to find new developers offshore. What's not to like?"

Though Carol was a little staggered by her boss's take-no-prisoners zeal, she wondered how hard she could push the guild without triggering a strike. On the flip side, what minor concessions could she offer that might yield a deal saving both Detonation's numbers and its freedom to manoeuvre online?

Carol asked Emilio whether she had any wiggle room to build the raises back up closer to the original offer.

He grimaced. "We could afford it—just barely—but Wall Street will kill us if we don't win more givebacks."

"They'll also punish us if SEG walks out," she said.

He laughed. "No chance of that in this economy. They'd be insane."

"You have no idea, Emilio. Who knows how long they could hold out? They live on ramen and Red Bull."

Should Detonation Media blow up or make nice with the SEG?

KEYWORDS

Knowledge Worker: Knowledge worker (also referred to as intellectual worker or brain worker) is someone who is employed due to his or her knowledge of a subject matter, rather than their ability to perform manual labour.

Knowledge Age: In the Knowledge Age, wealth is based upon the ownership of knowledge and the ability to use that knowledge to create or improve goods and services. Product improvements include cost, durability, suitability, timeliness of delivery, and security.

LAN: Local area network. A type of network. There are other two types of networks, namely, MAN, WAN.

IT: Automated data processing resources, including applications, databases, technologies and everything needed for IS development and IT operations.

IT Architecture: An integrated framework for evolving/maintaining/acquiring IT to achieve strategic and information resources management goals.

Chief Knowledge Officers: The chief knowledge officer is responsible for creating the vision of what is possible and designing the framework for realising the results.

INDIVIDUAL ASSIGNMENT

(a) "High attrition rate of knowledge worker is a threat for knowledge organisation"—Explain.
(b) The Knowledge Workers' Strike

The case given here is a fictional case study and considers how much influence employee unions can exert on companies' decisions in today's down economy. Traditionally, just three experts are invited to comment on the case. Make the class an interactive session, and contribute your own solution.

The case study by Jon Healey is adapted from "The Knowledge Workers' Strike", the July—August 2009 *Harvard Business Review*.

EXERCISE

1. Collect information on the job description of the CKO. Find out what percentage of firms with KM initiatives have CKOs and what are their duties and responsibilities.

GROUP ASSIGNMENT

Divide the class into two teams and provide a scenario that provokes a genuine learning for a knowledge engineer based on the job description of knowledge engineers.

QUESTIONS FOR DISCUSSION

Part A

1. What do you understand by the term 'knowledge worker'? Explain in your own words.
2. Explain the Peter Drucker's view on "knowledge worker".
3. Describe the personality attributes of a knowledge worker.
4. Explain briefly the relationships between technology and knowledge worker.
5. Explain the concept of hierarchy of knowledge worker in detail.
6. What are the different roles played by knowledge workers?
7. Identify the role of knowledge workers and knowledge developers with examples.
8. Enumerate the attributes of knowledge developer.
9. In what way did the knowledge system affect the relationships between knowledge workers in the organisation?

SUGGESTED READINGS

Alan Liu. The Laws of Cool: Knowledge Work and the Culture of Information, University of Chicago Press, 2004.

Davenport, Thomas H. and Laurence Prusak, *Working Knowledge*, Harvard Business School Press Boston, MA, 1998.

Drucker, Peter F., Management: Tasks, Responsibilities, Practices. Harper & Row, New York, 1973.

Sheridan, William. How to Think Like a Knowledge Worker, United Nations Public Administration Network, New York, 2008.

WEBSITES

University of Wolverhampton (2002). *A Review of the Concept of Organisational Learning* URL: http://www.wlv.ac.uk/PDF/uwbs_WP004_02_Wang_Ahmed.pdf [27th April, 2008]

1000Ventures.com (Undated). Learning Organisation—*Converting Learning by the People Within Your Organisation into Learning by the Organisation Itself* URL: http://www.1000ventures.com/business_guide/im_learning_org.html [27th April, 2008]

http://cio.ittoo

lbox.com/groups/strategy-planning/it-portfolio-management-sp/

http://www.pateo.com/art6pf.html

The University of Edinburgh (Undated). *Learning Organisation—The Definition* URL:http://www.see.ed.ac.uk/~gerard/MENG/MEAB/learning_organisation/definition.html [27th April, 2008]

Pearn, M. (1997). A question of survival, in Royal Society of Arts, For Life—A vision of learning for the 21st century, London

The Ohio State University (1995). *The Learning Organisation: Myths and Realities* URL: http://www.cete.org/acve/docgen.asp?tbl=archive&ID=A028 [27th April, 2008]

CHAPTER 4

Knowledge Management System
Life Cycle (KMSLC)

OBJECTIVE

At the end of this lesson, you would be able to understand:

- The concept of KMSLC.
- Evaluation of existing infrastructure.
- How to Form a KM Team?
- Designing the KM Blueprint.
- Testing the KM System.
- Implementing the KM System.
- Practice Quality Assurance.
- Identify the Training Users.
- How to Manage Change?
- And the Post System Evaluation.

INTRODUCTION

> We have a hunger of the mind which asks for knowledge of all around us,
> and the more we gain, the more is our desire, the more we see,
> the more we are capable of seeing.
> —Maria Mitchell

The building of knowledge management can be viewed as a life cycle that begins with a master plan and justification and ends with a system structured to meet KM requirements for the entire company. The life cycle begins when a Knowledge Management System is determined to be doable, affordable and practicable with value added for company profitability and growth. This lesson will help you to understand the KMSLC in depth.

EVALUATING THE EXISTING INFRASTRUCTURE

The basis of KM System is satisfying a need for improving the productivity and potential of employees and the company as a whole. To do so, we need to gain familiarity with various components making up the KM strategy and supporting technology. Identifying and evaluating the current knowledge environment makes it easier to point out the critical missing gaps and justify the formation of a new KM environment. The psychology behind evaluating the current knowledge infrastructure is giving the perception that the current way of doing things is not conveniently abandoned in preference for brand new systems.

The following diagram 4.1 depicts the stages in Knowledge Management System Life Cycle (KMSLC).

KM Systems are developed in order to satisfy the need for improving productivity and potential of employees and the company as a whole. The existing knowledge infrastructure is evaluated so that it can give the perception that the present ways of doing things are not just abandoned in preference for a new system.

> *The learning and knowledge that we have, is, at the most,*
> *but little compared with that of which we are ignorant.*
>
> —Plato

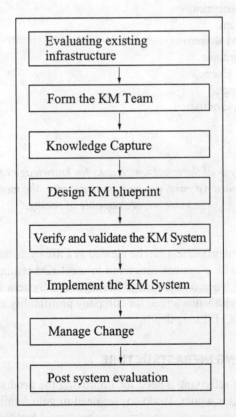

Fig. 4.1 Stages in Knowledge Management System Life Cycle

System Justification: It involves answers to the following questions:

- Is existing knowledge going to be lost through retirement, transfer, or departure to other organisations?
- Is the proposed KM system needed in multiple locations?
- Are experts available and willing to support the building of the proposed KM system?
- Does the concerned problem need years of proper experience and cognitive reasoning to solve?
- While undergoing knowledge capture, would it be possible for the expert to articulate how the problem will be solved?
- How critical is the knowledge that is to be captured?
- Are the involved tasks non-algorithmic in nature?
- Would it possible to find a champion within the organisation?

Scoping: The term scoping means limiting the breadth and depth of the project within the financial, human resource, and operational constraints.

Feasibility: Feasibility study involves addressing the following questions:

- Is it possible to complete the project within the expected timeframe?
- Is the project affordable?
- Is the project appropriate?
- How frequently the system would be consulted and at what associated cost?

The traditional approach used to conduct a feasibility study can be used for building a KM system. This involves the following tasks:

- Forming a knowledge management team.
- Preparing a master plan.
- Performing cost/benefit analysis of the proposed system.
- Quantifying system criteria and costs.

User Support

- Is the proposed user aware of the fact that the new KM system is being developed? How is it perceived?
- How much involvement can be expected from the user while the building process continues?
- What type of users' training will be needed when the proposed system is up and running?
- What kind of operational support should be provided?

Role of Strategic Planning

- As a consequence of evaluating the existing infrastructure, the concerned organisation should develop a strategic plan which should aim at advancing the objectives of the organisation with the proposed KM system in mind.

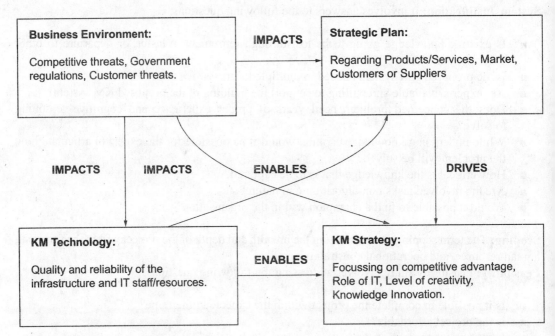

Fig. 4.2 Matching business strategies with KM strategies. (*Source*: Elias M. Awad, Hassan M. Ghaziri, Knowledge Management, Pearson Education Inc., Prentice Hall, 2005).

- Areas to be considered:
  - Vision
  - Resources
  - Culture

FORMING A KM TEAM

Forming a KM team usually means

- Identifying the key units, branches, and divisions, etc. as the key stakeholders in the prospective KM system.
- Strategically, technically, and organisationally balancing the team size and competency.

Factors impacting team success:

- Quality and capability of team members (in terms of personality, experience, and communication skill).
- Size of the team.
- Complexity of the project.
- Team motivation and leadership.
- Promising only that what can be actually delivered.

Capturing Knowledge

> *Children love to be alone, because alone is where they know themselves,*
> *and where they dream*
> — Roger Rosenblatt

- Capturing knowledge involves extracting, analysing and interpreting the concerned knowledge that a human expert uses to solve a specific problem.
- Explicit knowledge is usually captured in repositories from appropriate documentation, files, etc.
- Tacit knowledge is usually captured from experts, and from an organisation's stored database(s).
- Interviewing is one of the most popular methods used to capture knowledge.
- Data mining is also useful in terms of using intelligent agents who may analyse the data warehouse and come up with new findings.
- In KM Systems development, the knowledge developer acquires the necessary heuristic knowledge from experts for building the appropriate knowledge base.
- Knowledge capture and knowledge transfer are often carried out through teams.
- Knowledge capture includes determining feasibility, choosing the appropriate expert, tapping the expert's knowledge, retapping knowledge to plug the gaps in the system, and verify/validate the knowledge base.

CHALLENGES IN KM SYSTEMS DEVELOPMENT

There are four main challenges in KM systems development:
1. Changing Organisational Culture
2. Knowledge Evaluation
3. Knowledge Processing
4. Knowledge Implementation

1. Changing Organisational Culture involves changing an individual's attitude and behaviour.
2. Knowledge Evaluation involves the assessing of the worth of information (where and how many publications it had gone, etc.)
3. Identification of techniques to acquire, store, process and distribute information involves Knowledge Processing.
4. What is Knowledge Implementation?
5. Once when an orgnisation learns, commits to change and innovates, then the knowledge is implemented. It is a must to extract as much information as may have an impact on specific tasks. Lastly, lessons learned from feedback can be stored for the future to help others who are facing the same situation.

Let us look into a few stages of Conventional Systems Life Cycle and KM System Life Cycle. Figure 4.3 gives a clear differentiation of both the systems.

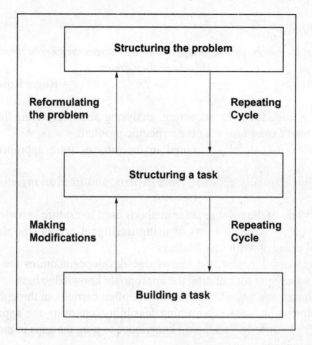

Fig. 4.3   An Overview of Rapid Prototyping

Key Differences

1. The systems analyst gathers data and information from the users and the users depend on analysts for the solution.
2. The knowledge developer gathers knowledge from people with known knowledge and the developer depends on them for the solution.
3. The main interface for the systems analyst is associated with novice users who know the problem but not the solution.
4. The main interface for the knowledge developer is associated with the knowledgeable person who knows the problem and the solution.
5. Conventional systems development is primarily sequential, whereas KMSLC is incremental and interactive.
6. In case of conventional systems, testing is usually done towards the end of the cycle (after the system has been built), whereas in KMSLC, the evolving system is verified and validated from the beginning of the cycle.
7. Systems development and systems management is much more extensive for conventional information systems than it is for KMSLC.
8. The conventional systems life cycle is usually process-driven and documentation-oriented whereas KMSLC is result-oriented.
9. The conventional systems development does not support tools such as rapid prototyping since it follows a predefined sequence of steps.
10. KMSLC can use rapid prototyping incorporating changes on the spot.

ATTRIBUTES	USER	EXPERT
Dependence on System	High	Low
Ambiguity Tolerance	Low	High
Cooperation	Required	Not Required
Knowledge about the problem	High	Average
User of the System	Yes	No
Contribution	Information	Expertise/Knowledge
Availability	Yes, Readily available	No, not readily available

Fig. 4.4 A Comparison between Users and Experts

Key Similarities

- Both the system cycles start with a problem and end with a solution.
- The early phase in case of conventional systems development life cycle starts with information gathering. In KMSLC the early phase needs knowledge capture.
- Verification and validation of the conventional systems testing is similar to KM system.
- In both the systems, analyst and the knowledge developer need to choose the appropriate tools for designing their intended systems. A brief overview of both users and experts along with their attributes are listed in Figure 4.5.

Role of Rapid Prototyping

- In most cases, knowledge developers use iterative approach for capturing knowledge.
- For example, the knowledge developer may start with a prototype (based on the somehow limited knowledge captured from the expert during the first few sessions).
- The following can turn the approach into rapid prototyping:
  - Knowledge developer explains the preliminary/fundamental procedure based on rudimentary knowledge extracted from the expert during the past few sessions.
  - The expert reacts by saying certain remarks.
  - While the expert watches, the knowledge developer enters the additional knowledge into the computer-based system (that represents the prototype).
  - The knowledge developer again runs the modified prototype and continues adding additional knowledge as suggested by the expert till the expert is satisfied.
- The spontaneous and iterative process of building a knowledge base is referred to as rapid prototyping.

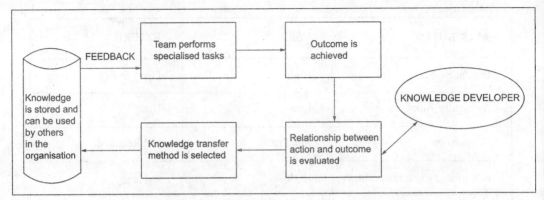

Fig. 4.5 Matching Business Strategies with KM Strategies. (*Source:* Elias M. Awad, Hassan M. Ghaziri, Knowledge Management, Pearson Education Inc., Prentice Hall, 2005).

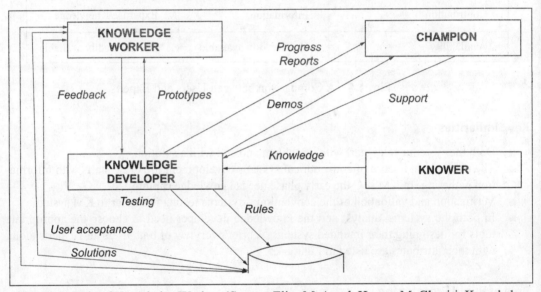

Fig. 4.6 Role of Knowledge Worker. (*Source:* Elias M. Awad, Hassan M. Ghaziri, Knowledge Management, Pearson Education Inc., Prentice Hall, 2005).

Expert Selection

The expert must have excellent communication skills to be able to communicate information understandably and in sufficient detail.

Some common questions that may arise in case of expert selection:

- How to know that the so-called expert is in fact an expert?
- Will he/she stay with the project till its completion?
- What backup would be available in case the expert loses interest or quits?
- How is the knowledge developer going to know what does and what does not lie within the expert's area of expertise?

The Role of the Knowledge Developer

> *The greatest gift is a passion for reading. It is cheap, it consoles,*
> *it distracts, it excites, it gives you knowledge of the world and*
> *experience of a wide kind. It is a moral illumination.*
> — Elizabeth Hardwick

- The knowledge developer can be considered the architect of the system.
- He/she identifies the problem domain, captures knowledge, writes/tests the heuristics that represent knowledge and coordinates the entire project.
- Some necessary attributes of a knowledge developer:
  - Communication skills.
  - Knowledge of knowledge capturing tools/technology.
  - Ability to work in a team with professional/experts.
  - Tolerance for ambiguity.
  - To be able to think conceptually.
  - Ability to frequently interact with the champion, knowledge workers and knowers in the organisation.

DESIGNING THE KM BLUEPRINT

This phase indicates the beginning of designing the IT infrastructure/ Knowledge Management infrastructure. The KM Blueprint (KM system design) addresses a number of issues.

- Aiming for system interoperability/scalability with existing IT infrastructure of the organisation.
- Finalising the scope of the proposed KM system.
- Deciding about the necessary system components.
- Developing the key layers of the KM architecture to meet an organisation's requirements. These layers are:
  - User interface
  - Authentication/security layer
  - Collaborative agents and filtering
  - Application layer
  - Transport internet layer
  - Physical layer
  - Repositories

TESTING THE KM SYSTEM

This phase involves the following two steps:

- ***Verification Procedure:*** Ensures that the system is right, i.e., the programmes do the task that they are designed to do.

- *Validation Procedure:* Ensures that the system is the right system—it meets the user's expectations, and will be usable on demand.

IMPLEMENTING THE KM SYSTEM

- After capturing the appropriate knowledge, encoding in the knowledge base, verifying and validating; the next task of the knowledge developer is to implement the proposed system on a server.
- Implementation means converting the new KM system into actual operation.
- Conversion is a major step in case of implementation.
- Some other steps are post implementation review and system maintenance.

QUALITY ASSURANCE

It indicates the development of controls to ensure a quality KM system. The types of errors to look for:

- Reasoning errors
- Ambiguity
- Incompleteness
- False representation

TRAINING USERS

- The level/duration of training depends on the user's knowledge level and the system's attributes.
- Users can range from novices (casual users with very limited knowledge) to experts (users with prior IT experience and knowledge of latest technology).
- Users can also be classified as tutors (who acquire a working knowledge in order to keep the system current), pupils (unskilled workers who try to gain some understanding of the captured knowledge), or customers (who are interested to know how to use the KM system).
- Training should be geared to the specific user based on capabilities, experience and system complexity.
- Training can be supported by user manuals, explanatory facilities, and job aids.

MANAGING CHANGE

If we value the pursuit of knowledge, we must be free to follow wherever that search may lead us. The free mind is no barking dog to be tethered on a 10-foot chain.
—Adlai Stevenson

The author and founder Dow decided to become a pioneer in the area of Intellectual Capital Management (ICM) and realised that it had to undergo a number of changes. Dow established in 1897 a structured business model that, to a great extent, followed the old organisational models.

Before implementing any new initiative, Dow had to make sure that its vision, structure, and culture would not defeat change. Fortunately for Dow, the culture was right with its long-term and historical commitment to management of inventions, with the first invention management group being formed as early as 1958, and the first patent department in 1928.

The successful implementation of new technologies is dependent on many factors including the efficient management of intellectual capital. Furthermore, recent research indicates that intellectual assets and resources can be utilised much more efficiently and effectively if organisations apply knowledge management techniques for leveraging and enhancing their human resources.

This facilitated the perceiving of intellectual assets and capital as enablers of value creation and maximisation. Despite the value of this new awareness, more than a progressive vision is needed towards viewing intellectual capital. Visionary leadership, strategic planning, intellectual Capital Management champions, committed managers and employees, and effective teams and programmes are all needed for the transformation.

In the Knowledge Management stage, Dow has a matrix organisational structure wherein each business group maintains its autonomy to a considerable extent. As a result, though the KM initiatives are led by the centralised top management, the extent of implementation, attention, and resources allocated to this initiative are up to the vice-president (VP) of each business group. Dow's Knowledge Management System is led by the knowledge management director, who reports to the chief information officer (CIO), and supervises a group of senior executives that form the Knowledge Management Group. The KM Group is an 11-member executive team entrusted to manage knowledge across Dow's 23 businesses, with a budget of $15 million over five years. It is responsible for supporting the information stewards, who in turn champion KM initiatives in each of the business groups. The information stewards report to the senior manager of the KM Group and to the VP of each of the business groups.

Implementation means change, and organisational members usually resist change. The resistors may include:

- Experts
- Regular employees (users)
- Troublemakers
- Narrow-minded people

Resistance can be seen in the form of following personal reactions:

- Projection, i.e., hostility towards peers.
- Avoidance, i.e., withdrawal from the scene.
- Aggression.

POST SYSTEM EVALUATION

Key questions to be asked in the post implementation stage:

- How the new system improved the accuracy/timeliness of concerned decision-making tasks?
- Has the new system caused organisational changes? If so, how constructive are the changes?
- Has the new system affected the attitudes of the end users? If so, in what way?

- How the new system changed the cost of business operation? How significant has it been?
- In what ways has the new system affected the relationships between end users in the organisation?
- Does the benefit obtained from the new system justify the cost of investment?

A NEW MODEL FOR KM SYSTEM LIFE CYCLE

A model and framework that has been designed by Mustafa Sagsan created a new Knowledge Management System model for KM activities to be initiated in a simple way. The following Figure 4.7 gives us a clear understanding of the various stages in KMSLC.

In accordance with the knowledge management literature, five basic processes can be considered for managing knowledge. These can be defined as creating, sharing, structuring, using, and auditing in turn what is called "knowledge management life cycle" model. This model makes us understand knowledge management processes in hierarchical order. Each model is explained in the following paragraphs.

1. *Knowledge Creating*

Knowledge Creating is the first stage of managing organisational knowledge and this requires moving to a place where all forms of knowledge can be created and processed. In other words, in

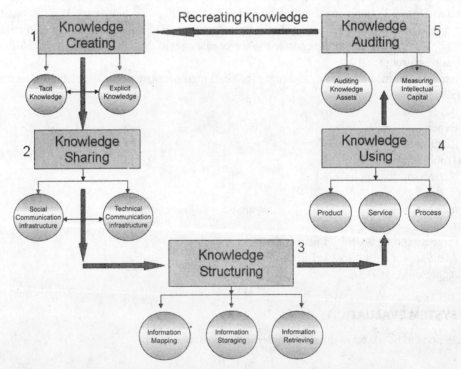

Fig. 4.7   A New Model of Knowledge Management Life Cycle

this stage, knowledge exploration takes place and knowledge can be processed in an organisation leading to focus on individual, group, and department.

There are too many knowledge creators in the place where knowledge can be processed due to the fact that organisation cannot create collective knowledge by itself. Thus, organisational partici-pants create knowledge through their intuition, ability, skills, behaviours, and work experiments. 'Key players, departments and their interactivity can play a critical role in creating knowledge in organisation' (Nonaka, 1996).

Two forms of knowledge can appear while creating knowledge. These are tacit and explicit know-ledge which are embedded in an organisation's products, services and work processes after creating. "The explicit knowledge can be defined as words, diagrams or photographs that cannot convey in-formation that can be understood by direct pointing, or demonstrating, or feeling" (Collins, 2001). Explicit knowledge is technical or academic data or information that is described in formal language, like manuals, mathematical expressions, copyright and patents. It is gained through formal education or structured study and codifies, stores, hierarchy of databases and accesses with high quality, reliable, fast information retrieval systems (Smith, 2001). Therefore, explicit knowledge is easy to structure and retrieve.

Another form of knowledge is tacit, which is completely individual and collective (Polanyi, 1967). Tacit knowledge is a personal form of a knowledge, which individuals can only obtain from direct experience in a given domain. It is held in a non-verbal form, and therefore the holder can-not provide a useful verbal explanation to another individual. Individuals and firms might choose to keep their knowledge tacit in order to prevent its transfer and diffusion and thereby, maintain a competitive advantage.

There are some barriers that occur at knowledge creation stage (Krogh, Ichijo ve Nonaka, 2000). First is at individual and the second is at organisational level. The first barrier contains beliefs that people cannot easily adapt to organisation enough and the second is the need for a legitimate lan-guage, organisational stories, procedures and company's paradigm (Berger ve Luckmann, 1967).

2. Knowledge Sharing

The second important stage of knowledge management life cycle is knowledge sharing. Çapar (2005) emphasises the ways and tools for effective knowledge sharing as follows:

- Formal social communication network,
- Informal social communication network,
- Teamwork,
- Communities of practices,
- Organisational learning,
- Rumours and,
- Formal structured technological communication networks (e-mail, mobile communications, teleconferences, videoconferences, etc.).

Knowledge sharing involves creating knowledge by individuals and groups with their interactivity and connectivity in organisations. Knowledge sharing is carried out by social and technical com-munication channels. As Çapar argues that constructing these channels effectively depends on the stability and durability of organisational infrastructure. If organisational infrastructure is suitable for aligning the knowledge management system infrastructure, successful knowledge sharing can be carried out.

a. Social communication channel

The social communication channel requires an effective interactivity between workers in informal ways. The main purpose of this infrastructure is not only converting tacit knowledge into explicit forms at the individual level, but also transmitting message from bottom to up and up to bottom in appropriate positions at the organisational level (Miller, 1999).

Three types of communication can be constructed while designing social communication channel: oral communication, written communication, and non-verbal communication. The chief means of conveying messages is oral communication. Speeches, formal one-on-one and group discussions, and the informal rumour mill or grapevine are popular forms of oral communication.

Generally, the written communication comprises memos, letters, electronic mail, fax transmissions, organisational periodicals, notices placed on bulletin boards, or any other device that is transmitted via written words or symbols. Non-verbal communication entails body movements, the intonations or emphasis we give the words, facial expressions, and the physical distance between the sender and receiver (Robbins, 2003). Knowledge Management takes into consideration all three forms of organisational communication because effective knowledge management system requires all forms of knowledge.

b. Technical communication channel

Technical communication channel refers to information and communication technology. Information networks, technical communities of practice, internet, web-based networks, intranets, and extranets should be considered in this context. Participants can share their expertise knowledge through e-mail, in-group computerised communication networks, databases, telephone conversations (Davenport and Prusak, 2001). Technical communication infrastructure, which is known as formal communication networks, provide in sharing, structuring, classifying and organising explicit/tacit knowledge in the environment. The best technological channel for the best knowledge management application allows knowledge flow continuously, mapping information correctly, distributes data sources equally, exchanges information timely and contains intelligence agents and network mining. Notwithstanding designing effective channel in technical perspective permits the construction of a good community of practice, that is a team of knowledge workers who share a common interest in a specific area of competence and are willing to work together.

To conclude, knowledge can be shared by both social and technical communication channels effectively. But it is considered that knowledge sharing is based on volunteering and reciprocity. For this reason, before constructing these two channels for knowledge sharing, participants can be encouraged by reward systems through verbal communication style. For example, the knowledge workers who can share their tacit and explicit knowledge can be evaluated for a good performance in an organisation. Reward system and performance appraisal are necessary for successful knowledge sharing which is also required by trust system because "participants feel they are being treated fairly for the intelligence, creativity, innovation, experience and passion they bring to their work".

In knowledge sharing, a reward system and performance appraisal are necessary for successful knowledge sharing which is also required by trust system because "participants feel they are being treated fairly for the intelligence, creativity, innovation, experience and passion they bring to their work.

3. Knowledge Structuring

Knowledge mapping or structuring is the third stage and this is frequently processed by technical communication channel which "includes structuring databases, organising data for analysing, taxonomy of data, clustering/managing databases" (Awad and Ghaziri: 2004).

Knowledge structuring separates data and information through certain types of classification tools and enables retrieving this information timely. Mapping, storing and retrieving information are the three important components of knowledge structuring.

First is mapping information that refers to determining organisational information sources and what participants know. In other words, mapping knowledge puts forward determining textual/ graphical, audio/visual, tacit/explicit forms of knowledge and finding suitable information sources in organisations. A good knowledge mapping benefits from second hand information to the first hand and making knowledge inventory available to overall organisation.

Second is information storing that contains knowledge repositories such as databases, data warehouses, and information centres and indicates electronic environment of organisational memory. Third is the most critical factor in structuring knowledge that is called information retrieval. At this stage, knowledge is stored and retrieved via information retrieval systems such as surrogates, user interface, Boolean logic, Fuzzy logic, Vector query, and Extended Boolean logic.

4. Knowledge Using

Organisations use knowledge for three reasons: 1) Knowledge can be used for determining an organisation's work processes and making strategies for sustainable competitive advantage. 2) Knowledge can be used for designing and marketing product. 3) Knowledge plays a critical role in an organisation's services quality (Nonaka, 1995).

Also, Alavi emphasised that knowledge can be used through three basic mechanisms: Directives that refer to a specific set of rules, standards, procedures, and instructions developed through the conversion of the specialist's tacit knowledge to explicit and integrated knowledge for efficient communication to non-specialist. Organisational routines refer to the development of task performance and coordination patterns, interaction protocols and process specifications that allow individuals to apply and integrate their specialised knowledge without the need to articulate and communicate what they know to others. Self-contained task teams refer to task uncertainty and complexity prevent the specification of directives and organisational routines, teams of individuals with prerequisite knowledge and specialty are formed for problem solving (Alavi, 2001:122). Like knowledge structuring, knowledge using is also based on information technology. For this reason, if individuals would like to use information effectively, they should be information literate.

5. Knowledge Auditing

Knowledge auditing means what amount of knowledge can be used in an organisation's products, services and processes. This knowledge management life cycle stage refers to the capacity of information processing in organisations. In other words, what amount of information and knowledge are created, shared, stored, and used in an organisation at a certain time helps us to determine the information capacity in organisations.

The knowledge audit provides value when company is doing one or more of the following:

- devising a knowledge-based strategy,
- architecting a knowledge management blueprint or roadmap,
- planning to build a knowledge management system,
- planning research and development,
- seeking to leverage its 'people assets',
- facing competition from knowledge intensive competitors that are far ahead on the learning curve,
- striving to strengthen its own competitive weakness,
- looking for direction for planning a market entry or exit strategy (Tiwana, 2000:242–43).

Another critical factor for auditing knowledge in an organisation is measuring intellectual capital, intangibles such as information, knowledge and skills that can be leveraged by an organisation to produce an asset of equal or greater importance than land, labour and capital.

This life cycle model motivates the Chief Knowledge Officer about how knowledge management should succeed. The model brings us to reinvestigate what new management style gains competitive advantage and survive organisational capability in uncertain environment.

This new business model is applied in some companies like Andersen Consulting, Boeing, British Petroleum, Buckman Laboratories, Chaparral Steel, Chase Manhattan Bank, Chrysler, Coca-Cola, CSIRO, Dai-Ichi Pharmaceuticals, Dow Chemical, Ernst & Young, Ford, GM, HP, Hoeschst-Celanese, Owens-Corning, Sandia National Laboratories, Sematech, Senco Products, Sequent Computer, Skandia, Teltech, Texas Instruments and 3M.

SUMMING UP

The building of knowledge management can be viewed as a life cycle that begins with a master plan and justification and ends with a system structured to meet KM requirements for the entire company.

KM systems are developed in order to satisfy the need for improving productivity and potential of employees and the company as a whole. The existing knowledge infrastructure is evaluated so that it can give the perception that the present ways of doing things are not just abandoned in preference for a new system.

Evaluating the existing infrastructure is basic to KMSLC and it includes system justification, scoping, feasibility, strategic planning, capturing knowledge and prototyping. Quality assurance is an integral part of KMSLC.

CASE

Acumen Technologies Holdings is a global communication solutions provider. Having been in the market for more than 15 years, it has made its presence felt as a single stop shop for total communication solutions. The company had its footprint in more than 30 countries. The technology offering of

Acumen was diverse. Though the company had grown as a leader, there were always competitions from large scale and small scale players.

The company over the years had acquired more than 10 companies. Either it was to add a new technology to the offering or a strategic one to build the account. The operation method of company was unique to each location. This was more so because, though Acumen acquired companies from different countries, the acquired companies' operations were limited to one or few countries.

The company recently had a change on top. The new CEO comes out with a very aggressive growth plan. The company had a major restructuring. Technological groups were created with separate P&L. Acumen has had a healthy growth of around 20% year on year. The restructuring expected a growth of more than 35%.

With new group heads in each SBU, the company was buzzing with activities. Each SBU head came out with his own plans to meet the targets. It was just a wait of time to make it large.

A quarter passes by. All the SBU heads were happy that they had done very good representation in multiple bids. CEO calls for a review. CEO was impressed to know the number of representations. But how many business conversions? Where is the growth? None.

Before the formation of SBUs, Acumen was able to acquire at least 3 to 4 customers in a quarter. The creation of SBUs, predominantly for growth, has backfired. Was there a fault in judging capabilities? SBUs, however, were buzzing with activities. A record number of proposals were made in a quarter. But still no conversions! What went wrong?

A committee consisting of senior members from each SBU was formed to investigate. After a few sittings the report was ready. Shocking outcome.

As each SBU was seen as an independent P&L, it was virtually a competition among SBUs to get that piece of business. SBUs failed to leverage on overall organisation's potential. In a stunning revelation, on a couple of occasions, two SBUs were bidding for the same project at international level, to their embarrassment, without their knowledge until that point.

The committee also exposed how creation of SBUs acted as a double edged sword. It killed its own business.

The committee continued with a revised task now. To revamp the system.

Questions:

Identify the problems in the field of Knowledge Management in Acumen Technologies and provide alternatives by applying KMSLC stages to solve the issues.

Source: The case is created by Mr. Bharath C, HR Manager, Aricent Technologies.

KEYWORDS

KMSLC: The building of Knowledge Management can be viewed as a life cycle that begins with a masterplan and justification and ends with a system structured to meet KM requirements for the entire company.

Scoping: The term scoping means limiting the breadth and depth of the project within the financial, human resource, and operational constraints.

Knowledge Capture: Capturing knowledge involves extracting, analysing and interpreting the concerned knowledge that a human expert uses to solve a specific problem.

QUESTIONS FOR DISCUSSION

1. Briefly explain the concept of KMSLC.
2. What is coping? What system infrastructure is required to build a strong KMSLC? Explain.
3. What are the factors impacting team success? Explain.
5. What is knowledge capture? Explain.
5. How should be designed a KM blueprint?
6. Write short notes on: (i) Prototyping (ii) Expert Selection (iii) Quality Assurance KM System implementation (iv) Managing Change (v) Testing the KM System.

INDIVIDUAL ASSIGNMENT

True or False

 (i) KM Systems are developed in order to satisfy the need for improving productivity.
 (ii) Forming a KM team usually means identifying the key units, branches, divisions, etc.
 (iii) Capturing knowledge involves extracting, analysing and interpreting the concerned knowledge that a human expert uses to solve a specific problem.

Answers

 (i) True
 (ii) True
 (iii) True

GROUP ASSIGNMENT

1. Assess the current state of the practice of Knowledge Management with a live example.
2. Here is a simple example and pleasing demonstration of how something can change when experienced in a new context, particularly when the warmer spring season approaches. The facilitator or the classroom teacher should take his\her tea/coffee break outside along with students, and ask them if their tea/coffee tastes different, compared to how it normally tastes indoors. The demonstration is clearest if first students pour the drink and take a few sips indoors, and then walk outside, so as to compare the indoor and outdoor taste. Strangely the taste is quite different, sometimes remarkably different. This is probably due to the fresh air being smelled and tasted along with the drink. I am open to better explanations. The effect also works with cold drinks.

   Taste is not the only characteristic altered, for example, in cold weather the drink cools far quicker. Small and insignificant though it is, the drink experience and memory is altered by the different outside environment. The indoor cup of tea or coffee is perceived to be different because of the outdoor context and situation.

   Everything in life – especially concerning human attitude – alters according to context. This is only an example. In a similar way write down 10 situations where you find a change and write five steps for each situation by applying Knowledge Management concepts for each situation.

SUGGESTED READINGS

Alavi, M. and Leidner, D., Knowledge Management and Knowledge Management Systems: Conceptual Foundations and Research Issues, *MIS Quarterly*, 25(1): 107-136, 2001.

Allee, V. Knowledge Networks and Communities of Practice, *OD Practitioner*, Vol. 32, No:4. [Çevrimiçi: http://www.odnetwork.org/odponline/vol32n4/knowledgenets.html], 14.05.2006.

Augier, M. ve Shariq, S. ve Vendelø, M., "Understanding Context: Its Emergence, Transformation and Role in Tacit Knowledge Sharing", *Journal of Knowledge Management*, 5 (2): 125-136, 2001.

Awad, M.A. ve Ghaziri, H.M., *Knowledge Management*, Pearson Education, Prentice Hall, Upper Saddle River, New Jersey, 2004.

Berger, P. ve Luckmann, T., *The Social Construction of Reality*, Penguin, New York, 1967.

Collins, H. M., "Tacit Knowledge, Trust and the Q Sapphire", *Social Studies of Science*, Vol. 31, No. 1: 71-85, 2001.

Davenport, T. H. ve Prusak, L., *İş Dünyasında Bilgi Yönetimi: kuruluşlar ellerindeki bilgiyi nasıl yönetirler?*, İstanbul: Rota, 2001.

Dictionary of Philosophy of Mind, Tacit Knowledge, [Online], web address: http://www.artsci.wustl.edu/~philos/MindDict/tacitknowledge.html, [17th May, 2003].

Jensen, M. C. and Meckling, W. H., Specific and General Knowledge and Organisational Structure. In Myers, P.S. (ed.), *Knowledge Management and Organisational Design*, Butterworth-Heinemann, Newton, MA, pp. 17-38, 1996.

Krogh, G. V.; Ichijo, K. ve Nonaka, I. *Enabling Knowledge Creation: How to Unlock the Mystery of Tacit Knowledge and Release the Power of Innovation*, Oxford: Oxford University Press, 2000.

Meyer, C., *Relentless Growth: How Silicon Valley Innovation Strategies Can Work in Your Business*, Free Press, 1997.

Miller, P., "How Communication Can Add Spice to Knowledge Management", *Strategic Communication Management*, April/May: 12-15, 1999.

Nonaka, I. ve Takeuchi, H., *The Knowledge Creating Company: How Japanese Companies Create the Dynamics of Innovation*, Oxford University Press, New York, 1995.

Polanyi, M, *The Tacit Dimension*. Garden City, Anchor Books, NY, 1967.

Robbins, S.P., *Organisational Behavior*. Pearson Education, Prentice Hall, Upper Saddle River, New Jersey, 2003.

Sağsan, M., "The Cognitive Dimension of Tacit Knowledge Based on HIP and SIP: Can it be Managed by CEO?", 3rd European Knowledge Management Summer School, Knowledge Management in Action bildirileri içinde, San Sebastian, İspanya. [Çevrim içi], Elektronik, 2003.

Tiwana, A., *The Knowledge Management Toolkit: Practical Techniques for Building Knowledge Management System*. Prentice Hall PTR, Upper Saddle River, NJ, 2000.

WEBSITES

www.knowledgeboard.com
http://www.episcopalpeacefellowship.org/

CHAPTER 5

Knowledge Creation and Knowledge Architecture

OBJECTIVE

At the end of this lesson, you would be able to understand:

- The concept of knowledge creation.
- KM architecture
- Different layers of KM architecture.
- Nonaka's model of knowledge creation and sharing.

INTRODUCTION

The ability to perceive or think differently is more important than the knowledge gained.
— David Bohm

Organisations of all types are in dire need of the skills of information professionals. With information production growing exponentially, who else is so well-placed to organise it for later retrieval when required? We don't exactly stand out on the CEO's radar yet, but information and knowledge management is in such confusion in many organisations that the bells are going to ring sometime soon. And that means that the CEOs are going to understand the significant costs of failing to manage information and knowledge.

One of the latest areas in industry right now is that of Knowledge Management and the development of KM architecture. Driven by tremendous pressures for service quality, speed to market, and innovation, and by the availability of a new generation of exciting information management tools, companies are employing new technologies to leverage the intellectual assets of knowledge workers. New software/hardware technology hits the market daily, e.g., advertising capabilities like intelligent search, document management, data mining, groupware, call centre customer support and telesales, enterprise management, information retrieval, graphic data display, etc.

This effort to harness the knowledge-creating capability of the organisation is one of the key elements of the Information Revolution that is redefining the competitive landscape of business. This lesson will help you understand the process of knowledge creation and knowledge architecture.

KNOWLEDGE

"With everything else dropping out of the competitive equation, knowledge has become the only source of long-run sustainable competitive advantage,

but knowledge can only be employed through the skills of individuals.
The value of an individual's knowledge depends
upon the smartness with which it is used in the entire system."
—Lester Thurow

What is Knowledge?

Though knowledge has been defined in the first chapter, let us have an insight into what knowledge is from a different perspective. A simple definition of knowledge is the ability to make quality decisions on information and data. There are many other definitions for knowledge, for example:

- Knowledge is the process of knowing
- Knowledge is a superior level of information in the value chain
- Knowledge is the means by which we create information and data in a social context.

How is Knowledge different from Data and Information?

There are many definitions for differentiating data, information and knowledge; one such is given below:

- Data = attributes, events, transactions
- Information = data which is organised to convey meaning to many people
- Knowledge = data and information which is organised to convey experience in a reusable fashion.

For example, the reporting of daily oil production volumes may be classified as data. Summarising this data into a production decline curve produces information. Knowledge is the ability to make a business decision based on this information.

Are there different types of Knowledge?

The answer is YES. There are equally numerous knowledge classifications. Quinn, Anderson and Finklestein define four types of knowledge below. The interesting aspect of this definition is that processes and technology can address the first three points. The final point of 'caring why' emphasises the human element that differentiates KM.

- Cognitive Knowledge—Know What
- Advanced Skill—Know How
- Systems Understanding—Know Why
- Self-motivation—Care Why.

Another knowledge classification is taken from Hope & Hope (Harvard Business School):

- Explicit—skills and facts that can be written down and taught to others

■ Tacit—skills, experience and native talent that people cannot easily describe.

This illustrates the fact that not all knowledge can be written down on paper or captured electronically on computers. Written knowledge often requires human support (for example, in the form of training). Just because someone reads a manual, it does not mean that they understand the content.

What is Knowledge Management and how it is designed?

Knowledge Management is a term applied to any initiative involving people, processes and technology that leverages the knowledge within an organisation to achieve business results. KM practice requires vision and organisational communities aided by leadership.
Knowledge Management as a business activity with two primary aspects:

■ Treating the knowledge component of business activities as an explicit concern of business reflected in strategy, policy, and practice at all levels of the organisation.
■ Making a direct connection between an organisation's intellectual assets—both explicit [recorded] and tacit [personal know-how]—and positive business results.—Knowledge Praxis

Regarding the design (architecture), let us look into few information models of KM Architecture available.

Knowledge Architecture: Basic Model

There is a basic theme that underlies all KM techniques (see Figure 5.1). You learn while doing the work, then record and share the results, which in turn are reused in later work cycles. Innovation can occur anywhere in the process. The following section looks at some techniques developed for 'learning', 'sharing' and 'innovating' components of this model.

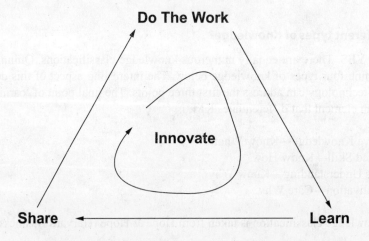

Fig. 5.1   Basic Model of Knowledge Architecture

Learning and Recording

Training courses, on-the-job training and mentoring from colleagues, seminars and conferences are just some of the traditional ways by which an employee can learn. Many companies move their employees from one position to the next, from one country to the next, every 2–3 years. This is designed to maximise their opportunities for learning.

It seems that the majority of companies do not record or capture a significant proportion of the useful knowledge they generate. The increased use of technology (e.g., webcam, multimedia, information capture applications) to support organisational processes is enabling more information to be recorded electronically, which is in itself causing information overload for employees. It is important that the standards and processes for recording information are in place before the appropriate knowledge sharing strategy is implemented.

Sharing Knowledge

Knowledge sharing is synergistic. It is not sharing a piece of cake that each member can eat. It is trying to take a small piece but in turn giving a bigger piece to others. Synergistic means "working together", moving towards a win-win situation collaboratively. Figure 5.2 gives a clear picture of how knowledge is shared.

Sharing knowledge is not about giving people something, or getting something from them. That is only valid for information sharing. Sharing knowledge occurs when people are genuinely interested in helping one another develop new capacities for action; it is about creating learning processes.

Sharing Tacit Knowledge

> *"Communication is human nature—Knowledge sharing is human nurture!"*
> —Alison Tucker

Sharing knowledge within an organisation is arguably the biggest problem to be addressed by KM. Processes like project 'post-mortems' are vital to share the lessons learnt throughout the organisation. Forming networks of people in knowledge communities (groups of people with a common interest) and teams (a group of people with a common goal) can also help tacit knowledge exchange. Videoconferencing and web technology are being increasingly used in support of these networks.

Sharing Explicit Knowledge

The owner-ship strategy	This is the traditional way of sharing knowledge. The information owner decides when to make it available and to whom. When reports were only available in paper form this was the only way to share knowledge. The method was classically used in the 1970s and 1980s by the large middle management tier, which fostered interdepartmental rivalry and a 'knowledge is power' philosophy. Although some organisations still practice this in the virtual domain, the main issue is 'how does one person know what is or isn't of value to another?'

The pull strategy	If we answer the above question, we find that the individual is the only person who knows what is or isn't important to them. Office noticeboards, document management systems and traditional web technology are examples of a 'pull' strategy where the user has to actively search for information they require. A weakness in the pull strategy is that it needs active information management with users having to seek out the information.
The push strategy	Both paper and e-mail are examples of 'push' strategies. This allows specific information to be delivered to specific people. Delivery agents search and deliver information on the user's behalf, obeying a defined sets of rules. They gather information from disparate sources (e.g., document management systems, e-mail, file systems, web) and push it to the desktop based on interests from a user's profile. In this way when a user creates or updates information, other users with similar interests are immediately notified. The interfaces to these information sources, user profiles and delivery agents are called 'information portals'. These portals deliver a customised view of information that may be collected from a number of sources matching the users' interest. Imagine all the information that interests you from a newspaper, or series of newspapers presented to you electronically through a single interface.

Revolutionising Knowledge Sharing

Leading-edge individuals and institutions are on the threshold of major advances in their capacity to acquire, assimilate, utilise, reflect on, and share knowledge. Between now and 2010, the elements of e-knowledge, e-knowing, and e-knowledge commerce will mature, using technologies that are largely developed and that await deployment and widespread use. Academia will need to become far more reflective about knowledge—the forms, uses, and sharing—if it is to be a vanguard participant.

The knowledge climate of colleges and universities will need to change if they are to move from a culture of knowledge hoarding to one of knowledge sharing. In institutions where this happens, learners, faculty, staff, and other stakeholders will derive greater value from a set of genuinely new experiences. In "Rethinking the Knowledge-based Organisation," Michael H. Zack asserts that the degree to which an enterprise is knowledge-based depends not on the nature of its programmes, products, and services but primarily on how it is organised and how it functions. True knowledge-based enterprises leverage their knowledge assets in every aspect of their activities and try to cultivate the process of knowledge.

Using knowledge to create knowledge—Innovation

"An individual without information cannot take responsibility; An individual who is given information cannot help but take responsibility."
—Jan Carlson Former Chairman, SAS Airlines

The ability to use knowledge to create new knowledge is of vital importance to all organisations because of the efficiency and effectiveness benefits. Innovation could be described by the following equation:

$$\text{Innovation} = \text{Learning Opportunities} \times \text{Experience} \times \text{Proximity to Business} \times \text{Freedom}$$

Ideas are commonly generated in an environment of accelerated learning and proximity to the business. People need the freedom to express and challenge traditional ways of working and should be encouraged to think 'out of the box'. The traditional way of working in a hierarchical structure, following instruction after instruction, is in fact alien to our nature. The ability to think differently is not something we need to learn, but something we need to relearn. Watching a child experiment, learn and innovate tells us this.

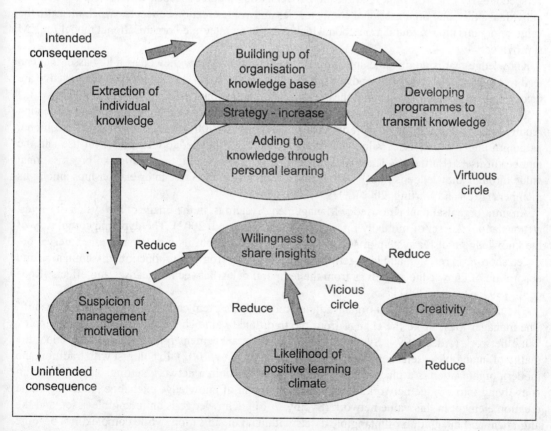

Fig. 5.2   Knowledge Creation and Transfer in an Organisation

KNOWLEDGE CREATION

The knowledge economy has sparked considerable interest in Knowledge Management [KM] over the last decade. This interest has encouraged numerous scientific disciplines to address knowledge issues in a variety of different ways. The result is the proliferation of models and concepts developed by different schools of thought. Effective intra-organisational KM suggests: 1) a need for the integration of these various models, concepts and perspectives to service the overall knowledge needs and interests of organisations and 2) a holistic approach to KM that leverages the different human and technical aspects presently under consideration in many organisations.

Since all of these concepts and models aim to increase the value of goods and services produced by organisations, a need exists to assess them using value creation measurement tools and techniques. Such an approach will help in the achievement of a certain level of maturity in KM through which the appropriate choice of KM tools and mechanisms support the integration of organisational resources.

The literature on KM and value creation is reviewed to determine possible connections among the various models and concepts and determine how KM can be assessed from a value creation perspective. By establishing a relationship between knowledge concepts, which form the basis of individual skills, and organisational competencies and value creation concepts, which measure the value of organisation, a foundation upon which to build an integrated organisational model for KM is provided.

Knowledge that is unique and specific to an organisation is now viewed as a key asset that can lead to a sustainable competitive advantage (Nonaka et al., 2000). Information and knowledge are recognised as driving forces behind the creation of organisational value (Cuganesan, 2009).

The designation of knowledge as an organisational asset in need of development and protection requires a paradigm shift on the part of managers (Edvinsson, 2001). In contrast with the traditional paradigm under which asset value depreciates over time, knowledge increases with use and the number of users (Barthelme-Trapp and Vincent, 2001). As a result, the creation of organisational value through knowledge is linked to the presence of strong, effective interrelationships among its members (Russ and Darling, 2000).

An intra-organisational Knowledge Management System is, in the image of the system it serves, a [translation] "...set of mutually interrelated units" (Durand, 2002). The dynamic complexity of the knowledge transfer system arises, among other things, from its non-linearity, the interval between short-term reaction and long-term response resulting from the production, dissemination and absorption of knowledge as well as from the temporal delay between the causes and effects (Roos et al., 1997; Sterman, 2001).

The management of an intra-organisational knowledge system calls for another paradigm shift. The manager must make the change from the traditional value chain to a dynamic and complex value network (Allee, 1999; Sveiby, 2001). Modern management principles need to reflect the reality of intangible assets that propel the new economy (Lev, 2002). In contrast with tradition, the modern organisation is a place where value is created within a network setting. The value chain is evolving into a value network. Strategic management of knowledge exchange is the key value creation element in this value network (Sveiby, 2001). Knowledge is an intangible asset, and the alignment and integration of intangible assets within an organisation, while complex, has become a crucial issue in value creation (Kaplan and Norton, 2004).

Administration of an organisational Knowledge Management System requires the sustainable integration of various theoretical concepts and approaches relating to Knowledge Management (Glot and Berrell, 2003). The following are the ways how knowledge can be created in an organisation.

- Knowledge update can mean creating new knowledge based on ongoing experience in a specific domain and then using the new knowledge in combination with the existing knowledge to come up with updated knowledge for knowledge sharing.
- Knowledge can be created through teamwork.
- A team can commit to perform a job over a specific period of time.
- A job can be regarded as a series of specific tasks carried out in a specific order.
- When the job is completed, then the team compares the experience it had initially (while starting the job) to the outcome (successful/disappointing).
- This comparison translates experience into knowledge.
- While performing the same job in future, the team can take corrective steps and/or modify the actions based on the new knowledge they have acquired.

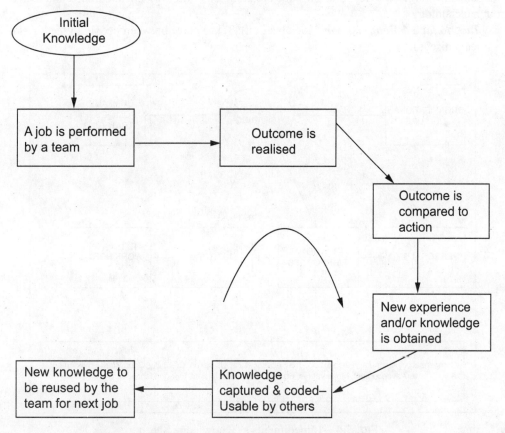

Fig. 5.3   Knowledge Creation/Knowledge Sharing via Teams

- Over time, experience usually leads to expertise where one team (or individual) can be known for handling a complex problem very well.
- This knowledge can be transferred to others in a reusable format.
- There exist factors that encourage (or retard) knowledge transfer.
- Personality is one factor in case of knowledge sharing.
- For example, extrovert people usually possess self-confidence, feel secure, and tend to share experiences more readily than the introvert, self-centred, and security-conscious people.
- People with positive attitudes, who usually trust others and who work in environments conducive to knowledge sharing tend to be better at sharing knowledge.
- Vocational reinforcers are the key to knowledge sharing.
- People whose vocational needs are sufficiently met by job reinforcers are usually found to be more likely to favour knowledge sharing than the people who are deprived of one or more reinforcer.

NONAKA'S MODEL OF KNOWLEDGE CREATION & TRANSFORMATION

In 1999, Nonaka coined the terms *tacit knowledge* and *explicit knowledge* as the two main types of human knowledge. The key to knowledge creation lies in the way it is mobilised and converted through technology.

- *Tacit to tacit communication* (Socialization): Takes place between people in meetings or in team discussions.

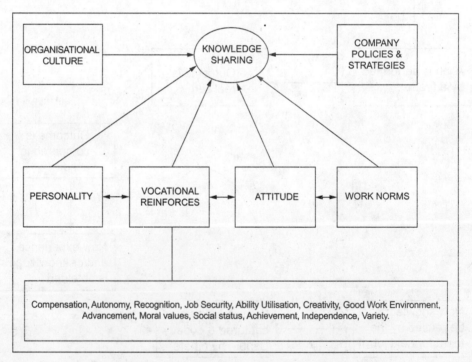

Fig. 5.4 Impediments to Knowledge Sharing

Organisational Knowledge Creation (Nonaka)

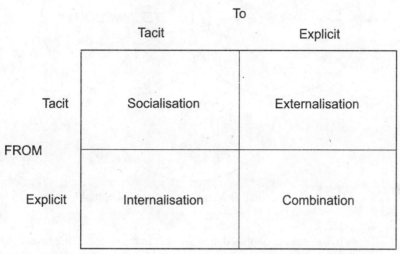

Fig. 5.5 Nonaka's Organisational Knowledge Creating

- *Tacit to explicit communication* (Externalisation): Articulation among people through dialogue (e.g., brainstorming).
- *Explicit to explicit communication* (Communication): This transformation phase can be best supported by technology. Explicit knowledge can be easily captured and then distributed/transmitted to worldwide audience.
- *Explicit to tacit communication* (Internalisation): This implies taking explicit knowledge (e.g., a report) and deducing new ideas or taking constructive action. One significant goal of Knowledge Management is to create technology to help the users derive tacit knowledge from explicit knowledge.

KNOWLEDGE ARCHITECTURE

Knowledge Architecture is the application of information architecture to Knowledge Management. That is, using the skills for defining and designing information spaces to establish an environment conducive to managing knowledge.

Borrowing a metaphor from physics, you can think of the difference between information architecture and knowledge architecture in terms of energy. Information architecture tends to focus on designing spaces for existing or predefined information. What might be called kinetic information. For example, one branch of information architecture focuses on findability, with little or no concern about how the content itself comes into being.

Knowledge architecture, on the other hand, deals with potential information. So, rather than determining the best way to use existing content, the knowledge architect is designing "spaces" that

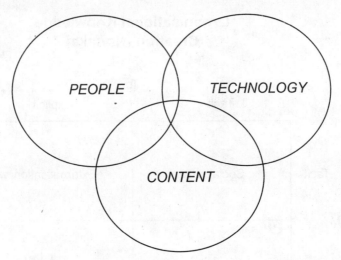

Fig. 5.6 Knowledge Management, a conceptual view

encourage knowledge to be created, captured, and shared. In this respect, the actual content doesn't matter as much as the life cycle—how and when it gets created and how best to get it to the right people quickly. For example, collaboration strategies may focus on the structure and set up of team spaces or discussion forums—how they get created, how they operate, how people find them and vice versa. But the actual tasks and topics discussed in those spaces are up to the teams that use them and may not be determined long after the strategy is completed and in place.

Finally, KA can be put in a nutshell as:

■ Knowledge architecture can be regarded as a prerequisite to knowledge sharing.
■ The infrastructure can be viewed as a combination of people, content, and technology.
■ These components are inseparable and interdependent.

The People Core

■ By people, here we mean knowledge workers, managers, customers, and suppliers.
■ As the first step in knowledge architecture, our goal is to evaluate the existing information/ documents which are used by people, the applications needed by them, the people they usually contact for solutions, the associates they collaborate with, the official e-mails they send/ receive, and the database(s) they usually access.
■ All the above stated resources help to create an employee profile, which can later be used as the basis for designing a Knowledge Management System.
■ The idea behind assessing the people's core is to do a proper job in case of assigning job content to the right person and to make sure that the flow of information that once was obstructed by departments now flows to the right people at the right time.
■ In order to expedite knowledge sharing, a knowledge network has to be designed in such a way as to assign people authority and responsibility for specific kinds of knowledge content, which means:

- Identifying knowledge centres:
  - After determining the knowledge that people need, the next step is to find out where the required knowledge resides, and the way to capture it successfully.
  - Here, the term knowledge centre means areas in the organisation where knowledge is available for capturing.
  - These centres support to identify expert(s) or expert teams in each centre who can collaborate in the necessary knowledge capture process.
- Activating knowledge content satellites
  - This step breaks down each knowledge centre into some more manageable levels, satellites, or areas.
- Assigning experts for each knowledge centre:
  - After the final framework has been decided, one manager should be assigned for each knowledge satellite who will ensure integrity of information content, access, and update.
  - Ownership is a crucial factor in case of knowledge capture, knowledge transfer, and knowledge implementation.
  - In a typical organisation, departments usually tend to be territorial.
  - Often, fight can occur over the budget or over the control of sensitive processes (this includes the kind of knowledge a department owns).
  - These reasons justify the process of assigning department ownership to knowledge content and knowledge process.
  - Adjacent/interdependent departments should be cooperative and ready to share knowledge.

The Technical Core

- The objective of the technical core is to enhance communication as well as ensure effective knowledge sharing.
- Technology provides a lot of opportunities for managing tacit knowledge in the area of communication.
- Communication networks create links between necessary databases.
- Here the term technical core is meant to refer to the totality of the required hardware, software, and the specialised human resources.
- Expected attributes of technology under the technical core: accuracy, speed, reliability, security, and integrity.
- Since an organisation can be thought of as a knowledge network, the goal of knowledge economy is to push employees towards greater efficiency/productivity by making best possible use of the knowledge they possess.
- A knowledge core usually becomes a network of technologies designed to work on top of the organisation's existing network.

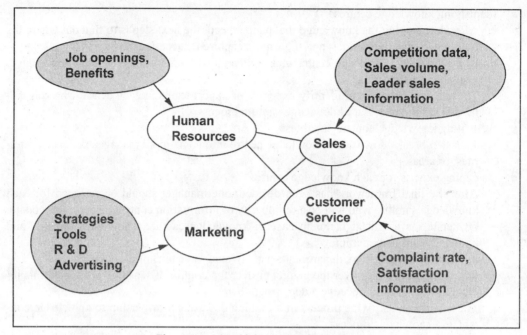

Fig. 5.7   Identifying Knowledge Centre

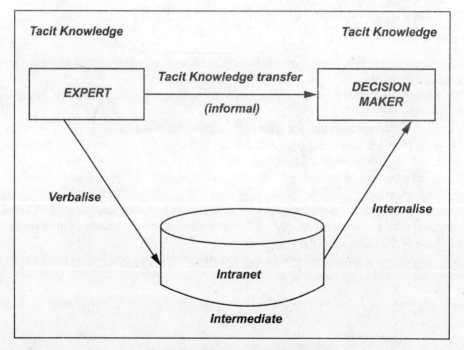

Fig. 5.8   Transfer of Knowledge

LAYERS OF KM ARCHITECTURE

The User Interface (Layer 1): User interface design focuses on consistency, relevance, visual clarity, navigation, and usability.

- Usually a web browser represents the interface between the user and the KM system.
- It is the top layer in the KM system architecture.
- The way the text, graphics, tables, etc. are displayed on the screen tends to simplify the technology for the user.
- The user interface layer should provide a way for the proper flow of tacit and explicit knowledge.
- The necessary knowledge transfer between people and technology involves capturing tacit knowledge from experts, storing it in the knowledge base, and making it available to people for solving complex problems.
- Features to be considered in case of user interface design:
  - Consistency
  - Relevance

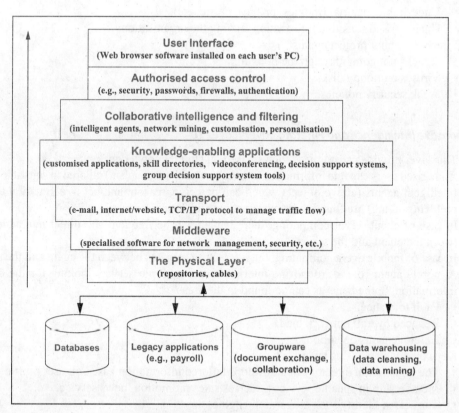

Fig. 5.9   Layers of KM Architecture

- Visual clarity
- Usability
- Ease of Navigation

Authorised Access Control (Layer 2)

- This layer maintains security as well as ensures authorised access to the knowledge captured and stored in the organisation's repositories.
- The knowledge is usually captured by using internet, intranet of extranet.
- An organisation's intranet represents the internal network of communication systems.
- Extranet is a type of intranet with extensions allowing specified people (customers, suppliers, etc.) to access some organisational information.
- Issues related to the access layer: access privileges, backups.
- The access layer is mostly focused on security, use of protocols (like passwords), and software tools like firewalls.
- Firewalls can protect against:
  - E-mails that can cause problems.
  - Unauthorised access from the outside world.
  - Undesirable material (movies, images, music, etc).
  - Unauthorised sensitive information leaving the organisation.
- Firewalls cannot protect against:
  - Attacks not going through the firewall.
  - Viruses on floppy disks.
  - Weak security policies.

Collaborative Intelligence and Filtering Layer (Layer 3)

- This layer provides customised views based on stored knowledge.
- Authorised users can find information (through a search mechanism) tailored to suit their needs.
- Intelligent agents (active objects which can perceive, reason, and act in a situation to help problem solving) are found to be extremely useful in some situations.
- In case of client/server computing, there happens to be frequent and direct interaction between the client and the server.
- In case of mobile agent computing, the interaction happens between the agent and the server.
- A mobile agent roams around the internet across multiple servers looking for the correct information. Some benefits can be found in the areas of:
  - Fault tolerance.
  - Reduced overall network load.
  - Heterogeneous operation.
- Key components of this layer:
  - The registration directory that develops tailored information based on user profile.
  - Membership in specific services, such as sales promotion, news service, etc.
  - The search facility such as a search engine.

- In terms of the prerequisites for this layer, the following criteria can be considered:
  - Security.
  - Portability.
  - Flexibility.
  - Scalability.
  - Ease of use.
  - Integration.

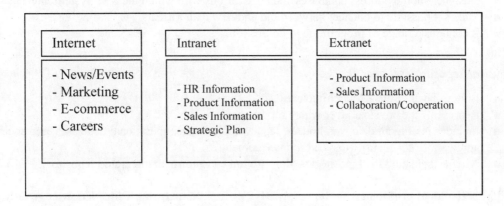

Collaborative Intelligence and Filtering (Layer 3)

- *Personalised* views based on stored knowledge.
- *Groupware* to facilitate both sync- and asynchronous interaction and discussion.
- *Intelligent agents* reduce search time for needed information.

Knowledge-Enabling Application (Layer 4)

- Referred to as value-added layer.
- Creates a competitive edge for the learning organisation.
- Provides knowledge bases, discussion databases, automation tools, etc.
- Ultimate goal: show how knowledge sharing could improve the employees.
- This creates a competitive edge.
- Most of the applications help users to do their jobs in better ways.
- They include knowledge bases, discussion databases, decision support, etc.

Transport Layer (Layer 5)

- Most technical layer to implement
- Includes LANs, WANs, intranets, extranets, and the internet.
- Ensures that the company will become a network of relationships.
- Considers multimedia, URLs, graphics, connectivity speeds, and bandwidths search tools, and consider managing of network traffic.

- This is the most technical layer.
- It ensures to make the organisation a network of relationships where electronic transfer of knowledge can be considered routine.

Middleware (Layer 6)

- Focus on interfacing with legacy systems and programmes residing on other platforms.
- Designer should address databases and applications with which the KM System interfaces.
- Makes it possible to connect between old and new data formats.
- It contains a range of programme to do this job.

Physical Repositories (Layer 7)

- Bottom layer in the KM architecture.
- Represents the physical layer where repositories are installed.
- Includes intelligent data warehouses, legacy applications, operational databases, and special applications for security and traffic management.
- After establishing the repositories, they are linked to form an integrated repository.

What is the ideal profile of a senior knowledge executive such as a Chief Knowledge Officer (CKO) or the Organisational Knowledge Architect (OKA)?

There are some significant differences in the profile of an ideal CKO and OKA.

A CKO needs to be able to take an appropriate place among the other CKO level individuals in the organisation. This means a span of control appropriate to that level. It means maturity and corporate experience. It means organisational and people skills. A CKO needs to understand knowledge and information management the same way that a CIO needs to understand IT, a CFO needs to understand accounting, a COO needs to understand manufacturing. They need to be able to see the big picture, to hire the right people below them, to have a good feel of when to trust the direction that these people are doing the right thing and when to give guidance.

Generally, the CKO is a VP over a 200-person organisation which includes a Knowledge Management group as well as groups like educational services, pre-sales technical support, competitive intelligence, and process analysis.

An Organisational Knowledge Architect needs considerably deeper understanding of the details and constraints. Any kind of design work requires knowledge of the details.

An architect also needs to be able to gather user requirements; evaluate those needs with respect to available technologies, resources and existing environment; choose the best solution; design it; and, if necessary, oversee the development. This implies that the architect must be skilled at listening to needs and elicting information and able to have those discussions at all levels of the corporation. They must be able to mediate between competing needs, evaluate the value of solutions to the corporation, and design to meet the overall goals of the organisation.

The technology skills are needed for a CKO because you can't really separate the communication of knowledge from the underlying technology medium. While the architect needs to focus on current and near-future technologies, one can't ignore older technologies and we can't limit our scope to traditional IT technologies.

The architect needs to be able to look into the future and divine the technology directions that need to be planned for. An architect needs to be able to pick the winners at a reasonably long range.

The architect needs to be comfortable playing with new technologies; reading standards document, research papers and presentations; and so forth. They need to be able to contribute to the advanced technology community in a way that gives them entry to the early discussions of new ideas.

The architect needs to have a detailed understanding of current technologies, particularly those currently in use in their environment, and how those technologies are deployed. One must know it for design reasons. They also need to know it because situations arise with some frequencies that call on you to do something. There is also the matter of maintaining the respect of the coders who are executing your designs. If someone has specified that the results of a certain database query will appear on a web page, one has to know better how to write that SQL if one had to and better know how those results are going to make it onto the web page.

The Knowledge Architect also needs to be able to work with the "keepers of the technology." Creating great, new, cutting edge tools doesn't mean anything if you can't get them implemented and there can be lot of reasons why they may not be. Technology environments in major companies are complex and lots of issues need to be resolved before embarking on projects. IT professionals tend to think a lot about support and maintenance issues, not just how cool the project is.

A OKA also needs to know the business. They need to understand how the business operates; what their industry and the competitive environment is like; how their specific business works; how it is positioned in the industry; how it relates to the channel partners, vendors, etc.; what its corporate culture is; how the major corporate information flows: the product development life cycle, the sales-fulfilment flow, etc.

The architect needs to understand the information needs of different parts of the business and how they differ. We need to know who the producers of information are and where the real demand for information is. We need to know who shouldn't see information and at what points in the information life cycle information should be accessible to different audiences.

They need to understand the legal implications of information flow including complying with copyright laws, handling non-disclosure information, preserving intellectual property rights, complying with export laws as they apply to information, maintaining appropriate records and audit trails, and many other issues.

Specific skills that are used almost daily include data modelling, usability testing and heuristic analysis, graphic design, classification/categorisation development, project management, technology skills mentioned above, and mediation.

Finally, knowledge architects don't have plenty of traditional information architecture/content management responsibilities as well—such as taxonomies, website structures, search interfaces, etc. But what sets them apart from other information architects is their focus on the design of spaces and the processes that support the exchange of knowledge being exchanged, rather than the knowledge itself.

THE FUTURE OF KNOWLEDGE ARCHITECTURE

1. Knowledge Architecture is the building block knowledge practice for creating world-class schooling in thousands of schools across India.
2. Knowledge Architecture is the critical link between business models and human behaviour within large organisational systems.

3. Knowledge Architecture is the enabler for rapid capacity creation in communities and social systems.

Can you become a Knowledge Architect?
Knowledge Architects need to be–

- Team players.
- Capable of working with a range of specialists.
- Focused on serving the target community.

Most important, great knowledge architects must love knowledge and have a desire to serve human beings, and bring these two great passions together into a single force in their lives.

SUMMING UP

This effort to harness the knowledge-creating capability of the organisation is one of the key elements of the Information Revolution that is redefining the competitive landscape of business. Knowledge update can mean creating new knowledge based on the ongoing experience in a specific domain and then using the new knowledge in combination with the existing knowledge to come up with updated knowledge for knowledge sharing.

In 1999, Nonaka coined the terms *tacit knowledge* and *explicit knowledge* as the two main types of human knowledge. The key to knowledge creation lies in the way it is mobilised and converted through technology.

KM architecture comprises people, process and technology. KM architecture has different levels – user interface, authorised access control, collaborative intelligence and filtering, knowledge enabling application, transport layer, middleware and the physical layer.

CASE

How not to do it

For very many years the UK government department responsible for business was called the DTI - Department for Trade and Industry.

The DTI was formed in 1970. It was a merger of the Board of Trade and the Ministry of Technology.

The name DTI was effectively a brand. It was a government department, but in all other respects it was a massive branded organisation, offering various services to businesses, and to regions and countries also.

The DTI had a logo, a website. It had staff, a massive target audience (of billions globally), customers (effectively, tens of millions), a huge marketing and advertising spend, including national TV campaigns, posters, information brochures, and every other aspect of branding which normally operates in the corporate world.

The organisation's name 'the DTI', was an obvious and recognised abbreviation of 'Trade' and 'Industry', and this described very clearly what the department was responsible for.

Not surprisingly, the name DTI developed extremely strong brand recognition and reputation, accumulated over a period of 27 years, surviving at least two short-lived attempted name changes during that period (each reverting to DTI due to user critical reaction)—until the name (brand) was finally killed off in 2007.

For more than a generation, millions and millions of people recognised the name DTI and knew it was the British government's department for business. Many people also knew the website—if not the exact website address, they knew it was 'www.dti.... (something or other)'.

Simply, tens of millions of people in the UK, and also around the world recognised the DTI as British government's department for business.

For people in business, this is a very substantial advantage for any organisation to have. In corporations, this sort of brand 'equity' is added into balance sheets, and can be valued at many million pounds.

Then in 2007 the government finally forced through a name change, and the DTI was replaced, with, wait for it...

The Department for Business Enterprise and Regulatory Reform - BERR.

Twenty-seven years of brand equity and reputation gone, just like that.

BERR became instantly the most forgettable, least logical, and most stupid departmental brand in the entire history of government department naming and branding cock-ups.

No one knew what it stood for, no one could remember what it was called, and no one could understand what it was supposed to be doing even when it was explained.

Even the term 'business enterprise' was a nonsense in itself. What is business if it's not enterprise? What is enterprise if it's not business?

And what is 'regulatory reform' in the context of business and enterprise? Hardly central to international trade. It was a bit like renaming Manchester United Football Club the Trafford Borough Playing Fields, Caterers and Toilets.

Not surprisingly BERR didn't last long, and duly in 2009 the government changed the name again to BIS—(the department for) Business, Innovation and Skills. Let's see how long this name lasts. I'll give it a year or two at most.

It's only taxpayers' money, so the enormous costs and wastage caused by this recklessness and poorly executed strategy are not scrutinized like they would be in a big company.

You can perhaps begin to imagine the costs, losses and other fallouts caused by changing such a well-established organisational name and presence, twice in two years.

The case study does, however, provide a wonderful example of renaming/rebranding gone wrong on a very grand scale.

Frame a KM Architecture for the above case.

INDIVIDUAL ASSIGNMENT

1. **True or False**
   (i) Knowledge can be created through teamwork.
   (ii) Extrovert people generally don't have self-confidence.
   (iiii) Nonaka coins the term 'tacit knowledge' and 'explicit knowledge'.
2. Explain how an academic institution can create knowledge.

ANSWERS

1.
(i)   True
(ii) False
(iii) True

Exercise # 1—Information Disaster

Clear your mind. Think about the "boxes" that you referred to in your last class of Knowledge Management. Specifically, visualise the contents of projects on servers or in the "CDs/DVDs in filing cabinets and paper drawings in boxes stored offsite by services like Iron Mountain" that is mentioned.

Now, imagine that your building burns down. What type of information artifacts would you lose?

Task—Write down at least 10 information artifacts you would lose.

If you are an architect who specializes in residential design, you probably carry around a library of unit plans which you have built over time. If you are a job captain, you probably have a checklist (at least a mental one) for transferring BIM models between members of the design team. As an HR professional, you probably have a set of guidelines for your technical staff, which you tell them before they interview new staff.

KEYWORDS

The People Core: By people, here we mean knowledge workers, managers, customers, and suppliers.

The Technical Core: The technical core is to enhance communication as well as ensure effective knowledge sharing.

Content Core: Identifying the knowledge centre.

Socialisation: Takes place between people in meetings or in team discussions.

Externalisation: Articulation among people through dialogue (e.g., brainstorming).

Communication: This transformation phase can be best supported by technology. Explicit knowledge can be easily captured and then distributed/transmitted to worldwide audience.

Internalisation: This implies taking explicit knowledge (e.g., a report) and deducing new ideas or taking constructive action. One significant goal of knowledge management is to create technology to help the users derive tacit knowledge from explicit knowledge.

QUESTIONS FOR DISCUSSION

1. What do you understand by knowledge creation? Briefly explain the knowledge creation process.
2. Explain the Nonaka's Knowledge Creation process.
3. What is knowledge architecture? Briefly explain the components of knowledge architecture.
4. Explain the different layers of KM architecture.

INTERNET EXERCISE

1. How does Knowledge Management support knowledge architechture? Identify products or systems on the web that help organisations accomplish knowledge management architecture. Start with *brint.com, decision–support.net,* and *knowledge management. Ittoolbox.com.* Report your findings in the class.

GROUP ASSIGNMENT

Search the internet for vendors of Knowledge Management suites, enterprise knowledge portals, and out-of-the-box Knowledge Management solutions. Identify the major features of each product (use three from each), and compare and contrast their capabilities.

SUGGESTED READINGS

Awad, M. Elias & Ghaziri, Hassan, *Knowledge Management,* Pearson Education, 2009.

Barnes, Stuart ed., *Knowledge Management Systems Theory and Practice,* Thomson Learning, 2002.

Clifford Lynch, "The Afterlives of Courses on the Network: Information Management Issues for Learning Management Systems," *ECAR Research Bulletin,* Vol. 2002, No. 23 (November 26, 2002).

Elias M. Awad, Hassan M. Ghaziri, *Knowledge Management,* Pearson Education Inc., Prentice Hall, 2004.

Frappaoli, Carl, *Knowledge Management,* Wiley, 2006.

Michael H. Zack, "Rethinking the Knowledge-based Organisation," *MIT Sloan Management Review* 44, No. 4 (summer 2003): 67–71.

Norris, Mason and Lefrere, *Transforming e-Knowledge,* 18–27, deals with the many aspects of the changing knowledge experience in words and pictures.

Stephen Denning, Michel Pommier, and Lesley Schneier, "Are There Laws of Knowledge Management?" (February 14, 2002), paper presented at "Connecting the Future: Global Summit of Online Knowledge Networks," Adelaide, March 4–5, 2002.

The notion of *value on investment* is more fully explored in two sources: Donald M. Norris, "Value on Investment in Higher Education," *ECAR Research Bulletin,* Vol. 2003, No. 18 (September 2, 2003); and Donald M. Norris and Mark A. Olson, *The Business Value Web: Resourcing Business Processes and Solutions in Higher Education* (Washington, D.C.: NACUBO, July, 2003).

Tiwana, Amrit, *The Knowledge Management Toolkit,* Pearson Education, 2009.

WEBSITES

<http://www.educationau.edu.au/globalsummit/papers/denning.htm> (accessed July 21, 2003).

http://www.businessballs.com/market.htm#organisational_philosophy_in_planning

CHAPTER 6

Codification

OBJECTIVE

At the end of this lesson, you would be able to understand:

- The concept of codification.
- Definition.
- Importance of codification.
- Modes of knowledge creation.
- Different techniques and procedures of codification.

> *I am enough of an artist to draw freely upon my imagination.*
> *Imagination is more important than knowledge.*
> *Knowledge is limited. But imagination encircles the world.*
> —Albert Einstein

INTRODUCTION

Hansen et al. (2000) describes codification as knowledge that "...is extracted from the person who developed it, then made independent of that person, and reused for various purposes". Codification is that process that creates knowledge storehouses. When conducting an internet search on "Knowledge Management", it is codification that provides 7,88,000 hits. Codification provides a valuable KM process capability. Without codification, the ability to allow explicit knowledge transfer is very limited.

There are two limitations in using codification. They are:

1. Under utilisation of codification.
2. Over utilisation.
   1. Underutilisation of codification results in crippling the spread and use of information throughout the organisation. This may lead to reinventing the things or information again and again.
   2. Overutilisation results in information overload, which is a direct result of codifying and storing in an electronic database, all the company's procedures, policies, processes and references. But it so happens that if any one individual wants any information from the intranet (company's shared information), one may get an enormous amount of data as the information is overloaded. Information overload creates the condition where,

as Cross & Baird (2000) point out, "People usually take advantage of databases only colleagues direct them to a specific point in the database".

Codification comes in many forms, depending on the type of knowledge and its specificity. A common way of displaying knowledge processes is via knowledge maps. Others refer to the process as storyboarding knowledge. Essentially, the goal is to link KM projects to identifiable corporate objectives that add value to the company's bottom line. The overall emphasis is on intellectual capital, company users, and the consumer. This lesson will make you understand the concept of knowledge codification and different techniques for codifications.

DEFINITION

Codification is converting tacit knowledge to explicit knowledge in a usable form for organisational members. From an information system view, it is converting undocumented to documented formation. Regardless of the view, codification is making corporate-specific knowledge (tacit and explicit) visible, accessible, and usable for value-added decision making, no matter what form it may take.

MODES OF KNOWLEDGE CONVERSION

There are four modes of knowledge conversion. They are:

- Conversion from tacit to tacit knowledge produces socialisation where knowledge developer looks for experience in case of knowledge capture.
- Conversion from tacit to explicit knowledge involves externalising, explaining or clarifying tacit knowledge via analogies, models, or metaphors.
- Conversion from explicit to tacit knowledge involves internalising (or fitting explicit knowledge to tacit knowledge.
- Conversion from explicit to explicit knowledge involves combining, categorising, reorganising or sorting different bodies of explicit knowledge to lead to new knowledge.

CODIFYING KNOWLEDGE

An organisation must focus on the following before codification:

- What organisational goals will the codified knowledge serve?
- What knowledge exists in the organisation that can address these goals?
- How useful is the existing knowledge for codification?
- How would someone codify knowledge?

Codifying tacit knowledge (in its entirety) in a knowledge base or repository is often difficult because it is usually developed and internalised in the minds of human experts over a long period of time.

CODIFICATION TOOLS AND PROCEDURE

Knowledge Map

The term "Knowledge Mapping" may seem to be a new concept, but it is not. We practise knowledge mapping in our daily lives but we do not document it and if at all we document our routines, we may not be doing it in a systematic way. Knowledge mapping is a process where a record is maintained from where you can get the knowledge or by whom it is possessed and who is expert in it. For example, if you want any object in your home, you can easily find it because you have all the information about where it is and within a short period of time you can allocate it. This is because a map is set about your home in your mind.

Knowledge maps are mind maps that are used to document knowledge and "how" to alternatives. A knowledge map stimulates both the sides of the brain and is easy to update when new knowledge comes in.

A knowledge map portrays a perspective of the players, sources, flows, constraints and sinks of knowledge within an organisation. It is a navigation aid to both explicit (codified) information and tacit knowledge, showing the importance and the relationships between knowledge stores and the dynamics. The final 'map' can take multiple forms, from a pictorial display to yellow pages directory, to linked topic or concept map, to inventory lists or a matrix of assets against key business processes.

Definitions of Knowledge Mapping

Knowledge mapping is an important practice consisting of survey, audit, and synthesis. It aims at tracking the acquisition and loss of information and knowledge. It explores personal and group competencies and proficiencies. It illustrates or "maps" how knowledge flows throughout an organisation. Knowledge mapping helps an organisation to appreciate how the loss of staff influences intellectual capital, to assist with the selection of teams, and to match technology to knowledge needs and processes. —**Denham Grey**

"Knowledge mapping is a process by which organisations can identify and categorise knowledge assets within their organisation – people, processes, content, and technology. It allows an organisation to fully leverage the existing expertise resident in the organisation, as well as identify barriers and constraints to fulfilling strategic goals and objectives. It is constructing a road map to locate the information needed to make the best use of resources, independent of source or form" —**Wesley Vestal (2003).**

Knowledge map describes what knowledge is used in a process, and how it flows around the process. It is the basis for determining knowledge commonality, or areas where similar knowledge is used across multiple processes. Fundamentally, a process knowledge map contains information about the organisation's knowledge. It describes who has what knowledge (tacit), where the knowledge resides (infrastructure), and how the knowledge is transferred or disseminated (social). —**IBM Global Services**

A knowledge map is the intellectual infrastructure for KM initiatives. The basis for it consists of multiple taxonomies for content repositories, dynamic categorisation of people, their expertise, and the communities they belong to, and finally a set of taxonomies for the variety of tasks that are performed within and by the company communities.

The taxonomies of content, people, and tasks then have to be mapped across the three components in order to provide a foundation for the integration of such KM enterprise projects as knowledge retrieval, for both document based knowledge and the tacit knowledge located within the minds of the companies' experts.

It is also the foundation for collaboration, both for capturing the knowledge that is generated in those collaborative communities, and for providing the framework within which knowledge facilitators or knowledge managers will operate as they provide services for those collaborative communities. For this let us have a look into how the knowledge maps (K-Maps) can be created for a specific task.

There are *four basic steps* of how knowledge maps can be created.

1. The outcomes of the entire process, and their contributions to the key organisational activities
2. Logical sequences of all the activities needed to achieve the goal
3. Specific knowledge required for each task
4. Manpower required for undertaking each task/activity.

After following the steps, what does the map show for a particular task? The knowledge map will show the sources, flows constraints and sinks of knowledge within an organisation. It will also show the knowledge gap and the paths of knowledge exchange.

The **principles** to be followed in K-Mapping are that

- There should be senior management support because of the power, scope and impact of the K-Map.
- Experts should identify and track the knowledge in all forms.
- Tracking of knowledge could be in any form like tacit, explicit, formal, informal, codified, internal, external and permanent knowledge.
- Identifying and tracking of knowledge should be accurate and current data should be produced.

Benefits of K-Mapping

The knowledge map methodology is proven to be effective in helping experts/employees transform their thinking, resulting in significant improvement in corporate performance. The main benefits of knowledge mapping are listed below:

- Most of the experts are engaged in dynamic and energising process as the process connects all experts.
- Different senses are used in the process like:
  - Seeing complex concepts made simple.
  - Reading the data and questions for discussion.

- • Touching exercise cards and placing them where they fit into the metaphor.
- • Talking about first premises and business realities.
- • Listening to the opinions of others and correcting theirs for a better understanding.
- It helps to find the key sources of knowledge creation.
- Knowledge mapping process helps to encourage reuse and prevent reinvention.
- Aids in retrieving critical information quickly.
- Helps in highlighting the experts' expertise.

Knowledge Mapping Tools

Visual concept

It is a visual thinking software; providing a medium for all kinds of creative and systems thinking. It enables ideas to be developed as a basis of planning, designing, authoring, organising, relating, mapping, scenario building and countless other activities. It enables one to easily structure ideas and print them out, communicate them, transfer them and relate them to other visual maps with links to ideas expressed in any Windows environment. It also helps one capture large amounts of information and creates knowledge maps either as ideas occur or as they are extracted from audits, meetings, lectures or texts. The software acts as an outliner to automatically develop clearly structured stories, essays and reports. By mapping interrelationships, one can greatly increase the organisational capacity to understand complex issues. On a corporate network, Visual Concept comes to the fore as a medium for sharing and developing ideas.

Concept mapping

Concept maps are tools for organising and representing knowledge. The fundamental idea propounded by David Ausubel – an expert on learning psychology is that, learning takes place by the assimilation of new concepts and propositions into existing concept propositional frameworks held by the learner. The basic idea is similar to that of a knowledge map. They include concepts–usually enclosed in circles or boxes of some type–and relationships between concepts or propositions, indicated by a connecting line between two concepts. Words on the line specify the relationship between the two concepts.

Concept mapping is also sometimes called taxonomy. It is a method of hierarchically organising and classifying content. This involves labelling pieces of knowledge and relationships between them. A concept can be defined as any unit of thought, any idea that forms in our mind [Gertner, 1978]. Often, nouns are used to refer to concepts [Roche, 2002]. Relations form a special class of concepts [Sowa, 1984]: they describe connections between other concepts. One of the most important relations between concepts is the hierarchical relation (subsumption), in which one concept (superconcept) is more general than the other concept (subconcept) like Natural Resource Management and Watershed Management.

This mapping should be able to relate similar kind of projects and workshops conducted by two different departments, making them more integrated.

Social Network Mapping

This shows networks of knowledge and patterns of interaction among members, groups, organisations, and other social entities like who knows whom, who goes to whom for help and advice, from where the information enters and leaves the groups or organisations, which forums and communities of practice are operational and generating new knowledge.

Competency Mapping

With this kind of mapping, one can create a competency profile with skill, positions, and even the career path of an individual. And, this can also be converted into the organisational yellow pages which enable individuals to find the needed expertise in people within the organisation.

Process-based Knowledge Mapping

This shows knowledge and sources of knowledge for internal as well as external organisational processes and procedures. This includes tacit knowledge (knowledge in people such as know-how, and experience) and explicit knowledge (codified knowledge such as that in document).

Decision Table

Decision table is a table of contingencies to be considered in the definition of a problem, together with the actions to be taken. It is sometimes used in place of a flow chart for programme documentation.

Decision tables are precise but still a compact way of modelling a complicated logic. Unlike the control structures found in the programming languages there are many independent conditions designed here in decision table with several actions.

- It is another technique used for knowledge codification.
- It consists of some conditions, rules, and actions.

A phone card company sends out monthly invoices to permanent customers and gives them discount if payments are made within two weeks. Their discounting policy is as follows:

"If the amount of the order of phone cards is greater than $35, subtract 5% of the order; if the amount is greater than or equal to $60 and less than or equal to $35, subtract a 4% discount; if the amount is less than $60, do not apply any discount."

An example of a decision table for their discounting decisions, where the condition alternatives are 'Yes' and 'No' is given for reference in Figure 6.5.

Structure of Decision Table

A decision table is typically divided into four quadrants, as shown below:

The four quadrants	
Conditions	Condition alternatives
Actions	Action entries

Each decision corresponds to a variable, relation or predicate whose possible values are listed among the condition alternatives. Each action is a procedure or operation to perform, and the entries specify whether (or in what order) the action is to be performed for the set of condition alternatives the entry corresponds to. Many decision tables include in their condition alternatives **don't care** symbol, a hyphen. Using don't cares can simplify decision tables, especially when a given condition has little influence on the actions to be performed. In some cases, entire conditions thought to be important initially are found to be irrelevant when none of the conditions influence which actions are performed

The following is a balanced decision Table 6.1 for reference. An example of working condition of a printer is given:

Table 6.1 Decision Table for Working Condition of Printer

Printer troubleshooter									
		Rules							
Conditions	Printer does not print	Y	Y	Y	Y	N	N	N	N
	A red light is flashing	Y	Y	N	N	Y	Y	N	N
	Printer is unrecognised	Y	N	Y	N	Y	N	Y	N
Actions	Check the power cable				X				
	Check the printer-computer cable	X			X				
	Ensure printer software is installed	X			X		X		X
	Check/replace ink	X	X				X	X	
	Check for paper jam			X		X			

Of course, this is just a simple example (and it does not necessarily correspond to the reality of printer troubleshooting), but even so, it demonstrates how decision tables can scale to several conditions with many possibilities.

Decision Tree

A Decision Tree is a pictorial representation of a decision situation, normally found in discussions of decision making under uncertainty or risk. It shows decision alternatives, states of nature, probabilities attached to the state of nature, and conditional benefits and losses. The tree approach is most useful in a sequential decision situation.

For example, assume ABC Corporation wishes to introduce one of the two products to the market this year. The probabilities and present values (PV) of projected cash inflows follow:

Products	Initial Investment	PV of Cash Inflows	Probabilities
A	$225,000		1.00
		$450,000	0.40
		200,000	0.50
		−100,000	0.10
B	80,000		1.00
		320,000	0.20
		100,000	0.60
		−150,000	0.20

An example of decision tree analysing the two products follows:

DECISON TREE

	Initial Investment (1)	Probability (2)	PV of Cash Inflow (3)	PV of Cash Inflow (2 x 3) = (4)
		0.40	$450,000	$180,000
	$225,000	0.50	$200,000	100,000
		0.10	-$100,000	10,000
Product A		Expected PV of Cash Inflows		$270,000

Choice A or B

		0.20	$ 320,000	$ 64,000
Product B	$ 80,000	0.60	$100,000	60,000
		0.20	-$150,000	30,000
		Expected PV of Cash Inflows		$ 94,000

For Product A:

Expected NPV = expected PV - 1 = $270,000 – $225,000 = $45,000

For Product B:

Expected NPV = $94,000 – $80,000 = $14,000

Based on the expected net present value, the company should choose product A over product B. In short, a decision tree is:

- Knowledge codification technique.
- A decision tree is usually a hierarchically arranged semantic network.

A decision tree consists of three types of nodes:

1. Decision nodes—commonly represented by squares.
2. Chance nodes—represented by circles.
3. End nodes—represented by triangles.

A decision tree is drawn from left to right. It has burst nodes (splitting paths) but no sink nodes (converging paths). When the decision trees are drawn manually they grow big because of the converging paths.

A decision tree for the phone card company discounting policy (as discussed above) is shown in Figure 6.1.

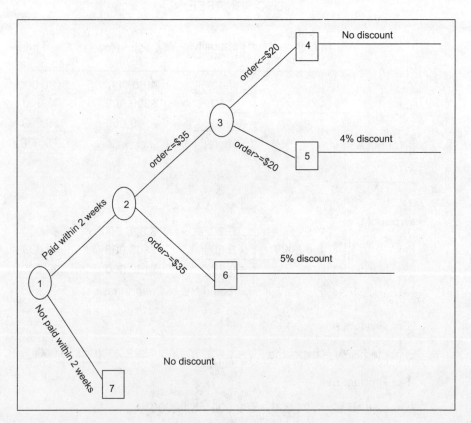

Fig. 6.1 Decision Tree

Advantages of Decision Tree

The decision tree has several advantages. A few of them are as follows:

- They are simple to understand and interpret. It can be explained in detail by looking at the diagram.
- Important insights can be generated based on experts describing a situation and their preferences for outcomes.
- If a result is given by a model then the explanation of the model is easily replicated by simple maths.
- Decision trees can be combined with other decision techniques.
- Decision tree is a useful tool for helping an individual choose between several courses of action.
- It has an effective structure within which one can explore options, and investigate the possible outcomes while choosing the options.
- It helps the experts to form a balanced picture of risks and rewards associated with each possible course of action.

Frames

A frame is a structure or a codification scheme for organising knowledge through previous experience. It handles a combination of declarative and operational knowledge, which makes it easier to understand the problem domain. A frame represents knowledge about an entity in the real world, such as an employee, a person, or person type.

A frame is like a cookbook recipe: Its "slots" contain both the ingredients for the recipe and the procedural details ("cook over medium heart", "toast until brown") to make the data operational or to fill the slots, within or between frames. The idea is to catalogue the requirements for membership of certain elements of a knowledge scheme. In other words, it is a data structure with a name, a type, and a set of attributes, called slots.

Frames have two key elements:

- A slot is a specific object being described as an attribute of an entity. For example, in a personnel knowledge base, some of the slots are "instructor", "unique feature of employee verification", and "training certification".
- A facet is the value of an object or a slot.

Case-Based Reasoning

- It is reasoning from relevant past cases in a way similar to humans' use of past experiences to arrive at conclusions.
- Case-based reasoning is a technique that records and documents cases and then searches the appropriate cases to determine their usefulness in solving new cases presented to the expert.
- The aim is to bring up the most similar historical case that matches the present case.

■ Adding new cases and reclassifying the case library usually expands knowledge.
■ A case library may require considerable database storage as well as an efficient retrieval system.

Knowledge-Based Agents

■ An intelligent agent is a programme code which is capable of performing autonomous action in a timely fashion.
■ They can exhibit goal directed behaviour by taking initiative.
■ They can be programmed to interact with other agents or humans by using some agent communication language.
■ In terms of knowledge-based systems, an agent can be programmed to learn from the user behaviour and deduce future behaviour for assisting the user.

SUMMING UP

Codification is converting tacit knowledge to explicit knowledge in a usable form for organisational members. From an information system view, it is converting undocumented into documented information. Regardless of the view, codification is making corporate-specific knowledge (tacit and explicit) visible, accessible, and usable for value-added decision making, no matter what form it may take.

There are various codification techniques: knowledge mapping, decision table, decision tree, frame name a few.

There are various knowledge capturing techniques available, e.g., onsite observation, brain storming, consensus decision making, repertory grid, NGT, Delphi method, concept mapping, blackboard, etc.

Onsite observation is the process of observing, interpreting and recording problem-solving behaviour while it takes place. Brainstorming is unstructured approach to generating ideas about a problem. Electronic brain storing is a computer-aided approach to dealing with multiple experts. Protocol analysis is thinking aloud the method. Consensus decision making is the clear agreement regarding the best solution to a problem. NGT provides an interface between consensus and brainstorming. Delphi method is a survey of experts. Concept mapping is a network of concepts, consisting of nodes and links. In blackboarding it is assumed that all participants are experts with unique experience and all have an equal chance at contributing to the solution, via the blackboard.

CASE STUDY

KM Initiatives at BaaN

BaaN is a world leader in powerful, innovative, easy-to-use business software. They are at the cutting edge of business technology used by industry leaders all over the world, promoting collaboration between customers and suppliers, linking people and processes across the world, and using the internet to make business faster and more cost-effective. They have turned towards knowledge management, in keeping with the demands of time. Two departments, viz. 'knowledge transfer' and 'knowledge development' are projected for this purpose. Their main objective is to empower the members with skills necessary to meet the external world. They have a centralised database system and it is christened as "SCOPUS". Intranet facility is provided for the members with their password authorising them to use the system.

One of the features of BaaN is the encouragement provided to the employees for knowledge management. "ASK HER" is one such technique that provides a chance to the employees to make use of public folders and register their doubts and genuine problems. Longer duration training programmes are provided for new recruits. The others receive short or mini programmes to update their knowledge.

BaaN's attempts to multiply knowledge could be seen in the well-maintained library for the purpose. They contain technical as well as non-technical printed material and is used by those employees who crave for knowledge.

"SPANDANA" known as 'reaction' is keenly felt in their monthly meetings. The people talk and they talk openly and freely with the management. They are helpful in extending the sharing of the knowledge which is considered a rich source of knowledge. The meetings also make the people come out of their shell and express their genuine concern for aspects that the organisation stands for. Sharing of knowledge, beyond doubt highlights the brighter side of the employees' vast experiences in a particular field, their updated knowledge, their concern for the system and their sense of responsibility.

Periodic seminars and discussions help both in documentation and multiplying the knowledge, thus leading to an effective Knowledge Management.

Source: Published Reading Material on Knowledge Management, National Conference, Informatica- 2003, Institute of Public Enterprise, Hyderabad.

LESSON & ACTIVITY

1. Allen and Hamilton have suggested that, amazingly, up to 84% of all knowledge management programmes fail. What do you make of this statement, and what can organisations do to increase the likelihood of success?
2. "Even though there are many knowledge capturing techniques available, however, capturing knowledge is really tough and very challenging"—Explain.

KEYWORDS

Brainstorming: It is an unstructured method to generate ideas about a problem.

Protocol analysis: Here experts talk loudly while solving a problem.

Consensus decision making: Clear agreement regarding the best solution to a problem.

NGT: Panel of experts become a nominal group whose meetings are structured in order to effectively pool individual judgment.

Delphi method: A survey of experts.

Codification: It is converting tacit knowledge to explicit knowledge in a usable form for organisational members.

Knowledge Map: A knowledge map portrays a perspective of the players, sources, flows, constraints and sinks of knowledge within an organisation.

Decision Table: It is another technique used for knowledge codification. It consists of some conditions, rules, and actions.

Frames: A frame is a structure or a codification scheme for organising knowledge through previous experience. It handles a combination of declarative and operational knowledge, which makes it easier to understand the problem domain. A frame represents knowledge about an entity in the real world, such as an employee, a person, or person type.

Decision Tree: It is also a knowledge codification technique. A decision tree is usually a hierarchically arranged semantic network.

QUESTIONS FOR DISCUSSION

1. What do you understand by knowledge codification?
2. Explain the importance of knowledge codification.
3. Define codification.
4. Write short notes on: (i) Knowledge Mapping (ii) Decision Tree (iii) Frames (iv) Decision Table.
5. Explain briefly codification tools and procedures.

SUGGESTED READINGS

A Thothathri Raman, *Knowledge Management*, Excel Book, New Delhi, 2003.

A. L. Delbecq and A. H Vande Ven, "A Group Process Model for Problem Identification and Program Planning," *Journal of Applied Behavioral Science* VII (July/August, 1971), 466–91 and A. L. Del becq A. H. Vande Ven, and D. H. Gustafson, *Group Techniques for Program Planners* (Glenview, Illinois: Scott Foresman and Company, 1975).

Bartlett, Christopher A., The Knowledge-Based Organisation, In *The Knowledge Advantage* (Ruggles), 1999.

Elias M. Awad, Hassan M. Ghaziri, *Knowledge Management*, Pearson, New Delhi, 2006.

Erickson, T. D. and Simon, H. A., Protocol Analysis: Verbal Reports as Data. Cambridge, USA: The MIT Press, 1985.

Jaspers, M.W., Steen, T., van den Bos, C. & Geenen, M., The Think Aloud Method: A Guide to User Interface Design, Int J. Med. Inform., 73(11–12): 781–95, 2004.

K. R. Vedros, "The Nominal Group Technique is a Participatory, Planning Method in Adult Education" (Ph.D. dissertation, Florida State University, Tallahassee, 1979)

Malhotra, Yogesh, "Knowledge Management and New Organisation Forms: A New Framework for Business Model Innovation", *Information Resources Management Journal, Jan–Mar 2000*.

M. D. Dunnette, J. D. Campbell, and K. Jaastad, "The Effect of Group Participation on Brainstoming Effectiveness for Two Industrial Samples", *Journal of Applied Psychology*, XLVII (February, 1963), 30–37.

Preece, J., Rogers, Y. & Sharp, H., Interaction Design: Beyond Human-Computer Interaction, New York: John Wiley & Sons, 2002.

Prusak, L., "Where did knowledge management come from*?*" *IBM Systems Journal*, Volume 40, Number 7, 2001.

Smith, Peter A.C., McLaughlin, Moira. "Knowledge Management: People are Important!" *Journal of Knowledge Management Practice,* January 2004.

Thomas, J. C., Kellogg, W. A., and Erickson, T. "The Knowledge Management Puzzle: Human and Social Factors in Knowledge Management"*, IBM Systems Journal,* Volume 40, Number 7, 2001.

Warier Sudhir, *Knowledge Management,* Vikas Publications, 2003.

CHAPTER 7

Knowledge Capturing Techniques

OBJECTIVE

At the end of this lesson, you would be able to understand:

- Various techniques for knowledge capturing.
- Onsite observation.
- Brainstorming.
- Consensus decision making.
- Repertory grid.
- Nominal group technique.
- Delphi method.
- Concept mapping.
- Blackboarding.
- The concept of capturing knowledge.

INTRODUCTION

"Knowledge management will never work until corporations
realize it's not about how you capture knowledge
but how you create and leverage it."
—Etienne Wenger

In the previous lesson, we have understood codification and in this lesson we will know more about knowledge capturing techniques and their characteristics.

TECHNIQUES COVERED

- Onsite Observation (Action Protocol)
- Brainstorming (Conventional & Electronic)
- Consensus Decision Making
- Repertory Grid
- Nominal Group Technique
- Delphi Method
- Concept Mapping
- Blackboarding

ONSITE OBSERVATION

It gives live exposure to the engineer through participant observation while working at the site. Observation of behaviour knowledge developer to seek knowledge of the expert within the working world. In comparison to the interview, observation places the knowledge developer closer to the actual steps and procedures used by the expert to solve the problem. One problem with this capture technique is that some experts do not like to be observed. They prefer to talk about their thought process rather than show them in practice. Sometimes, experts fear that observation will give away years of experience in one quick look.

The features can be summarised as follows:

- Process of observing, interpreting, and recording problem-solving behaviour while it takes place.
- More listening than talking.
- Some experts do not like to be observed.
- Fear of 'giving away' expertise is a concern.
- Process can be distracting to others in the setting.

BRAINSTORMING

Unlike onsite observation, which focuses on the work of a single expert, brainstorming is an unstructured approach to generating ideas about a problem, inviting two or more experts into a session in which discussions are carried out and a variety of opinions are tossed around. The primary goal of this process is to think up creative solutions to problems. In brainstorming, all possible solutions are considered equally. The emphasis is on the frequency of responses during the session. Anything related to the topic can be brought up, and everything is valued. Questions can be raised for clarification, but no evaluation is made at the moment.

The features can be listed as follows:

- Unstructured approach to generating ideas about a problem.
- All possible solutions considered equally.
- Emphasis is on the frequency of responses during the session.
- Idea generation, followed by idea evaluation.

ELECTRONIC BRAINSTORMING

A relatively new development in brainstorming is a computer-aided approach to deal with multiple experts. Desks in a U-Shaped layout hold PCs networked through a software tool that serves as a catalyst in the meeting, promotes instant exchange of ideas between experts and sorts and condenses those ideas into an organised format. Such a tool also allows experts to elaborate and vote on ideas.

- Computer-aided approach to dealing with multiple experts.
- Begin with a pre-session plan that identifies objectives and structures the agenda.
- Allows two or more experts to provide opinions through PCs asynchronously.
- Protects shy experts and prevents tagging comments to individuals.

Rules for Brainstorming

- No criticism, evaluation, judgment, or defence of ideas during the brainstorming session.
- No limit on 'wild' ideas, no matter how outrageous or impractical they seem. Every idea is to be expressed.
- Quantity is more desirable than quality.
- 'Piggybacking'—building on ideas—is encouraged.
- Everyone must be encouraged to participate.
- Record all ideas.
- Choose 'top 5 ideas'—combine similar ideas where appropriate.
- Individually rank ideas.
- Decide, as a group, which idea will be enacted first.
- Begin the brainstorming process again as necessary.

PROTOCOL ANALYSIS

Suppose you want to understand the diagnostic process of a medical expert; the knowledge he or she uses; and the cognitive actions he or she takes. How would you go about it? One obvious approach is to ask the expert questions about diagnosis. Chances are the expert will not find it easy to answer questions. One of the authors found out that his orthopaedic surgeon is more used to doing the job than explaining it. The surgeon tried to explain diagnosing a diabetic foot in terms of the formal procedure he learned in medical school, which is not quite the diagnosis he follows with each patient. The alternative is to observe an examination of a real patient and then listen to the spoken protocol.

The features can be listed as follows:

- Think-aloud method.
- Expert keeps talking, speaking out loud while solving a problem.
- Effective source of information on cognitive processes.
- Makes expert cognisant of the processes being described.
- Similarity / Difference to onsite Observation.

CONSENSUS DECISION MAKING

Decision making involves making a choice from the available or generated alternatives. When a decision is made face-to-face every member is a potential contributor to the process of decision making, which involves understanding the problem or the issue, breaking into meaningful components, which indicates the real problems on which decisions are required. In the process of decision making the group may range between two extremes. On one extreme may be the main consent of getting one's own point of view accepted. Consensus does not necessarily mean unanimity. It means sharing of differences, listening to each other, accepting the final choice in spite of the differences, which may still exist. As a result of consensus all members of the group don't come to the same conclusion. The difference may continue. The commitment to the implementation of the solution is assured.

The features can be listed as follows:

- Clear agreement regarding the best solution to a problem.
- As a tool, it follows brainstorming.
- Procedure ensures fairness and standardisation in the way experts arrive at a consensus.
- Can be tedious and take hours.
- The rigidity of the consensus method can be a problem for many experts.

NOMINAL GROUP TECHNIQUES (NGT)

In some problem domains, more than one expert might be available as a source of knowledge for building the KM system. However, for situations in which several experts have overlapping expertise, each expert's opinion must be interpreted in line with the problem domain. In fact, a single expert is used precisely to avoid potential contradictions between experts and possible misinterpretations on the part of the knowledge developer. The nominal group technique and Delphi method have been shown to mitigate some of the process losses associated with multiple experts.

The features are listed as follows:

- Provides an interface between consensus and brainstorming.
- Panel of experts becomes a "nominal" group whose meetings are structured in order to effectively pool individual judgment.
- An idea writing or idea generation technique.

NGT Procedure

- Each expert is asked to list the pros and cons of the problem or alternate solutions.
- A list of all pros and cons is compiled.
- Each expert is given the list and asked to rank them on the basis of their priorities.
- Knowledge developer leads a discussion on the relative ranks in the hope of getting possible solutions.
- A group discussion is followed to choose the "best" solution from the alternatives.

NGT (Advantages)

- Effective in multiple expert knowledge capture, especially when minimizing differences in status among experts.
- In NGT, each expert has an equal chance to express ideas parallelly by with other experts in the group.
- With discussion proceeds in sequential order, NGT can be a more efficient and productive approach than brainstorming.

NGT (Drawbacks)

- Technique can be time-consuming.
- Has been known to promote impatience among experts who must listen to discussions with other experts.
- With experts sharing their expertise, the best solution can be adopted.
- NGT is ideal in situations of uncertainty regarding the nature of the problem.

DELPHI METHOD

- A survey of experts.
- A series of questionnaires used to pool experts' responses in order to solve a difficult problem.
- Each expert's contributions shared with the rest of experts by using the results of one questionnaire to construct the next questionnaire.

Delphi Method (Pros and Cons)

Pros

- Anonymous response.
- Controlled feedback.
- Statistical group response.

Cons

- Experts often lack the necessary knowledge on which to base final judgment.
- Poorly designed questionnaire could cause all kinds of problems.

BLACKBOARDING

Imagine bringing a group of experts together in a room with a large blackboard. The experts work together to solve a problem, using the blackboard as their work space. Initial data is written on the blackboard for all to see. Each expert has an equal chance to contribute to the solution via the blackboard. The process of blackboarding continues until the problem has been solved.

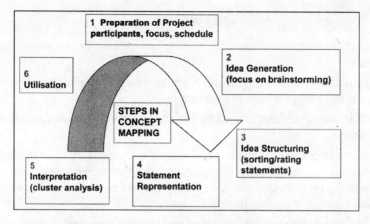

Fig. 7.1   Steps in Concept Mapping

One important assumption of a blackboard system is that all participants are experts, but they have acquired their own expertise in situations different from those of the other experts in the group. Because each expert's experience is unique, no one need feel either inferior or superior in offering a possible solution. The essence of this technique is the independence of expertise in an atmosphere that discourages compliance or intimidation.

The features are listed as follows:

- Participants share a common language for interaction.
- Flexible representation of information.
- Efficient storage and location of information.
- Organised participation.
- Iterative approach to problem solving.

SUMMING UP

There are various knowledge capturing techniques available, e.g., onsite observation, brainstorming, consensus decision making, repertory grid, NGT, Delphi method, concept mapping, blackboard, etc.

Onsite observation is the process of observing, interpreting and recording problem-solving behaviour while it takes place. Brainstorming is unstructured approach to generating ideas about a problem. Electronic brain storing is a computer-aided approach to dealing with multiple experts. Protocol analysis is the thinking aloud method.

Consensus decision making is the clear agreement regarding the best solution to a problem. NGT provides an interface between consensus and brainstorming. Delphi method is a survey of experts. Concept mapping is a network of concepts, consisting of nodes and links. In blackboarding it is assumed that all participants are experts with unique experiences and all have an equal chance at contributing to the solution, via the blackboard.

KEYWORDS

Codification: It is converting tacit knowledge into explicit knowledge in a usable form for organisational members.

Knowledge Map: A knowledge map portrays a perspective of the players, sources, flows, constraints and sinks of knowledge within an organisation.

Decision Table: It is another technique used for knowledge codification. It consists of some conditions, rules, and actions.

Frames: A frame is a structure or a codification scheme for organising knowledge through previous experience. It handles a combination of declarative and operational knowledge, which makes it easier to understand the problem domain. A frame represents knowledge about an entity in the real world, such as an employee, a person, or person type.

Decision Tree: It is also a knowledge codification technique. A decision tree is usually a hierarchically arranged semantic network.

Brainstorming: It is an unstructured method to generate ideas about a problem.

Protocol Analysis: Here experts talk loudly while solving a problem.

Consensus decision making: Clear agreement regarding the best solution to a problem.

NGT: Panel of experts becomes a nominal group whose meetings are structured in order to effectively pool individual judgment.

Delphi Method: A survey of experts.

QUESTIONS FOR DISCUSSION

1. Write short notes on: (i) Knowledge mapping (ii) Decision Tree (iii) Frames (iv) Decision table.
2. Explain briefly codification tools and procedures.
3. Name a few techniques of knowledge capturing.
4. Explain conventional and electronic brainstorming methods in detail.
5. What is blackboarding? Explain its characteristics.
6. Write short notes on: (i) NTG (ii) Repertory Grid (iii) Concept mapping (iv) Delphi Method.

SUGGESTED READINGS

A. Thothathri Raman, *Knowledge Management,* Excel Books, New Delhi, 2003.

Bartlett, Christopher A., The Knowledge-Based Organisation, in *The Knowledge Advantage* (Ruggles), 1999.

Elias M. Awad, Hassan M. Ghaziri, *Knowledge Management,* Pearson Education Inc., Prentice Hall, 2004.

Elias M. Awad, Hassan M. Ghaziri, *Knowledge Management,* Pearson, New Delhi, 2006.

Malhotra, Yogesh, "Knowledge Management and New Organisation Forms: A New framework for Business Model Innovation", *Information Resources Management Journal,* Jan–Mar, 2000.

Prusak, L. "Where did knowledge management come from?" *IBM Systems Journal* Volume 40, Number 7, 2001.

Savage, Charles M., 5th Generation Management, Digital Press, 1990.

Smith, Peter A.C., McLaughlin, Moira, "Knowledge Management: People are Important! In *Journal of "Knowledge Management Practice"*, January 2004.

Stuart Barnes (ed.), Knowledge Management Systems Theory and Practice, Thomson Learning, 2002.

Thomas, J. C., Kellogg, W. A., and Erickson, T., "The Knowledge Management Puzzle: Human and Social Factors in Knowledge Management", *IBM Systems Journal*, Volume 40, Number 7, 2001.

Warier Sudhir, *"Knowledge Management"*, Vikas Publications, 2003.

CHAPTER 8

Capturing Tacit Knowledge

OBJECTIVE

At the end of this lesson, you would be able to understand:

- The concept of capturing knowledge.
- The concept of tacit knowledge.
- Capturing tacit knowledge.
- Technique of capturing tacit knowledge.
- Interview as capturing tacit knowledge.
- Concept of prototyping interview.
- Measuring the value of Knowledge Management.
- What to measure? How to measure?
- Common measurement approaches.

> *A person who graduated yesterday and stops studying today*
> *is uneducated tomorrow.*
> —Anonymous

INTRODUCTION

The concept of tacit knowing comes from scientist and philosopher Michael Polanyi. It is important to understand that he wrote about a process (hence tacit knowing) and not a form of knowledge. However, his phrase has been taken up to name a form of knowledge that is apparently wholly or partly inexplicable.

Capturing tacit knowledge and converting it into rules that the computer can use is a costly business. It requires an extensive time commitment from the domain expert and the special skills of the knowledge developer. At times, the expert might list interest in the project and even feel like quitting. Perhaps the knowledge developer and the expert just never seem to hit it off their interpersonal chemistry, or the knowledge developer may use the wrong tool or approach.

Working with experts in capturing their tacit knowledge is not a straightforward routine. For example, the methods or tools chosen for knowledge capture depend on the temperament, personality, and attitude of the expert and whether the knowledge automation system is being built around a single expert or multiple experts. Another important factor is whether one or more knowledge developers will be involved in the building process.

Before beginning the knowledge capture process, a knowledge developer needs to have an understanding of the expert's level of expertise. The knowledge developer can look at several indicators of expertise as well as specific qualifications to determine whether someone is an expert. One of the most important indicators is the expert's communication skills.

This lesson will help you understand the basics of tacit knowledge and various capturing techniques.

HISTORY AND DEFINITION

The 19th century German physiologist Hermann von Helmholtz suggested that we derive understanding primarily through experience. It was Michael Polanyi who coined the term tacit knowledge and cemented the idea that not all knowledge could be transferred through explicit learning. In 1991, Ikujiro Nonaka took this theory and designed principles for large business training procedures.

By definition, tacit knowledge is knowledge that people carry in their minds and is, therefore, difficult to access. Often, people are not aware of the knowledge they possess or how it can be valuable to others. Tacit knowledge is considered more valuable because it provides context for people, places, ideas, and experiences. Effective transfer of tacit knowledge generally requires extensive personal contact and trust.

Nonaka, 1994, defines "explicit" or codified knowledge as one that is transmittable in formal, systematic language. On the other hand, "tacit" knowledge has a personal quality, which makes it hard to formalise and communicate. Tacit knowledge is deeply rooted in action, commitment, and involvement in a specific context.

Tacit knowledge is not easily shared. One of Polanyi's famous aphorisms is: "We know more than we can tell." Tacit knowledge consists often of habits and culture that we do not recognise in ourselves. In the field of knowledge management the concept of tacit knowledge refers to knowledge which is only known to an individual and which is difficult to communicate to the rest of the organisation. Knowledge that is easy to communicate is called explicit knowledge. The process of transforming tacit knowledge into explicit knowledge is known as codification or articulation.

A review of the literature reveals as many definitions of knowledge capture as there are authors. Some of the definitions are interesting:

- Knowledge developer–An 'applied brain drain'.
- A 'manual craft that depends on the skill and effectiveness of the knowledge developer'.
- The 'transfer of problem-solving expertise from some knowledge source to a repository or a programme'.
- The 'process by which knowledge management system developers discover the knowledge that company experts use to perform the task of interest'.
- An investigative experiment process involving interviews and protocol analysis in order to build a KM system.

Research has emphasised two areas of difficulty with regard to tacit knowledge.

1. Tacit knowledge is very difficult to identify in the practical sense, and
2. It is equally, if not more, difficult to isolate instances of tacit knowledge sharing as this discovery requires an explication of the tacit knowledge.

> *The store of wisdom does not consist of hard coins which keep their shape*
> *as they pass from hand to hand; it consists of ideas and doctrines whose*
> *meanings change with the minds that entertain them.*
>
> —John Plamenatz

TACIT KNOWLEDGE vs EXPLICIT KNOWLEDGE

There are a lot of differences that do exist between tacit and explicit knowledge. Let us first identify the differences between them.

Knowledge that can be passed on by explanation is considered explicit knowledge. Tacit knowledge requires hands-on training, and even then may not be learned. Tacit knowledge can be described as "know-how," while explicit knowledge can be described as "knowing-that." In some cases, explicit knowledge is how an apprentice is taught to help speed up the learning process. But tacit knowledge gained through experience and personal insight is what will transform the apprentice into an expert.

Example

Riding a bike is considered tacit knowledge. You can be told how to do it, but not well enough to do it correctly on the first try. Experience is what will teach you to ride a bike correctly. The ability to recognise someone's face instantly, even when presented with people who look similar, is tacit knowledge. Someone might describe a person to you, but if they're sat next to several other people who look similar (i.e., brown hair, brown eyes and medium skin), you will not 'recognise' that person by description alone. Language is mastered through tacit knowledge. Explicit teaching might give you grammatical rules and help you memorise some words, but immersion in the language is what allows you to master it.

Toyota's use of Quality Circles also provides an example of the tacit knowledge approach to creating new knowledge. At the end of each work week, groups of Toyota production workers spend one to two hours analysing the performance of their part of the production system to identify the actual or potential problems in quality or productivity. Each group proposes "countermeasures" to correct the identified problems, and discusses the results of countermeasures taken during the week to address problems identified the week before. Through personal interactions in such Quality Circle group settings, Toyota employees share their ideas for improvement, devise steps to test new ideas for improvement, and assess the results of their tests. This knowledge management practice, which is repeated weekly as an integral part of the Toyota production system, progressively identifies, eliminates, and even prevents errors. As improvements developed by Quality Circles are accumulated over many years, Toyota's production system has become one of the highest quality production processes in the world (Spear and Bowen, 1999).

Theories/speculation

Fred Dretske argued the limits of tacit knowledge versus implicit knowledge, stating that far more of what is attributed to tacit learning is actually implicit; those who have "know-how" on a certain subject have an implicit understanding of how to seek solutions to problems they are faced with and how to react to setbacks. Nonaka theorised that the work environment should be organised so the tacit knowledge of the individual worker could be amplified. Once the people that made up the "life" of the company experience a deeper understanding through their skills, the organisation can more effectively create "new knowledge."

> *Companies... have a hard time distinguishing between the*
> *cost of paying people and the value of investing in them.*
> —Thomas A. Stewart 1948

Misconceptions of Tacit Knowledge

To make wider use of the tacit knowledge of individuals, managers are urged to identify the knowledge possessed by various individuals in an organisation and then to arrange the kind of interactions between knowledgeable individuals that will help the organisation perform its current tasks, transfer knowledge from one part of the organisation to another, and/or create new knowledge that may be useful to the organisation. Let us consider some examples of current practice in each of these activities that are typical of the tacit knowledge approach.

Most managers of organisations today do not know what specific kinds of knowledge the individuals in their organisation know. This common state of affairs is reflected in the lament usually attributed to executives of Hewlett-Packard in the 1980s:

"If only we knew what we know, we could conquer the world." As firms become larger, more knowledge intensive, and more globally dispersed, the need for their managers to "know what we know" is becoming acute. Thus, a common initiative within the tacit knowledge approach is usually some effort to improve understanding of who knows about what in an organisation—an effort that is sometimes described as an effort to create "know who" forms of knowledge.

An example of such an effort is the creation within Philips, the global electronics company, of a "yellow pages" listing experts with different kinds of knowledge within Philips' many business units. Today on the Philips intranet one can type in the keywords for a specific knowledge domain —say, for example, knowledge about the design of optical pickup units for CD/DVD players and recorders—and the yellow pages will retrieve a listing of the people within Philips worldwide who have stated that they have such knowledge. Contact information is also provided for each person listed, so that anyone in Philips who wants to know more about that kind of knowledge can get in the touch with the listed individuals.

As new ways of developing explicit learning began to expand, many researchers overlooked how certain knowledge was adapted. They assumed that knowledge that was not explicitly learned was there all along. This overlooks the method for learning fundamental things, such as language. Long before a child is taught grammar, he/she utilizes grammatical rules to construct unique sentences. This type of learning is tacit, not explicit.

CAPTURING THE TACIT KNOWLEDGE

Expert Evaluation

- *Indicators of expertise:*
  - The expert commands genuine respect.
  - The expert is found to be consulted by people in the organisation, when some problem arises.

- The expert possesses self-confidence and he/she has a realistic view of the limitations.
- The expert avoids irrelevant information, and uses facts and figures.
- The expert is able to explain properly and he/she can customise his/her presentation according to the level of the audience.
- The expert exhibits his/her depth of the detailed knowledge and his/her quality of explanation is exceptional.
- The expert is not arrogant regarding his/her personal information.

■ *Experts' qualifications:*

The expert should

- know when to follow hunches, and when to make exceptions.
- be able to see the big picture.
- possess good communication skills.
- be able to tolerate stress.
- be able to think creatively.
- be able to exhibit self-confidence in his/her thoughts and actions.
- maintain credibility.
- operate within a schema-driven/structured orientation.
- use chunked knowledge.
- be able to generate enthusiasm as well as motivation.
- share his/her expertise willingly and without hesitation.
- emulate an ideal teacher's habits.

■ *Experts' levels of expertise:*

- Highly expert persons.
- Moderately expert problem solvers.
- New experts.

Capturing single vs multiple experts' tacit knowledge:

Advantages of working with a single expert:

■ Ideal for building a simple KM system with only few rules.

■ Ideal when the problem lies within a restricted domain.

■ The single expert can facilitate the logistics aspects of coordination arrangements for knowledge capture.

■ Problem related/personal conflicts are easier to resolve.

■ The single expert tends to share more confidentiality.

Disadvantages of working with a single expert:

■ Often, the experts' knowledge is found to be not easy to capture.

■ The single expert usually provides a single line of reasoning.

■ They are more likely to change meeting schedules.

■ The knowledge is often found to be dispersed.

Advantages of working with multiple (team) experts:

- Complex problem domains are usually benefited.
- Stimulates interaction.
- Listening to a multitude of views allows the developer to consider alternative ways of representing knowledge.
- Formal meetings are sometimes better environment for generating thoughtful contributions.

Disadvantages of working with multiple (team) experts:

- Disagreements can frequently occur.
- Coordinating meeting schedules is more complicated.
- Harder to retain confidentiality.
- Overlapping mental processes of multiple experts can result in a process loss.
- Often requires more than one knowledge developer.

The single greatest challenge facing managers in the developed countries
of the world is to raise the productivity of knowledge and service works.
—Peter F. Drucker 1909–2005

DEVELOPING RELATIONSHIP WITH EXPERTS

- *Creating the right impression:* The knowledge developer must learn to use psychology, common sense, and technical as well as marketing skills to earn the expert's respect and attention.
- *Understanding of the expert's style of expression.*
- *Preparation for the session:*
  - Before making the first appointment, the knowledge developer must acquire some knowledge about the problem and the expert.
  - Initial sessions can be most challenging/critical.
  - The knowledge developer must build the trust.
  - The knowledge developer must be familiar with project terminology and he/she must review the existing documents.
  - The knowledge developer should be able to make a quick rapport with the expert.
- *Deciding the location for the session:*
  - Protocol calls for the expert to decide the location.
  - The expert is usually more comfortable in having his/her necessary tools and information available close to him/her.
  - The meeting place should be quiet and free of interruptions.
- *Approaching multiple experts:*
  - Individual approach: The knowledge developer holds sessions with one expert at a time.

- **Approach using primary and secondary experts:**
  - The knowledge developer holds sessions with the senior expert early in the knowledge capture programme for the clarification of the plan.
  - For a detailed probing, he/she may ask for other experts' knowledge.
- *Small groups approach:*
  - Experts gather together in one place, discuss the problem domain, and usually provide a pool of information.
  - Experts' responses are monitored, and the functionality of each expert is tested against the expertise of the others.
  - This approach requires experience in assessing tapped knowledge, as well as cognition skills.
  - The knowledge developer must deal with the issue of power and its effect on the expert's opinion.

INTERVIEWING AS A TACIT KNOWLEDGE CAPTURE TOOL

- *Advantages of using interviewing as a tacit knowledge capture tool:*
  - It is a flexible tool.
  - It is excellent for evaluating the validity of information.
  - It is very effective in case of eliciting information regarding complex matters.
  - Often people enjoy being interviewed.
- *Interviews can range from the highly unstructured type to highly structured type.*
  - The unstructured types are difficult to conduct, and they are used in the case when the knowledge developer really needs to explore an issue.
  - The structured types are found to be goal-oriented, and they are used in the case when the knowledge developer needs specific information.
  - Structured questions can be of the following types:
    - Multiple-choice questions.
    - Dichotomous questions.
    - Ranking scale questions.
  - In semi-structured types, the knowledge developer asks predefined questions, but he/she allows the expert some freedom in expressing his/her answer.
- *Guidelines for successful interviewing:*
  - Setting the stage and establishing rapport.
  - Phrasing questions.
  - Listening closely/avoiding arguments.
  - Evaluating the session outcomes.

Reliability of the information gathered from experts:
- *Some uncontrolled sources of error that can reduce the information's reliability:*
  - Expert's perceptual slant.
  - The failure on the expert's part to remember exactly what had happened.
  - Fear of the unknown on part of the expert.
  - Problems with communication.
  - Role bias.

■ Errors on part of the knowledge developer: validity problems are often caused by the *interviewer effect* (something about the knowledge developer colours the response of the expert). Some of the effects can be as follows:
  • Gender effect
  • Age effect
  • Race effect
■ *Problems encountered during interviewing*
  • Response bias.
  • Inconsistency.
  • Problem with communication.
  • Hostile attitude.
  • Standardising the questions.
  • Setting the length of the interview.
■ *Process of ending the interview:*
  • The end of the session should be carefully planned.
  • One procedure calls for the knowledge developer to halt the questioning for a few minutes before the scheduled ending time, and to summarize the key points of the session.
  • This allows the expert to comment and schedule a future session.
  • Many verbal/non-verbal cues can be used for ending the interview.
■ *Issues:* Many issues may arise during the interview, and to be prepared for the most important ones, the knowledge developer can consider the following questions:
  • How would it be possible to elicit knowledge from the experts who cannot say what they mean or cannot mean what they say.
  • How to set up the problem domain.
  • How to deal with uncertain reasoning processes.
  • How to deal with the situation of difficult relationships with expert(s).
  • How to deal with the situation when the expert does not like the knowledge developer for some reason.

> *There is less to fear from outside competition than from inside inefficiency, miscalculation, lack of knowledge. Beat your competitors with the knowledge edge! Train your staff!*
> —Anonymous

RAPID PROTOTYPING IN INTERVIEWS:

■ Rapid prototyping is an approach to building KM systems, in which knowledge is added with each knowledge capture session.
■ This is an iterative approach which allows the expert to verify the rules as they are built during the session.
■ This approach can open up communication through its demonstration of the KM system.
■ Due to the process of instant feedback and modification, it reduces the risk of failure.
■ It allows the knowledge developer to learn each time a change is incorporated in the prototype.

- This approach is highly interactive.
- The prototype can create user expectations which, in turn, can become obstacles to further development effort.

INTRODUCTION TO MEASUREMENT OF KNOWLEDGE

Measurement is undoubtedly the least developed aspect of knowledge management, which is not surprising given the difficulties in defining it, let alone measuring it. In fact, some practitioners feel that measurement is premature at this stage and that trying to measure knowledge before you fully understand how knowledge is created, shared and used is likely to lead you to focus on the wrong things. Elaborate measurement systems, they say, cannot currently be justified because we simply do not yet know enough about the dynamics and impact of knowledge.

That being said, in practice, few organisations have the luxury of being allocated resources to implement something without being required to demonstrate its value. Without measurable success, enthusiasm and support for knowledge management is unlikely to continue. And without measurable success, you are unlikely to be able to know what works and what doesn't and therefore make an informed judgement regarding what to continue doing, and what to adjust.

WHAT TO MEASURE? COMMON MEASUREMENT APPROACHES

> *"Of central importance is the changing nature of competitive advantage—not based on market position, size and power as in times past, but on the incorporation of knowledge into all of an organisation's activities".*

—Leif Edvinsson, Swedish Intellectual Capital guru in

Corporate Longitude (2002)

There are a number of approaches that are increasingly being used to measure the value of, and progress in, knowledge and knowledge management in organisations. Some of the more common approaches are outlined here for the purpose of providing a general overview.

Measuring the impact of knowledge management on the organisation's performance

Given that the whole point of knowledge management is to improve the performance of your organisation and to help it to achieve its objectives, the best and most logical approach is tie-in measurement of knowledge management with your organisation's overall performance measurement systems. This can be done either at an organisational level, or for individual projects and processes.

However, one limitation of this approach is that if knowledge management practices are made an integral part of work, you cannot be sure of the relative contribution of those knowledge management practices to the success of a project or process, versus other factors. In view of this, O'Dell and Grayson (see Resources and References below) recommend a two-pronged approach that seeks to measure both outcomes and activities.

Measuring outcomes focuses on the extent to which a project or a process achieves its stated objectives. The success of the project or process serves as a proxy measure for the success of the knowledge management practices embedded in it. In other words, knowledge management is seen as an integral tool for improving a project or process, rather than as a separate thing. For example, outcomes might be measured in terms of the reduced cost of a process, improved efficiency, the reduction in time taken to do it, the improved quality of delivery, etc.

Measuring activities then shifts the focus onto the specific knowledge management practices that were applied in the project or process. What were the specific knowledge management activities behind this practice and what was their effect? In measuring activities, you are looking specifically at things like how often users are accessing, contributing to, or using the knowledge resources and practices you have set up. Some of these measures will be quantitative ('hard') measures such as the number and frequency of hits or submissions to an intranet site per employee. However, these measures only give part of the picture–they do not tell you why people are doing what they are doing. Hence, to complete the picture, you will also need qualitative ('soft') measures by asking people about the attitudes and behaviours behind their activities.

The balanced scorecard

An increasingly popular approach to measuring an organisation's performance, and one that is being widely adopted in knowledge management, is the balanced scorecard. The advantage of this approach in knowledge management terms is that it directly links learning to process performance, which in turn is linked with the overall organisational performance. Developed by Kaplan and Norton, the balanced scorecard focuses on linking an organisation's strategy and objectives to measure from four key perspectives: financial, customers, internal processes, and learning and growth. In contrast to traditional accounting measures, the balanced scorecard shifts the focus from purely financial measures to include three key measures of intangible success factors. These roughly equate to the three components of intellectual capital–namely, human capital (learning), structural capital (processes), and customer capital. The four perspectives can be framed as follows:

- *Financial:* How do we look to our 'shareholders' (or governing bodies)?
- *Customer:* How do our patients see us? Are we meeting their needs and expectations?
- *Internal processes:* What do we need to do well in order to succeed? What are the critical processes that have the greatest impact on our patients and our financial objectives?
- *Learning and growth:* How can we develop our ability to learn and grow in order to meet our objectives in the above three areas?

This knowledge management, which is about learning and growth, is measured as an integral and yet distinct part of overall organisational performance. The balanced scorecard approach can be applied to individual initiatives as well as to a whole organisation.

Return On Investment (ROI)

Most initiatives that require resources will be expected to show a return in investment–what benefits did we get to justify the costs involved–and knowledge management in usually no exception. The problem is that both the costs and the benefits of knowledge management can be notoriously difficult to pin down. While the costs associated with an investment in information technology can be

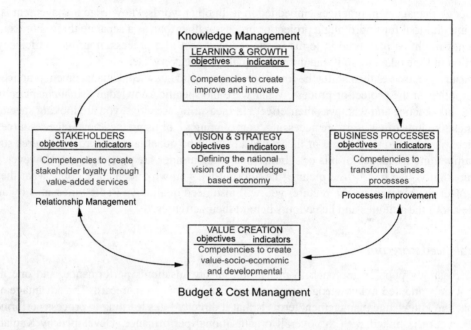

Fig. 8.1   Balanced Scorecard Measurement. (*Source:* United Nations, Department
of Social and Economic Affairs)

relatively straightforward to identify, other costs can be less so, such as for projects that involve an amalgam of resources from across the organisation, or those inherent in challenging an organisation's culture. On the benefits side, how do you measure things like increased knowledge sharing, faster learning or better decision making?

A number of approaches have been developed for showing financial returns on knowledge assets, such as that of Mark Clare and Arthur Detore (see Resources and References below). Such approaches tend to be rather complex, and are therefore probably more appropriate to organisations that are reasonably advanced in their knowledge management efforts, rather than just starting out.

The knowledge management life cycle

Some organisations measure the progress of their knowledge management activities in terms of their maturity–how far 'down the line' they are in implementing knowledge management practices and ways of working. The American Productivity and Quality Center has developed a framework known as Road Map to Knowledge Management Results: Stages of Implementation. The aim is to provide organisations with a map to guide them from getting started right through to 'institutionalising' knowledge management—embedding it in the organisation and making it an integral part of the way an organisation works. The map has five stages:

- Get started.
- Develop a strategy.

- Design and launch a knowledge management initiative.
- Expand and support.
- Institutionalise knowledge management.

Employee surveys

Given the importance of people in knowledge management, employee surveys can be a useful addition to your measurement toolbox. Surveys can be used to assess aspects of organisational culture and the extent to which people's opinions, attitudes and behaviours are, or are not, changing. Obviously, such surveys measure people's subjective perceptions and these may or may not reflect reality, but in many ways that can be their very benefit, as people's perceptions will determine their behaviour with respect to knowledge management. In order to be effective, it is vital that any such surveys are carried out by people with the required expertise, whether that be through in-house capabilities or by hiring external consultants.

HOW TO MEASURE?

Melissie Clemmons Rumizen outlines the following steps in developing measures:

1. Revisit your goals

Your starting point for measuring any knowledge management initiative will be the original goals of that initiative: what is it that you set out to achieve? Developing measures will often lead you to get clearer about how you define your goals in the first place; if your goals are not concrete and clear enough, then measuring your success or progress against them will be difficult. Hence, ensure that your goals define clearly what constitutes success in measurable terms.

2. Know the audience for your measures

In defining success, you will often find that different people have different ideas about what constitutes success. Managers who approve the allocation of resources will want to know about the returns on their investment. Users of the knowledge management initiative will want to know how it has benefited them and whether their participation has been worthwhile. Other beneficiaries of the initiative, such as patients, will want to know how they have gained.

3. Define the measures

Define what exactly you are going to measure, and what measurement approach or approaches you intend to take. Ensure that your measures are:

- Valid—they actually measure what they are intended to measure rather than something else.
- Reliable—they give consistent results.
- Actionable—they give information that can be acted upon if necessary.

4. Decide what data will be collected and how it will be collected

This is a process of 'putting the meat on the bones'—spelling out the details: what data will be collected, who will collect it, how, when, where, etc?

5. Analysing and communicating the measures

When analysing and presenting the results, be sure to refer back to your original goals and your audience. Aim to present results in a way that answers their questions in a meaningful way, rather than simply presenting facts and figures.

6. Review your combination of measures

Monitor and evaluate how your measures are working. Developing measures is a process of trial and error—don't necessarily expect to get it right the first time. Similarly, remember that as objectives and situations change over time, so will your measures need to.

Additional pointers emphasized by other practitioners include:

- Measuring for the sake of measuring is a waste of time—be sure that you are measuring for a specific purpose or purposes.
- Be sure that some kind of action or decision will be taken as a result of your measures.
- Don't try to measure everything; instead, focus on what is important. Trying to measure too much not only requires a great deal of work, it also tends to dilute the important issues.
- If your organisation already has a measurement system in place, then you can use those measures. If your knowledge management initiatives work, then you might assume that this will show up in your organisation's other performance measures. Of course, there is no guarantee that existing measures are good ones so you might like to look into them, but there are two major advantages to 'piggy-backing' on existing measures: first, they are already an accepted practice in the organisation, and second, they are most likely measuring things that are important to the organisation.

SUMMING UP

The concept of tacit knowing comes from scientist and philosopher Michael Polanyi. It is important to understand that he wrote about a process and not a form of knowledge. By definition, tacit knowledge is knowledge that people carry in their minds and is, therefore, difficult to access. Often, people are not aware of the knowledge they possess or how it can be valuable to others. Tacit knowledge is considered more valuable because it provides context for people, places, ideas and experiences.

There are various techniques for capturing the tacit knowledge, e.g., expert evaluation, interview, prototype interview, etc.

Measurement is undoubtedly the least developed aspect of knowledge management, which is not surprising given the difficulties in defining it, let alone measuring it. In fact, some practitioners feel that measurement is premature at this stage and that trying to measure knowledge before you fully understand how knowledge is created, shared and used is likely to lead you to focus on the wrong things. Elaborate measurement systems, they say, cannot currently be justified because we simply do not yet know enough about the dynamics and impact of knowledge.

There are a number of approaches that are increasingly being used to measure the value of, and progress in, knowledge and knowledge management in organisations. Some of the more common approaches are outlined here for the purpose of providing a general overview:

The balanced scorecard: An increasingly popular approach to measuring an organisation's performance, and one that is being widely adopted in knowledge management, is the balanced scorecard. The advantage of this approach in knowledge management terms is that it directly links learning to process performance, which in turn is linked with overall organisational performance. Developed by Kaplan and Norton, the balanced scorecard focuses on linking an organisation's strategy and objectives to measures from four key perspectives: financial, customers, internal processes, and learning and growth. In contrast to traditional accounting measures, the balanced scorecard shifts the focus from purely financial measures to include three key measures of intangible success factors. These roughly equate to the three components of intellectual capital—namely, human capital (learning), structural capital (processes), and customer capital.

Return on Investment (ROI): Most initiatives that require resources will be expected to show a return in investment—what benefits did we get to justify the costs involved—and knowledge management is usually no exception. The problem is that both the costs and the benefits of knowledge management can be notoriously difficult to pin down. While the costs associated with an investment in information technology can be relatively straightforward to identify, other costs can be less so, such as for projects that involve an amalgam of resources from across the organisation, or those inherent in challenging an organisation's culture. On the benefits side, how do you measure things like increased knowledge sharing, faster learning or better decision making?

The knowledge management life cycle: Some organisations measure the progress of their knowledge management activities in terms of their maturity—how far 'down the line' they are in implementing knowledge management practices and ways of working. The American Productivity and Quality Center has developed a framework known as Road Map to Knowledge Management Results: Stages of Implementation. The aim is to provide organisations with a map to guide them from getting started right through to 'institutionalising' knowledge management—embedding it in the organisation and making it an integral part of the way an organisation works.

Employee surveys: Given the importance of people in knowledge management, employee surveys can be a useful addition to your measurement toolbox. Surveys can be used to assess aspects of organisational culture and the extent to which people's opinions, attitudes and behaviours are, or are not, changing. Obviously, such surveys measure people's subjective perceptions and these may or may not reflect reality, but in many ways that can be their very benefit, as people's perceptions will determine their behaviours with respect to knowledge management. In order to be effective, it is vital that any such surveys are carried out by people with the required expertise, whether that be through in-house capabilities or by hiring external consultants.

GROUP ACTIVITY

Allen and Hamilton have suggested that—amazingly—up to 84% of all knowledge management programmes fail. What do you make of this statement, and what can organisations do to increase the likelihood of success?

"Even though there are many knowledge capturing techniques available but capturing knowledge is really tough and very challenging"—Explain.

Are there any differences in knowledge capturing between small organisations and large organisations?

INTERNET EXERCISE

Knowledge Disaster

Imagine that a couple of senior folks in your company have just told you that they are leaving. Not only are they leaving, but they are setting up shop across the street. Not only are they leaving and setting up shop across the street, but their first client is actually one of your best clients and oh...by the way...they are taking about ten of your best people with them. This is how most companies get started.

When companies are confronted with the question "What is your company's greatest asset?" the answer is some variant of "our people."

Think about the scenario described above. When those two or twelve people walk out of the door to start their new company, what types of "knowledge assets" would you lose? In other words, we've established that our people are our greatest assets, so what exactly is the impact of the disaster?

Group Task—As a team of four, write down at least 10 knowledge assets that you would lose.

KEYWORDS

Tacit Knowledge: Tacit knowledge is knowledge that people carry in their minds and is, therefore, difficult to access.

Rapid Prototype: Rapid prototyping is an approach to building KM systems, in which knowledge is added with each knowledge capture session.

Balance Scorecard: It focuses on three key measures of intangible success factors—human capital (learning), structural capital (processes) and customer capital.

Return on investment: Benefits we get to justify the cost involved.

Employees Survey: It is used to assess aspects of organisational culture and the extent to which people's opinions, attitudes and behaviours are or are not changing.

QUESTIONS FOR DISCUSSION

1. Explain the concept of tacit knowledge in your own words.
2. Define tacit knowledge.
3. Name a few techniques of capturing tacit knowledge. Explain briefly each of them.

4. What is expert evaluation? Explain.
5. Explain briefly the interviewing method as a tool for capturing tacit knowledge.
6. Discuss rapid prototype method.
7. Explain the importance of knowledge measurement.
8. Briefly explain the common techniques used to measure knowledge.
9. Write short notes on: (i) BSC (ii) ROI (iii) KMLC (iv) Employee survey.
10. Explain the process of measurement.
11. Explain the process of employee survey in measurement of knowledge.
12. Explain the importance of Balance Scorecard method in measuring knowledge.

SUGGESTED READINGS

A Report on Knowledge Management Services, Government Computer News (GCN), 21 May, 2001, IDC 19 May, 2001.

A Thothathri Raman, *Knowledge Management,* Excel Books, New Delhi, 2003.

Bartlett, Christopher A., The Knowledge-Based Organisation. In The Knowledge Advantage (Ruggles), 1999.

Clare, Mark and Detore, Arthur, Knowledge Assets: A Professional's Guide to Valuation and Financial Management. Harcourt Brace Professional Publishers, 2000.

Clemmons Rumizen Melissie., The Complete Idiot's Guide to Knowledge Management, Madison, WI: CWL Publishing Enterprises, 2002.

Corrall Sheila, *Knowledge Management: Are We in the Knowledge Management Business?,* Ark Publishing.

Dey Greg, Knowledge Management Update, IDC, 19 May, 2001.

Edvinsson, Leif and Malone, Michael S., Intellectual Capital: Realizing Your Company's True Value by Finding its Hidden Brainpower, Harper Business, 1997.

Elias M. Awad, Hassan M. Ghaziri, *Knowledge Management,* Pearson, New Delhi, 2006.

Kaplan, Robert and Norton, David., The Balanced Scorecard, Harvard Business School Press, 1996.

Malhotra, Yogesh, "Knowledge Management and New Organisation Forms: A New Framework for Business Model Innovation", *Information Resources Management journal,* Jan–Mar 2000.

Marwick, A. D., "Knowledge Management Technology", *IBM Systems Journal,* Volume 40, Number 2, 2001.

Mohanti, K. Santosh, and Chand, Mansh, "5iKM3—Knowledge Maturity Model", Tata Consultancy Services, 2004–05.

Nonaka, I., A Dynamic Theory of Organisational Knowledge Creation, *Organisation Science, (Providence,R.I.),* 5(1), 14–37, 1994.

O'Dell, Carla and Grayson, C. Jackson, *If Only We Knew What We Knew: The Transfer of Internal Knowledge and Best Practice.* The Free Press, New York, 1998.

Prusak, L., "Where did knowledge management come from? *IBM Systems Journal,* Volume 40, Number 7, 2001.

Savage, Charles M., *5th Generation Management,* Digital Press, 1990.

Smith, Peter A.C., McLaughlin, Moira. "Knowledge Management: People are Important!" In *Journal of Knowledge Management Practice,* January, 2004.

Smith, Peter A. C., McLaughlin, Moira, "Knowledge Management: People are Important! *Journal of Knowledge Management Practice"*, January, 2004.

Stenmark, D., Leveraging Tacit Organisational Knowledge, *Journal of Management Information Systems,* 17(3), 9–24, 2000.

Stuart Barnes, (ed.), *Knowledge Management Systems Theory and Practice,* Thomson Learning, 2002.

Terry, J., & Standing, C., The Value of User Participation in E-Commerce Systems Development. *Informing Science Journal,* 7, 31–45. Available at http://inform.nu/Articles/Vol7/v7p031-045-216.pdf

Tesch, R., *Qualitative Research: Analysis Types and Software Tools.* Falmer Press, New York, 1990.

Thomas, J. C., Kellogg, W. A., and Erickson, T. "The Knowledge Management Puzzle: Human and Social Factors in Knowledge Management", *IBM Systems Journal,* Volume 40, Number 7, 2001.

Warier, Sudhir, *Knowledge Management,* Vikas Publications, 2003.

CHAPTER 9

Global Dimension to Knowledge Management

OBJECTIVE

At the end of this lesson, you would be able to understand:

- The concept of knowledge economy.
- The driving forces behind global knowledge economy.
- Policy Economies.
- The reason for global momentum of knowledge economy.
- The World Bank Report.
- Global knowledge leadership.

> *Innovations are created primarily by investment in intangibles.*
> *When such investments are commercially successful, and are*
> *protected by patents or first-mover advantages, they are transformed*
> *into tangible assets creating corporate value and growth.*
> —Baruch Lev, Intellectual Capital guru in Intangibles (2001)

INTRODUCTION

Various observers describe today's global economy as one in transition to a 'knowledge economy', or an 'information society'. But the rules and practices that determined success in the industrial economy of the 20th century need rewriting in an interconnected world where resources such as know-how are more critical than other economic resources. This briefing highlights the recent thinking and developments and offers guidance on developing appropriate organisational strategies to succeed in the new millennium. This lesson will help you to understand the importance of knowledge and its competitive advantage in an integrated world-economy.

GROWING INTEREST

Over the past 15 years the term Knowledge Management has evolved to represent the changing nature of the workplace as a true paradigm shift in coining the phrase knowledge society. Peter Drucker convincingly argued that land, labour, and capital as the classical factors of production have largely been replaced by knowledge (Drucker, 1993), and that knowledge having become the resource, rather than *a resource*, is what makes our society post-capitalist.

The modern knowledge organisation has become a social environment designed by the specialists, to meet the needs of the market and the specialists, in the most efficient and quickest way possible.

In 1997, KM was the star of emerging technologies, a burning issue for business and technology leaders alike. Two years later, technology media lost interest. The next new thing, B2B mania, supplanted it with new killer applications.

KM did not die, it has been quietly smoldering within corporations. In practice, knowledge management is rising like the phoenix, with great velocity. It has morphed into a series of killer applications including portals, e-learning, e-analysis, and content management. Corporations such as Northrop Grumman, Hallmark, Pillsbury, Pfizer, and Buckman Labs have successful KM practices —and these are the companies that are willing to talk about their efforts.

Neef (1999) expanded the more micro-level view of knowledge management by commenting, "A knowledge-based revolution is taking place, and it comes in a matching set: knowledge management for organisations and the knowledge-based economy for nations themselves. Both are part of a major evolutionary economic movement which is beginning to reshape the global economic structure, and knowledge management should be seen as one of the most concrete and important set of practices and policies than an organisation can adopt, marking a significant step in an enterprise as evolution towards becoming a global, learning organisation that can survive in the knowledge based economy".

Call it KM, call it an Executive Information Portal, call it Content Management—it is still Knowledge Management: leveraging collective wisdom and experience to expedite innovation and responsiveness. KM enables taking informed action in previously unencountered/unknown circumstances. We speak of KM in terms of the practices and technologies which facilitate the efficient creation and exchange of knowledge on an organisation-wide level. When you extend this definition to include partners, suppliers and customers as well, you extend the KM practice into the Collaborative Commerce space. In the current economic climate, although companies are careful about undertaking new technology initiatives, they are realising that leveraging the already accumulated corporate intellectual property is by far the least costly way available to increase their competitive stature.

Knowledge, however, is both powerful and dangerous. In their rush to implement these new killer applications, many organisations often do not take the time to fully understand the complexities that belie successful Knowledge Management. Without this due diligence, a KM strategy can leave the organisation burning in this phoenix's ashes. I caution companies that a Knowledge Management implementation, under any name, is, at best, only partially about technology. A technology focus—such as a portal or content management can provide a focus. But, it is critical to first define the business imperative behind your KM initiative. Who benefits and how will they benefit? What are the business goals for the initiative and can they be measured?

Indeed, selecting the right mix of technology is the simplest of dilemmas. It is not at all like the automation of a structured and predictable application, (e.g., a document management system). Knowledge Management forces the designer, developer and knowledge participants to delve into processes that almost defy formal procedure and rules. Until a valid assessment is made of each of these factors within the organisation, attempts to initiate a knowledge-focused strategy are futile.

Various management writers have, for several years, highlighted the role of knowledge or intellectual capital in business. The value of high-tech companies such as software and biotechnology companies is not in physical assets as measured by accountants, but in their intangibles such as knowledge and patents. The last few years have a growing recognition by accounting bodies and international agencies that knowledge is a crucial factor of production. For example, the OECD has groups investigating 'human capital' and also the role of knowledge in international competitiveness. Several conferences in 1997, including one sponsored by the World Bank, have placed knowledge firmly at the heart of the economic agenda.

> *There are two ways to slide easily through life;*
> *to believe everything or to doubt everything;*
> *both ways save us from thinking.*
> —Alfred Korzybski

What is the knowledge economy all about?

> *All agree that the single most important key to development and to poverty*
> *alleviation is education. This must start with universal primary education*
> *for girls and boys equally, as well as an open and competitive system of*
> *secondary and tertiary education....Adult education, literacy, and lifelong*
> *learning must be combined with the fundamental recognition that education of*
> *women and girls is central to the process of development.*
> —James D. Wolfensohn, President of the World Bank, 1999

The remarkable economic growth that has occurred in the world over the past two centuries has been due, to a large extent, to the advancement of knowledge combined with an increase in human resources, both in number and capabilities, and an increase in savings which have been translated into physical capital. Two factors have been important in increasing knowledge. One is simply the growth of population. The other factor is rising real per capita income, which has made it possible for the world's population to specialize in the production of knowledge.

A larger population leads to greater creation of knowledge. That is because the larger the population, the greater the benefit from a given improvement in productivity resulting from new knowledge. With a larger population there are also more individuals capable of making a significant discovery or adding to existing knowledge. Since the distribution of talent or intelligence can be presumed to be the same today as was in the past, the sheer increase in the number of people implies that there are many more of us capable of advancing knowledge.

But it is not only that there are more of us available to add to the world's knowledge. With the improvements in agricultural productivity, the expansion of the cities, and the very large increase in real per capita incomes that have occurred over the past two centuries, institutions, namely, universities and research institutes, have been created specifically to advance and transmit knowledge. When 80 or 85% of the world's labour force was engaged in farming, a small percentage of a much smaller world population had the time and resources to devote to producing non-food products, such as clothing, tools, roads, and housing, let alone acquiring new knowledge and technology.

Not only are there about seven times as many people as there were in 1800, but a significant percentage of this much larger population now specializes in the creation of knowledge, compared to two centuries ago. The modern university, with many faculty devoting their time to research in science and graduate education, is a relatively recent creation dating to the middle of the 19th century.

Over the last two centuries, and especially in the last century, there has been an enormous increase in knowledge that has been transformed into technology and ways of utilizing resources more efficiently. This increase in knowledge has been complemented with improvements in the means of communicating that knowledge in an effective way, with the effect that knowledge has become much more accessible throughout the world, resulting in lower infant mortality rates, increased life expectancy, and higher per capita food supplies.

Knowledge is a public good. It is a 'public good' because, at the physical level, one can share it with others without losing it. Knowledge is not 'rival' in consumption, as are apples or oranges, for example. This is the difference from other fields such as land and machines. The latter are 'private' goods because, if I use a piece of land, it is not available to others, and the same is true of a machine. Knowledge is provided mostly privately by individuals.

Patents of ownership of ideas is increasingly becoming more critical than capital. The ownership of 'intellectual capital' is crucial to economic development. But in order to take advantage of knowledge, there is a need for appropriate institutions. It is important to differentiate the knowledge revolution from the service economy.

An economy of service is characterized by the production of services more than goods, and it is similar to a knowledge economy in that knowledge sectors often involve services (such as finance). The main difference between the service economy and the knowledge society is that in the latter the typical worker is highly skilled and generally well paid. Furthermore, the worker's knowledge resides in her/himself, rather than in the machines that complement labour. The knowledge economy helps create proper institutions in a society which centre around human creativity and diversity, rather than in fossil fuels to power economic growth.

Above all, knowledge workers are not homogeneous: knowledge is effective only if it is specialised. Because knowledge work is specialised, it is deeply splintered work, even in large organisations, according to management guru Peter Drucker. Moreover, the critical feature of a knowledge workforce is that its workers are not labour, they are capital. And what is decisive in the performance of capital is not what capital costs. It is not how much capital is being invested—or else the Former Union of Soviet Socialist Republics would have easily been the world's foremost economy. What is critical is the productivity of capital.

The former Union of Soviet Socialist Republics collapsed, in large part because the productivity of its capital investments was incredibly low. In many cases, it was less than one-third that of capital investments in market economies, and sometimes actually negative. Peter Drucker posits that no one paid any attention to the productivity of capital, because no one had that as his or her job, and therefore no one got rewarded if productivity went up. Private industry in the market economies teaches the same lesson.

In new companies, leadership can be obtained and maintained by innovation, Drucker continues, while in an established industry, what differentiates the leading company is the productivity of capital. The emergence of knowledge work and the knowledge worker, let alone their emergence as the chief source of capital in our knowledge-based society and economy, is as profound a change as the switch to a machine-driven economy was all those years ago, or perhaps an even a greater one.

Today, more than 50% of Gross Domestic Product (GDP) in the major OECD economies is based on the production and distribution of knowledge. Perhaps the knowledge economy's two most important characteristics are: its borderlessness, as knowledge can travel easily across borders; and due to the increasing need for specialization, its upward mobility bias through education and training programmes.

DRIVING FORCES

Individuals are becoming more and more aware of the fact that knowledge is a resource requiring explicit and specific management policies and practices to be acquired, processed and exploited efficiently as we are moving towards the knowledge driven economy. For example, one-third of the nation's growth is accounted for by the knowledge sectors. Some of the most dynamic developing countries are making a swift transition from traditional societies to knowledge-intensive societies. Knowledge sectors could flourish in those nations that have skilled labour. Governments, therefore, need to establish the institutions that could lead countries, particularly the developing ones, to leap-frog into the knowledge society.

The driving forces behind internalisation of KM can be listed as follows:

- *Globalisation*—markets and products are more global. Products by Nike and Virgin are known the world over. Today, even resourcing is becoming global. Thus, many companies outsource manufacturing and software development to distant locations.
- *Information/Knowledge Intensity*—efficient production relies on information and know-how; over 70% workers in developed economies are information workers; many factory workers use their heads more than their hands.
- *Networking and Connectivity*—developments such as the internet bring the 'global village' ever nearer.

The net result is that goods and services can be developed, bought, sold, and in many cases even delivered over electronic networks. Electronic commerce offers many advantages in terms of cost savings, efficiency and market reach over traditional physical methods. These developments are the driving force behind the growing importance of the knowledge worker and better knowledge management to have competitive advantage over others.

As per the World Bank report, four features of the knowledge economy have far-ranging implications for any individual's education and training programmes:

- *Knowledge is being developed and applied in new ways.*
  The information revolution has expanded networks and provided new opportunities for access to information. It has also created new opportunities for generating and transferring information. Knowledge networks and sharing of information have expedited innovation and

adaptation capacity. Changes in ICT have revolutionised the transmission of information. Semiconductors are getting faster, computer memories are expanding, and ICT prices are falling. Data transmission costs have fallen dramatically and continue to fall, bandwidth is growing, and internet hosts are expanding and multiplying. Cellular phone usage is growing worldwide, adding to the pace of and capacity for change and innovation.

■ *Product cycles are shorter and the need for innovation greater.*
In 1990 it took six years to go from concept to production in the automobile industry; today that process takes just two years. The number of patent applications is growing, and more and more international and multiple applications are being filed. Industrial countries filed 82,846 patent applications at the European Patent Office in 1997, a 37% increase over 1990 (OECD 2001).
■ *Trade is increasing worldwide, increasing competitive demands on producers.*
Countries that are able to integrate into the world economy may be able to achieve higher economic growth and improve health and education outcomes (World Bank 2002e).
■ *Small and medium-size enterprises in the service sector have become increasingly important players, in terms of both economic growth and employment.*

A knowledge economy rests on four pillars (World Bank Institute 2001):
■ A supportive economic and institutional regime to provide incentives for the efficient use of existing and new knowledge and the flourishing of entrepreneurship.
■ An educated and skilled population to create, share, and use knowledge.
■ A dynamic information infrastructure to facilitate the effective communication, dissemination, and processing of information.
■ An efficient innovation system of firms, research centres, universities, consultants, and other organisations to tap into the growing stock of global knowledge, assimilate and adapt it to the local needs, and create new technology.

GLOBAL KNOWLEDGE ECONOMY

When there is use of ideas rather than physical abilities, a knowledge-based economy is created. It depends on the application of technology rather than mere transformation of materials or the labour. The main concept is that knowledge can be developed and applied in many ways. Knowledge-based economy places more demand on ideas, knowledge and skills given by the workforce, to ensure that they perform these things on a daily basis. For developing the knowledge-based economy, a model of lifelong learning is needed as suggested by the reports of World Bank. Lifelong learning includes learning from childhood till retirement, and emphasis on learning throughout the life cycle of any individual.

Individuals have to be equipped according to the changing demands and this requires a new model of educational system and training methods that has to be carried on throughout the lifespan of an individual. Initially, the model includes the formal learning in schools, colleges and universities. Later the non-formal learning takes place (on-the-job learning process) and finally the informal learning where the skills are acquired from the senior members in the family and working environment.

It is important to note that the main component of the knowledge-based economy is the knowledge-based organisation, which presents some characteristics that clearly differentiate it from the traditional industrial economy. The focus on an enterprise has changed from Porter's environmental view to a resource-based view and during the last decade many authors within the resource-based view have paid particular attention to knowledge as the key resource within organisations. Thus, KM has become increasingly important for all organisations. The function of knowledge management is to allow an organisation to leverage its information resources and knowledge assets by remembering and applying experience.

Knowledge, and consequently its management, is currently being touted as the basis of future economic competitiveness. Knowledge, if properly utilised and leveraged, can drive organisations to become more innovative, competitive, and sustainable. KM is managing the corporation's knowledge through a systematically and organisationally specified process for acquiring, organising, sustaining, applying, sharing and renewing both the tacit and explicit knowledge of employees to enhance organisational performance and create value.

In holistic terms, KM must be seen as a strategy to manage organisational knowledge assets to support management decision making to enhance competitiveness, and to increase the capacity for creativity and innovation. The literature in KM distinguishes different types of knowledge in order to be able to propose its management. KM authors divide and typify knowledge in different ways. For example, some authors differentiate technical and strategic types. Some authors focus on issues related to problem solving knowledge in work practices and knowledge associated with coordination and tactical issues.

Various management experts have, for several years, highlighted the role of knowledge or IC in business and the need to leverage them to bring about tangible organisational benefits. The value of high-tech companies such as software and biotechnology companies lies, not in physical assets that are measured by conventional accountancy techniques but, in their intangibles such as knowledge and patents. The last few years have witnessed a growing recognition by accounting bodies and international agencies that knowledge is a crucial factor of production. The current global economy has been described by most of the industry observers as one in transition to a knowledge economy.

The knowledge economy differs from the traditional economy in several key respects:

- The economics is not of scarcity, but rather of abundance. Unlike most resources that deplete when used, information and knowledge can be shared, and actually grow through application.
- The effect of location is diminished. Using appropriate technology and methods, virtual marketplaces and virtual organisations can be created that offer benefits of speed and agility, of round the clock operation and of global reach.
- Laws, barriers and taxes are difficult to apply on solely a national basis. Knowledge and information 'leak' to where demand is highest and the barriers are lowest.
- Knowledge enhanced products or services can command price premiums over comparable products with low embedded knowledge or knowledge intensity.
- Pricing and value depends heavily on context. Thus, the same information or knowledge can have vastly different value to different people at different times.
- Knowledge, when locked into systems or processes, has higher inherent value than when it can 'walk out of the door' in people's heads.

- Human capital—competency—is a key component of value in a knowledge-based company, yet few companies report competency levels in annual reports. In contrast, downsizing is often seen as a positive 'cost cutting' measure.

These characteristics, so different from those of the physical economy, require new thinking and approaches by policy makers, senior executives and knowledge workers alike. To do so, though, requires leadership and risk taking, against the prevailing and slow changing attitudes and practices of existing institutions and business practice.

POLICY IMPLICATIONS

The evolving knowledge economy has important implications for policy makers of local, regional and national government as well as international agencies and institutions, e.g.:

- Traditional measures of economic success must be supplemented by new ones. Example: Nova Scotia has developed Knowledge Quotients for their economy.
- Economic development policy should focus not on 'jobs created' but rather on infrastructure for sustainable 'knowledge enhancement' that acts as a magnet for knowledge-based companies.
  Example: Sophia Antipolis in France is a hub for many knowledge-based businesses.
- Develop regulation and taxation for information and knowledge trading at international level, looking to future knowledge-based industries rather than traditional industries.
  Example: WIPO is seeking harmonisation of copyright legislation for online markets.
- Stimulate market development through new forms of collaboration.
  Example: Several EU programmes now focus on market development (rather than product development) and encourage participation by collaboration across national boundaries using electronic knowledge networking methods.

KNOWLEDGE NETWORKING

Organisations are looking for ways to generate more value from their assets. The two critical resources are people and information. Knowledge networking is a productive way combining a person's knowledge and skills to achieve personal and orgnisational objectives. It is difficult to define and describe what knowledge networking is. When knowledge is shared, developed or evolved in a dynamic phenomenon, then we call it as knowledge networking.

Knowledge networking is more than access to information, because it also delves into the unknown. It is more than using the rules and inferences of expert systems, because it is about knowledge that is evolving. Although it verges on simplification, it is the computer augmentation person-to-person communications resulting in the development of new knowledge.

GLOBAL KNOWLEDGE LEADERSHIP

"An individual without information cannot take responsibility; an individual who is given information cannot help but take responsibility."
—Jan Carlson-Former Chairman, SAS Airlines

Taking the long-term view, many stock markets are still higher than they were a year ago, and usually short-term corrections fade into history. But are the fundamentals in place for a return to sustained economic boom? In countries whose economies are in turmoil, one cannot overlook the fact that most have the latent resources needed to succeed in the new economy—knowledge and talent. It never fails to impress how the younger generation in these countries demonstrates a thirst for knowledge, and is so enthusiastic and energetic.

> *"The best executive is the one who has sense enough to pick good men to do what he wants done, and self-restraint enough to keep from meddling with them while they do it."*
>
> —Theodore Roosevelt

GLOBAL MOMENTUM FOR KNOWLEDGE STRATEGY

Clearly, knowledge is seen as the engine for value creation. What lies in the future is/must be grounded in values, competencies and the quality of relationships. Knowledge economy has an open access rather than knowledge being perceived and managed as a "private good". The reason being the bountiful nature of the resource and its quality to multiply as it is shared with others.

This new economy we are innovating works for the people creating a world free of poverty, disease and violence. It is an economy directed towards sustainable development, placing knowledge at the point of need or opportunity. It is an economy that is transnational in scope, balancing the local/national needs with a global scope. The driving mandate is one of creating a society with a better quality of life and increased standard of living worldwide. And the initiative begins with the individual, where knowledge resides!

> *Nobody can make you feel inferior without your consent.*
>
> —Eleanor Roosevelt

WORLD BANK REPORT

This report explores the challenges to education and training systems that the knowledge economy presents. It outlines policy options for addressing these challenges and developing viable systems of lifelong learning in developing countries and countries with transition economies.

It addresses four questions:

1. What does a national education and training system, including its formal and non-formal components, need to do to support knowledge-based economic growth?
2. How can developing countries and countries with transition economies promote lifelong learning, and what challenges do they face in doing so?
3. Given limited resources, what type of governance framework promotes lifelong learning for people in general and disadvantaged groups in particular?
4. How can financing of lifelong learning be inclusive, affordable, and sustainable?

The report provides a conceptual framework for education-related lending activities reflecting the latest knowledge and successful practices of planning and implementing education for lifelong learning. It encourages countries to look beyond traditional approaches to education and training and to engage in a policy dialogue on the pedagogical and economic consequences of lifelong learning.

Traditional learning

- The teacher is the source of knowledge.
- Learners receive knowledge from the teacher.
- Learners work by themselves.
- Tests are given to prevent progress until students have completely mastered a set of skills and to ration access to further learning.
- All learners do the same thing.
- Teachers receive initial training plus ad hoc in-service training.
- "Good" learners are identified and permitted to continue their education.

Lifelong learning

- Educators are guides to sources of knowledge.
- People learn by doing.
- People learn in groups and from one another.
- Assessment is used to guide learning strategies and identify pathways for future learning.
- Educators develop individualised learning plans.
- Educators are lifelong learners. Initial training and ongoing professional development are linked.
- People have access to learning opportunities over a lifetime.

Teacher training needs to change

This new learning context implies a different role for teachers and trainers. Teachers need to learn new skills and become lifelong learners themselves to keep up-to-date with new knowledge, pedagogical ideas, and technology. As learning becomes more collaborative, so too must teachers' professional development, which needs to promote professional networks and learning organisations within schools and institutions.

Another example that can be given regarding global knowledge networks is Shell. During the late 1990s, Shell's global exploration and production business saw a spontaneous explosion of computer-based knowledge networks, made possible by improving information technology and communications infrastructure. But walking the fine line between exponential knowledge growth and the chaos of information overload requires some experienced people, a robust process and enabling technology that truly delivers.

Working closely with facilitators and local network coordinators, the Organisational Performance and Learning team has been helping restructure, reinvigorate and expand our computer-based global networks. Spawned by the Well Delivery Value Creation team with its highly successful network, our exploration and production professional communities are rapidly joining facilitated global networks covering the wells, surface and subsurface areas of our business. In addition to these core technical networks more communities have sprung up in the past two years, such as commercial practice, procurement, benchmarking, competitive intelligence and knowledge sharing.

KNOWLEDGE MANAGEMENT—THE FUTURE

KM initiatives are on an upswing as managers at all levels within all organisations face mounting pressure to work smarter and faster while wrestling with the demands of advanced technology and a shrinking workforce. Practices of the bygone era are not applicable in the highly techno savvy environment and transient work force of today. KM techniques and technologies can help organisational workforce to examine their processes and improve their services to customers.

One of the biggest drivers of the KM movement is the issue of e-governance. Some countries and governments actually set deadlines for launching a host of online initiatives. One of the first states in India to come out with a comprehensive IT blueprint and a ten year plan to bring the benefits of e-governance and technology to the grass roots is Andhra Pradesh.

The use of the term "global knowledge economy" fails to acknowledge the uneven distribution of knowledge-based economic activity. Moreover, as currently constituted, the idea of a global knowledge economy, which focuses on knowledge as conceptualised in the commercial activities of advanced countries, overlooks the diversity of knowledge present in the world today.

The need of the hour, is the need to build knowledge bases that help government agencies and institutions to get a better understanding of things such as who are the recipients of those services, who are the providers, and where is the room for improvement and cost control. This would result in a significant investment in education driven by a nationwide push among schools systems to learn about the best practices that can lead to improved test results. There is also interesting work being done with criminal investigation knowledge bases that allow law enforcement officials to conduct pattern analyses in high crime areas. This has been funnelled by a worldwide realisation by organisations on the tremendous need to consolidate their knowledge assets; how their internal operations work and how that dovetails with their constituent bases.

We are in a knowledge economy. Individuals compete with people all over the world. In the private sector, it is no longer necessary to belong to any particular race, caste or creed. To impact the bottomline of an organisation and an individual's goals and aspirations, the very basic necessity is to provide them with the basic requirements. And yes, knowledge management is as important as food, water and air.

In many global companies, comprehensive knowledge management system is already in place. The only drawback is that it has to be nurtured by individuals in majority of the situations. For instance, majority of the knowledge base comprises employees' contribution such as case studies, lessons learned from projects, etc. Sure, I am not questioning the premise of a knowledge base, but the reality is not just about lessons learned after maths' successful projects.

What gets documented into a knowledge base is 'yesterday' in most of the organisations. We need Knowledge Management for tomorrow. It is also about what to anticipate in the real projects of today and clients and how to mitigate proactively for the unfavourable situations of tomorrow.

In the final analysis, it is all about transforming an unfavourable environment to a favourable landscape of immense opportunities that exceeds customer expectations in the competitive global world.

SUMMING UP

Various observers describe today's global economy as one in transition to a 'knowledge economy', or an 'information society'. But the rules and practices that determined success in the industrial economy of the 20th century need rewriting in an interconnected world where resources such as know-how are more critical than other economic resources. This briefing highlights recent thinking and developments and offers guidance on developing appropriate organisational strategies to succeed into the new millennium.

Globalisation, internet, etc. are the driving force behind the growing importance of the knowledge worker and better Knowledge Management to have competitive advantage over others.

Taking the long-term view, many stock markets are still higher than they were a year ago, and usually short-term corrections fade into history. But are the fundamentals in place for a return to sustained economic boom? In countries whose economies are in turmoil, one cannot overlook the fact that most have the latent resources needed to succeed in the new economy—knowledge and talent. It never fails to impress how the younger generation in these countries demonstrates a thirst for knowledge, and is so enthusiastic and energetic.

Clearly, knowledge is seen as the engine for value creation. What lies in the future is/must be grounded in values, competencies and the quality of relationships. Knowledge economy is having an open access rather than knowledge being perceived and managed as a "private good". The reason being the bountiful nature of the resource and its quality to multiply as it is shared with others.

CASE

WELLS GLOBAL NETWORK

Shell Offshore Inc's Deep Bo High Pressure High Temperature (HPHT) drilling team sought assistance when faced with a significant lost circulation challenge related to low pressure margins and higher pressures due to penetration of a high energy fault zone. A search of the Wells Global Network and LiveLink for best practices amongst Shell communities produced a potential solution. By applying a DiaSseal-M and Cement Squeeze technology which had previously proven to be successful in South Texas HPHT wells, a tremendous cost saving of $1.5 million was made whilst still meeting well objectives.

From the Philippines

Any suggestion how to properly remove swarf and fines from our (Shell Philippines) well (we are milling up one 6-1/4" DC which was/is stuck at liner hanger). The well will be completed using horizontal Cameron tree in the first half of 2001.

Any suggestion what to do with regard to the clean up:

> *NOW, before we take the Blow Out Preventer off. (Wednesday 6/9/2000...)—or LATER when tree is installed (danger of scoring seal areas when pulling tree bore protection sleeve*
> —Joan Horbeek, Shell Philippines

Answer-1 Wellbore Clean Up Option

We have had a lot of success in the last few months with the SPS well patroller system (inverted cup below screen section) in the subsea well engineering section in Expro. They also provide a number of other tools, i.e., scrapers, magnets, etc. which may or may not also be of use. Baker also have a 'super downhole' magnet which has also been used successfully here. **Neil Robertson, Shell Expro, UK.**

Answer-2 Cased hole cleaning

In addition to the SPS well patroller mentioned by Neil, we also had good success using Weatherford's venturi junk baskets, retrieving larger pieces of metallic junk (up to 6" long × 1" wide) following packer milling and liner cutting jobs. **Allan Garden, Shell Expro, UK.**

1. Find out the discrepancies found in this case.
2. Collect more facts regarding Shell Company with respect to the other international units.
3. Format a rough draft based on global knowledge economy issues referring to Shell.

INDIVIDUAL EXERCISE

- A truck dealer who has just learned about Knowledge Management thinks it could be ideal for separating tire-kickers from serious buyers. Would this be a typical KM application? Why?
- Name a global company and find out the Knowledge Management architecture of that company. (Browse net or refer magazine/journal/paper/book, etc.)

KEYWORDS

Globalisation: Moving towards a borderless world and integrated global economy.

Information/Knowledge Intensity: Efficient production relies on information and know-how; over 70% of the workers in developed economies are information workers; many factory workers use their heads more than their hands.

Networking and Connectivity: Developments such as the internet bring the 'global village' ever nearer.

Knowledge Economy: The economics is not of scarcity, but rather of abundance. Unlike most resources that deplete when used, information and knowledge can be shared, and actually grow through application.

QUESTIONS FOR DISCUSSION

1. Define knowledge economy.
2. What do you understand by knowledge economy?
3. Differentiate between a traditional economy and a knowledge economy.
4. What are the driving forces behind the global expansion of knowledge management?
5. Define and explain global knowledge leadership.
6. Explain the reason for momentum in knowledge economy.

SUGGESTED READINGS

A Thothathri Raman, *Knowledge Management,* Excel Books, New Delhi, 2003.

Bartlett, Christopher A., The Knowledge-Based Organisation, In *The Knowledge Advantage* (Ruggles), 1999.

Bergeron, Bryan., *Essentials of Knowledge Management,* Wiley, 2003.

Boughzala, Imed., *Trends in Enterprise Knowledge Management,* 2008.

Delbecq A. L. and VandeVen A. H., "A Group Process Model for Problem Identification and Program Planning," *Journal of Applied Behavioral Science,* VII, July/August, 1971, 466–91 and A. L. Del becq, A. H. VandeVen, and D. H. Gustafson, *Group Techniques for Program Planners* (Glenview, Illinois: Scott Foresman and Company, 1975).

Dunnette, M. D., Campbell, J. D., and Jaastad K., "The Effect of Group Participation on Brainstoming Effectiveness for Two Industrial Samples, *Journal of Applied Psychology,* XLVII, 30–37, Feb, 1963.

Elias M. Awad, Hassan M. Ghaziri, Knowledge Management, Pearson, New Delhi, 2006.

Erickson, T. D. & Simon, H. A., Protocol analysis: Verbal Reports as Data, The MIT Press, Cambridge USA, 1985.

Frappaoli, Carl., *Knowledge Management,* Wiley, 2006.

Jaspers, M.W., Steen, T., van den Bos, C. & Geenen, M., The Think Aloud Method: A Guide to User Interface Design, Int J. Med. Inform., 73(11–12): 781–95, 2004.

Joanne Roberts, "The global knowledge economy in question", *Critical Perspectives on International Business,* Vol. 5 Iss: 4, pp.285–303, 2009.

Preece, J., Rogers, Y. & Sharp, H., Interaction Design: Beyond Human-Computer Interaction. John Wiley & Sons, New York, 2002.

Savage, Charles M., 5th Generation Management, Digital Press, 1990.

Vedros K. R.,"The Nominal Group Technique is a Participatory, Planning Method in Adult Education" (Ph.D. dissertation, Florida State University, Tallahassee, 1979).

WEBSITES

http://www.nickmilton.com/2009/06/knowledge-management-exercises-and.html
http://www.changeup.org.uk/documents/regions/EastRegion-GuideToCapacityBuilding.pdf
http://www.iog.ca/Publications/policybrief6.pdf
http://en.wikipedia.org/wiki/Capacity_building
http://www.inwent.org/capacity_building/bei_inwent/index.php.en

http://www.recoftc.org/site/index.php?id=376
http://www.informationr.net/ir/7-1/paper112.html
http://www.informationr.net/ir/11-1/paper241.html
http://www.slideshare.net/mkconway/environmental-scanning-what-it-is-and-how-to-do-it
http://w3.atlcon.net/~mperla/cis8110/environmental_scanning.htm
http://www.providersedge.com/kma/km_articles_case_studies.htm

CHAPTER 10

Environment Scanning and KM

OBJECTIVE

At the end of this lesson, you would be able to understand:

- The concept of environmental scanning.
- Importance of environmental scanning.
- Different informations available in environment.
- Organisational learning.
- Framework for information seeking.

INTRODUCTION

> *"Sharing knowledge is not about giving people something, or getting something from them. That is only valid for information sharing. Sharing knowledge occurs when people are genuinely interested in helping one another develop new capacities for action; it is about creating learning processes."*
>
> —*Peter Senge*

Knowledge Management helps to spot, preserve, enhance and make more attractive the strategic knowledge of the firm. It becomes essential for the firm to make its knowledge base evolve. If not, the lack of creativity will cause a great damage. Information coming from the environment is necessary for the enhancement of the knowledge base. By "environment", we mean scientific and technical environment but obviously, we must keep in mind that some economic and geopolitical aspects cannot be separated from the scientific and technical aspects.

CHANGES IN ENVIRONMENT

Changes in the Global Economy

Since the 1970s, the waves of change rolling over business have altered the basis for competition in many industries, and have transformed the role of local enterprises in the global economy. Everywhere, businesses are now moving into the global arena to keep up with the competition, to keep abreast of new trends in technology, and to create and take advantage of developing business opportunities. [Daniels, 1994] The driving force for these changes emanate from a broader set of structural shifts in the world economy. Naisbitt [1996] predicts eight major shifts that would be the driving forces for an Asian renaissance. These are shifts from:

- nation-states to networks as the source of economic power.
- traditions to options as the basis for individual behaviour.

- export-led to consumer driven economies, fuelled by an emerging middle class with new expectations.
- government-controlled to market-driven economies, based on a new model of economic co-operation and coordination in the region.
- farms to supercities as the locus of new career opportunities.
- labour-intensive to high-technology as the basis for job creation.
- male dominance to the emergence of women as voters, workers, and consumers "in all aspects of Asian life in unprecedented ways".
- West to East as the axis of the global economy.

"You can't teach people everything they need to know. The best you can do is position them where they can find what they need to know when they need to know it"

—Seymour Papert

While these eight trends will bring prosperity to Asia, they also expose peripheral regions located far from the "supercities" to the threat of economic marginalisation. This pattern, combined with the falling real value of commodity raw materials, is a distinct threat to the Sabah economy. This is especially so where knowledge has become the underlying driving force of economic competitiveness. As Drucker [1995:236] argues: "the performance of an individual, an organisation, an industry, a country, in acquiring and applying knowledge will increasingly become the key competitive factor—for career and earnings opportunities of the individuals; for the performance, perhaps even the survival, of the individual organisation; for an industry; and for a country."

Changes in Technology and Its Use

The threat of rapid changes in an information age can be leveraged, to a certain extent, by the strategic deployment of information technology. However, technology itself is in a state of flux, adapting itself to the needs and requirements of the knowledge economy. The shifts in technology are best described by Tapscott [1995:96–118] as shown below.

Connectivity

The sustained success of Asia's economies is driving the growth of its telecommunications infrastructure at incredible rates. Last year, Asian markets installed more than 20 million new fixed lines and 14 million new cellular connections (about half of the new subscribers worldwide). Within five years, the installed base of fixed lines will be overtaken by the number of wireless lines, as digital technologies become more widely accepted and PCS, PHS, and wireless local loop technologies enter the marketplace.

One immediate impact of this trend will be a management development gap, as operators struggle to recruit and train staff to operate and manage their expanding wireless networks. Another impact will be rapidly falling costs, both for equipment and for subscriber services, as manufacturers and service providers zoom up the learning curve. This new digital mobility will enable "anywhere, anytime" contact with state workers, thus improving productivity and responsiveness to public needs.

Old Economy		New Economy	Implications
Analog	<	Digital	leading to the convergence between computing and telecommunications technologies
Traditional Semiconductor	<	Microprocessor	enabling exponential improvements in price-performance, power consumption, and portability
Host-Based	<	Client Server	allowing an enterprise to become a network, and a network to become the computer
Garden Path Bandwidth	<	Information Highway	enabling economical access via distributed multimedia tools to a vast array of services and information content
Dumb Access	<	Information Appliance	providing "smart on and off ramps for the information highway," at rapidly falling costs
Separate Data, Text, Voice, Image	<	Multimedia	facilitating high-quality human communications across great distances
Proprietary	<	Open	enabling interoperability among networks, the integration of solutions from multiple sources, and scalability within networks
Dumb	<	Intelligent	letting agents do your routine browsing and shopping instead of your fingers on the keyboard
Craft	<	Object Computing	providing more immediate solutions to emerging business problems
GUIs	<	MUDs, MUIs, and MOOs	creating collaborative environment to support the emergence of a new economy

The internet, in its role as the network of all networks, will connect perhaps 100 million host computers by the year 2000. Today, there are an estimated 62.5 million direct internet users in 135 countries around the world. The internet enables low cost publication of a wide range of information (of highly variable quality), resource sharing among academics, long-distance research by students and their teachers, and provides consumers with access to information about goods and services available from businesses. Internet technology, a variation on the client-server model, employs the TCP/IP network protocol and packet switching to improve the utilisation of limited capacity and to provide robustness in the event of component failure. The World Wide Web provides an easy-to-use interface to network resources through a browser such as Mosaic, Netscape or Internet Explorer. An Intranet applies these technologies within an organisation.

The major trends in this rapidly evolving arena include:

- The emergence of low cost "appliances" for network access, which will be widely used in homes.
- Rapid increases in available bandwidth resulting from heavy investments in network capabilities combined with efficiency improvements through data compression and other technological advances.

- Exponential growth in content as more individuals gain access to the medium.
- Changes in industry structure, both worldwide and locally, as the business model evolves and weaker players exit.

Changes in the Nation

If we agree that Malaysia today differs in significant ways from the new nation which emerged from the colonial era about 40 years ago, the Malaysia of 25 years from now will be simply unrecognisable. History shows that new technology is the source of change in other domains. Except for our new generation of technologies, this scenario is very similar to the current forces at work in Asia, and is especially relevant to Malaysia.

The Multimedia Super Corridor Initiative

The Malaysian government embarked on a policy to bring its people into the ranks of the developed world by the year 2020, now less than a quarter-century away. Within this broad initiative, it has recently formulated plans for a Multimedia Super Corridor (MSC), to support the Prime Minister's vision of an information-rich society. This goal will require the coordinated development and effective use of IT, and implies the development of an acculturation process that will enable its citizens to participate meaningfully in this transformation to a knowledge-based society. The resource elements of the IT 2020 vision include building the national capacity to produce and manage IT resources, developing sufficient manpower with the right skills and knowledge to put these resources to use, developing telecommunications and data services infrastructure and industries to provide connectivity at the national and international levels, continuing development of the local IT industry, and especially of the small and medium scale support industries on which the computer and telecommunication industries depend.

The Multimedia Super Corridor (MSC) project involves attracting and nurturing a cluster of enterprises to Peninsular Malaysia, which will develop seven flagship applications that embody its diverse thrusts. These include electronic government, multi-purpose card, smart schools, telemedicine, R&D cluster, worldwide manufacturing web, and borderless marketing.

While all these application areas are certainly relevant, the MSC Electronic Government project represents a strategic opportunity to link the Sabah initiative to the larger and technically deeper efforts emanating from the MSC. Its main thrusts are to offer efficient, high-quality administrative services to citizens and businesses.

- streamline internal government processes to improve service quality and reduce costs.
- strengthen data security while protecting privacy.
- strengthen democracy.

Business Culture

The industrial success of high-technology regions such as Silicon Valley is traditionally explained as a consequence of the size and flexibility of the labour force, breadth of supplier networks, excellence of educational services, and strength of nearby research institutions. Unfortunately, Sabah has none of these factors. While these factors are now present in the Silicon Valley, they have not always been: in 1960, San Jose was a farming community. In fact, it is difficult to explain why these regions grew so rapidly, while other areas with similar endowments failed to develop at an equal rate, or why other areas (such as Penang or Bangalore) have attracted high-technology industry.

DEFINITION

Environmental scanning is a process of gathering, analysing, and dispensing information for tactical or strategic purposes. The environmental scanning process entails obtaining both factual and subjective information on the business environments in which a company is operating or considering entering.

There are three ways of scanning the business environment:

■ Ad-hoc scanning: Short term, infrequent examinations usually initiated by a crisis.
■ Regular scanning: Studies done on a regular schedule (e.g., once a year).
■ Continuous scanning (also called continuous learning): Continuous structured data collection and processing on a broad range of environmental factors.

Most commentators feel that in today's turbulent business environment the best scanning method available is continuous scanning because this allows the firm to act quickly, take advantage of opportunities before competitors do and respond to environmental threats before significant damage is done.

Environmental scanning usually refers just to the macro environment, but it can also include industry, competitor analysis, marketing research (consumer analysis), new product development (product innovations) or the company's internal environment.

Macro environmental scanning involves analysing:

Economy

■ GDP per capita
■ economic growth
■ unemployment rate
■ inflation rate
■ consumer and investor confidence
■ inventory levels
■ currency exchange rates
■ merchandise trade balance, financial and political health of trading partners
■ balance of payments
■ future trends
■ political climate—amount of government activity
■ political stability and risk
■ government debt
■ budget deficit or surplus

- corporate and personal tax rates
- payroll taxes
- import tariffs and quotas
- export restrictions
- restrictions on international financial flows

Legal

- minimum wage laws
- environmental protection laws
- worker safety laws
- union laws
- copyright and patent laws
- anti-monopoly laws
- Sunday closing laws
- municipal licences
- laws that favour business investment

Technology

- efficiency of infrastructure, including: roads, ports, airports, rolling stock, hospitals, education, health care, communication, etc.
- industrial productivity
- new manufacturing processes
- new products and services of competitors
- new products and services of supply chain partners
- any new technology that could impact the company
- cost and accessibility of electrical power

Ecology

- ecological concerns that affect the firm's production processes
- ecological concerns that affect customers' buying habits
- ecological concerns that affect customers' perception of the company or product

Sociocultural

- demographic factors such as:
  - population size and distribution
  - age distribution
  - education levels
  - income levels
  - ethnic origins
  - religious affiliations

- attitudes towards:
  - materialism, capitalism, free enterprise
  - individualism, role of family, role of government, collectivism
  - role of church and religion
  - consumerism
  - environmentalism
  - importance of work, pride of accomplishment
- cultural structures including:
  - diet and nutrition
  - housing conditions

Potential suppliers

- Labour supply
  - quantity of labour available
  - quality of labour available
  - stability of labour supply
  - wage expectations
  - employee turnover rate
  - strikes and labour relations
  - educational facilities
- Material suppliers
  - quality, quantity, price, and stability of material inputs
  - delivery delays
  - proximity of bulky or heavy material inputs
  - level of competition among suppliers
- Service providers
  - quantity, quality, price, and stability of service facilitators
  - special requirements

Stakeholders

- Lobbyists
- Shareholders
- Employees
- Partners

Scanning these macro environmental variables for threats and opportunities requires that each issue be rated on two dimensions. It must be rated on its potential impact on the company, and rated on its likeliness of occurrence. Multiplying the potential impact parameter by the likeliness of occurrence parameter gives a good indication of its importance to the firm.

The gathering of large amount of information to measure and study the changes in the environment is known as environmental scanning. The environmental scanning is taken into business scenario. It is very important for any business to get the latest information about the environment to keep its business steady and stable. In large and small organisation, environmental scanning is a must. Environmental scanning, as the point of business, is businesses have to look what is going on around them, whether the market is saturating, or if there is a need for product innovation.

The benefits of environmental scanning for the businesses are that they can uncover many issues that have an effect on the organisations' mission and goals. They might use it to increase their profit ratio. One of the motives for environmental scanning could be that they know whether the market is going as they expected it to. One of the latest methods for environmental scanning, which are frequently used by the companies, is the computer intelligence. By using these processes the businesses get information about their rivals. So this is the latest technological way for keeping an eye on your business. Many of the third party services being provided to other companies include environmental scanning.

Environmental scanning is the seeking and use of information about events, trends and relationships in an organisation's external environment, the knowledge of which would assist the management in planning the organisation's future course of action.

$$ES = CI + KM$$

CI (Competitor information) = Being well informed, alert, vigilant about threats and opportunities.

KM = Creating new knowledge, understanding, and being innovative, proactive.

$$ES = IS + OL$$

IS = Information Seeking
OL = Organisational Learning

WHY SCAN?

There are basically four broad reasons why we scan the environment:

- Competitiveness
- Strategic Change
- Culture Change
- Early Warning

A CONCEPTUAL FRAMEWORK FOR ENVIRONMENT SCANNING

(**Source:** Information Research, Vol. 7, No. 1, October 2001, Chun Wei Choo Faculty of Information Studies, University of Toronto, Toronto, Canada)

- *Situational dimensions:* The effect of perceived environmental uncertainty. Managers who perceive the environment to be more uncertain will tend to scan more. Environmental uncertainty is indicated by the complexity, dynamism, and importance of the sectors comprising external environment.

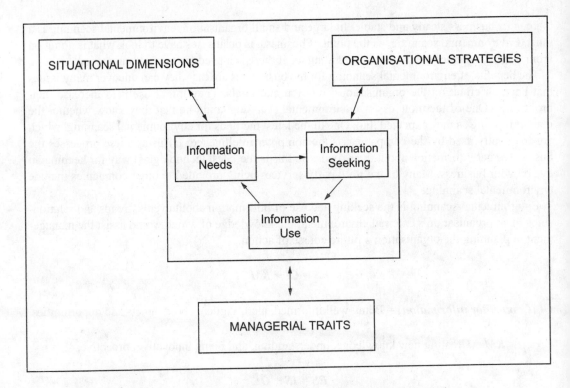

Fig. 10.1 A Conceptual Framework for Environment Scanning

- *Organisational strategy and scanning strategy.* An organisation's overall strategy is related to the sophistication and scope of its scanning activities. Scanning must be able to provide the information and information processing needed to develop and pursue the elected strategy.

- *Managerial traits:* Unanswered questions. Little is known with confidence about the effect of the manager's job-related and cognitive traits on scanning. Upper-level managers seem to scan more than lower-level managers. Functional managers scan beyond the limits of their specialisations.

- *Information needs:* The focus of environmental scanning. Most studies look at scanning in various environmental sectors: customers, competitors, suppliers, technology; social, political, economic conditions. Business organisations focus their scanning on market-related sectors of the environment.

- *Information seeking:* Source usage and preferences. Although managers scan with a wide range of sources, they prefer personal sources to formal, impersonal sources, especially when seeking information about developments in the fluid, market-related sectors.

- *Information seeking:* Scanning methods. Organisations scan in a variety of modes, depending on the organisation's size, dependence and perception of the environment, experience with scanning and planning, and the industry that the organisation is in.

- *Information use:* Strategic planning and enhanced organisational learning. Information from scanning is increasingly being used to drive the strategic planning process. Research suggests that effective scanning and planning is linked to improved organisational learning and performance.

ENVIRONMENTAL SCANNING AS INFORMATION SEEKING AND ORGANISATIONAL LEARNING

The monitoring of changes in the external environment in which an organisation operates in order to identify threats and opportunities for the future and maintain competitive advantage. The process of environmental scanning includes gathering information on an organisation's competitors, markets, customers, and suppliers; carrying out a PEST analysis of social, economic, technological, and political factors that may affect the organisation; and analysing the implications of this research. Environmental scanning may be undertaken systematically by a dedicated department or unit within an organisation or more informally by project groups and may be used in the planning and development of corporate strategy.

An organisation processes information to make sense of its environment, to create new knowledge, and to make decisions. Sense making is induced by changes in the environment that create discontinuity in the flow of experience engaging the people and activities of an organisation. People enact or actively construct the environment that they attend to by bracketing experience, and by creating new features in the environment. Organisational sense making can be driven by beliefs or by actions (Weick, 1995). In belief-driven processes, people start from an initial set of beliefs that are sufficiently clear and plausible, and use them as nodes to connect more and more information into larger structures of meaning.

People may use beliefs as expectations to guide the choice of plausible interpretations, or they may argue about beliefs and their relevance when these beliefs conflict with current information. In action-driven processes, people start from their actions and grow their structures of meaning around them, modifying the structures in order to give significance to those actions. People may create meaning to justify actions that they are already committed to, or they may create meaning to explain actions that have been taken to manipulate the environment.

An organisation possesses three kinds of knowledge: tacit knowledge, explicit knowledge and cultural knowledge. Tacit knowledge is the personal knowledge that is learned through extended periods of experiencing and doing a task, during which the individual develops a feel for and a capacity to make intuitive judgments about the successful execution of the activity.

Explicit knowledge is knowledge that is expressed formally using a system of symbols, and may be object-based or rule-based. Knowledge is object-based when it is represented using strings of symbols (documents, software code), or is embodied in physical entities (equipment, substances). Explicit knowledge is rule-based when the knowledge is codified into rules, routines, or operating procedures. Cultural knowledge consists of the beliefs an organisation holds to be true based on experience, observation, reflection about itself and its environment.

Over time, an organisation develops shared beliefs about the nature of its main business, core capabilities, markets, competitors, and so on. These beliefs then form the criteria for judging and selecting alternatives and new ideas, and for evaluating projects and proposals. In this way an organisation uses its cultural knowledge to answer questions such as 'What kind of an organisation are we?' 'What knowledge would be valuable to the organisation?' and 'What knowledge

UNDIRECTED VIEWING		ENACTING	
Sense Making	Waiting for important change	Sense Making	Create features in environment
Knowledge Creation	Little pre-existing knowledge	Knowledge Creation	Tacit knowledge: learn by doing
Decision Making	Coalition/Political mode	Decision Making	Anarchic/Process mode
CONDITIONED VIEWING		SEARCHING	
Sense Making	Driven by norms and beliefs	Sense Making	Determine objective reality
Knowledge Creation	Cultural knowledge: expectation, frames	Knowledge Creation	Explicit knowledge: hard data, formal models
Decision Making	Programmed/Rational mode	Decision Making	Process mode

Environmental Analysability — Unanalysable / Analysable

Passive — Active

Organisational Intrusiveness

Fig. 10.2   Environmental Learning as Organisational Learning

would be worth pursuing?' Organisations continuously create new knowledge by converting between the personal, tacit knowledge of individuals who develop creative insight, and the shared, explicit knowledge by which the organisation develops new products and innovations (Nonaka & Takeuchi, 1995).

Environmental scanning as information seeking and organisational learning

In the ensuing sections, we will analyse each mode of scanning by examining its characteristic information needs, information seeking, and information use behaviours. In addition, we analyse organisational learning processes by considering the sense making, knowledge creating and decision-making processes at work in each mode.

An organisation processes information to make sense of its environment, to create new knowledge, and to make decisions (Choo, 1998). Sense making is induced by changes in the environment that create discontinuity in the flow of experience engaging the people and activities of an organisation. People enact or actively construct the environment that they attend to by bracketing experience, and by creating new features in the environment (Weick, 1995). Organisational sense making can be driven by beliefs or actions (Weick, 1995). In belief-driven processes, people start from an initial set of beliefs that are sufficiently clear and plausible, and use them as nodes to connect more and more information into larger structures of meaning. People may use beliefs as expectations to guide the choice of plausible interpretations, or they may argue about beliefs and their relevance when these beliefs conflict with current information. In action-driven processes, people start from their actions and grow their structures of meaning around them, modifying the structures in order to give significance to those actions. People may create meaning to justify actions that they are already committed to, or they may create meaning to explain actions that have been taken to manipulate the environment.

An organisation possesses three kinds of knowledge: tacit knowledge, explicit knowledge and cultural knowledge. Tacit knowledge is the personal knowledge that is learned through extended periods of experiencing and doing a task, during which the individual develops a feel for and a capacity to make intuitive judgements about the successful execution of the activity. Explicit knowledge is knowledge that is expressed formally using a system of symbols, and may be object-based or rule-based. Knowledge is object-based when it is represented using strings of symbols (documents, software code), or is embodied in physical entities (equipment, substances). Explicit knowledge is rule-based when the knowledge is codified into rules, routines, or operating procedures. Cultural knowledge consists of the beliefs an organisation holds to be true based on experience, observation, reflection about itself and its environment. Over time, an organisation develops shared beliefs about the nature of its main business, core capabilities, markets, competitors, and so on. These beliefs then form the criteria for judging and selecting alternatives and new ideas, and for evaluating projects and proposals. In this way an organisation uses its cultural knowledge to answer questions such as 'What kind of an organisation are we?' 'What knowledge would be valuable to the organisation?' and 'What knowledge would be worth pursuing?' Organisations continuously create new knowledge by converting between the personal, tacit knowledge of individuals who develop creative insight, and the shared, explicit knowledge by which the organisation develops new products and innovations (Nonaka & Takeuchi, 1995).

Completely rational decision making requires information gathering and information processing beyond the capabilities of any organisation. In practice, organisational decision making departs from the rational ideal in important ways depending on: (1) the ambiguity or conflict of goals in the decision situation (goal ambiguity or conflict), and (2) the uncertainty about the methods and processes by which the goals are to be attained (technical or procedural uncertainty). In the boundedly rational mode, when goal and procedural clarity both are high, choice is guided by performance programmes (March & Simon, 1993). Thus, decision makers 'simplify' their representation of the problem situation; 'satisfice' rather than maximise their searches; and follow 'action programmes' or routinie procedures.

In the process mode (Mintzberg et al., 1976), when strategic goals are clear but the methods to attain them are not, decision making becomes a process that is highly dynamic, with many internal and external factors interrupting and changing the tempo and direction of the decision process. In the political mode (Allison & Zelikow, 1999), goals are contested by interest groups but procedural certainty is high within the groups: each group believes that its preferred alternative is best for the organisation. Decisions and actions are then the result of the bargaining among players pursuing their own interests and manipulating their available instruments of influence. In the anarchic mode (also known as the Garbage Can model of decision making) (Cohen et al., 1972), when goal and procedural uncertainty are both high, decision situations consist of independent streams of problems, solutions, participants, and choice opportunities arriving and leaving. A decision then happens when problems, solutions, participants, and choices coincide. When they do, solutions are attached to problems, and problems to choices by participants who are present and have the interest, time and energy to do so.

Undirected viewing

Undirected viewing, a term first used by Aguilar (1967), takes place when the organisation perceives the environment to be unanalysable and so does not intrude into the environment to understand it. Information needs are ill-defined and fuzzy, and much of the information obtained is non-routine or informal, usually gained through chance encounters. Since the environment is assumed to be unanalysable, the organisation is satisfied with limited, soft information and does not seek comprehensive, hard data. Information seeking is thus casual and opportunistic, relying more on irregular contacts and casual information from external, people sources. Information use is concerned primarily with reducing the high levels of environmental equivocality. Weick (1979) suggests that to resolve equivocality, organisations use assembly rules to shape data into a collective interpretation. The greater the equivocality, the fewer the number of rules activated because of uncertainty about what the information means. At the same time, arriving at a common interpretation requires many cycles of information sharing.

An example of undirected viewing might be a small firm that gathers information through pre-existing personal contacts with a limited number of buyers, suppliers, sales personnel, and associates in other companies. What information gets noticed and used depends on the frequency and intensity of cues that are entering the firm's awareness. Over time, a few of these signals build up in frequency and intensity, and so become 'noticed.' The advantage of undirected viewing is that the organisation need not expend resources on formalised scanning, but this saving incurs the risk of the organisation being surprised or caught off-guard.

During undirected viewing, sense making is characterized by informal bracketing. Bracketing of external signals is informal in that what the organisation notices depends on what subjective cues observers happen to be attending to at the time. Partly because multiple observers with different frames of reference may be involved, many cycles of sense making are required to reduce equivocality about what is going on in the environment. This may require many episodes of face-to-face communication, involving dialogue, negotiation and persuasion. Often, the issues or questions are not known beforehand, and the organisation has to identify or clarify the gaps of understanding. In some situations, issues are imposed by the external environment, as when government agencies, industry associations, consumer groups or other stakeholders bring forth areas of concern.

Knowledge that is used in undirected viewing is based on tacit beliefs that the complexity, opacity and dynamism of the environment are such as to render it unanalysable. These beliefs are shared by the organisation's members and can remain unspoken and unexamined. There is little by way of a stable stock of knowledge that can be called upon to interpret and make sense of changes in the environment. Decision making has to deal with high levels of uncertainty and ambiguity, and Daft & Weick (1983) suggested that coalition building may be necessary for the management to rally around a particular interpretation and a single course of action. Alternatively, a strong, powerful leader may choose the course of action. Overall, the modus of learning in undirected viewing is one of stimulus-and-response: the organisation maintains its status quo until a strong stimulus is recognised and necessitates a response.

Conditioned viewing

Conditioned viewing, again from Aguilar (1967), occurs when the organisation perceives the environment to be analysable but is passive about gathering information and influencing the environment. Information needs focus on a small number of relatively well-defined issues or areas of concern. These are often based on widely-accepted industry assumptions and norms. Information seeking makes use of standard procedures, typically employing internal, non-people sources, with a significant amount of data coming from external reports, databases, and sources that are highly respected and widely used in the industry. Thus, viewing is conditioned in the sense that "it is limited to routine documents, reports, publications, and information systems that have grown up through the years." (Daft & Weick, 1984: 289) Because the environment is assumed to be knowable, there is less need for equivocality reduction, with a greater number of rules that can be applied to assemble or construct a plausible interpretation.

During conditioned viewing, sense making is belief-driven, and there are fewer cycles of equivocality reduction. Over time, the organisation (or the industry it is in) has developed a set of assumptions and beliefs about the environment and uses them to define a number of areas of particular interest to structure or 'condition' the scanning activity. Fewer cycles of sense making are required to reduce equivocality because the organisation is starting from an initial set of clear, accepted beliefs, and it is already sensitised to known issues that are deemed critical for the organisation. Cultural knowledge plays an important role in conditioned viewing by supplying the assumptions and beliefs about the business and the environment that the organisation is in: who are its customers, competitors, stakeholders; what environmental sectors to watch out for; as well as what information sources to use.

These assumptions and beliefs may be part of the received knowledge that firms in the same industry share. They draw a frame of reference within which knowledge about the environment is created. Decision making in conditioned viewing is likely to resemble that of the boundedly rational model. Decisions are mostly programmed (March & Simon, 1993), following standard procedures and premises derived from past experience. Representation of the decision situation is simplified, search is 'satisficing', and procedures are structured by rules and routines. These rules may be adopted from standard industry practice or developed from the firm's own experience.

Overall, the modus of learning in conditioned viewing is for the organisation to use its existing knowledge about what is important in the environment to focus its scanning and action taking.

An illustration of conditioned viewing gone awry is provided by a recent analysis of the computer disk drive industry (Christensen, 1997). Several generations of disk drive manufacturers were highly focused on listening carefully to their largest customers, and failed to see how new technologies that were rejected by their best customers, had in fact appealing features for new customers, which expanded into new market segments. Thus, while one advantage of conditioned viewing is having established procedures and mental models to structure the scanning process, the disadvantage is that these rules and routines might miss detecting the emergence of new, possibly disruptive technologies or developments.

Enacting

Enacting takes place when the organisation perceives the environment to be unanalysable but then proceeds to intrude actively into the environment in order to influence events and outcomes. Information needs are those required for experimentation and testing the environment. This could involve identifying areas for fruitful intervention. Information seeking is from external sources and channels that the organisation has created through its intervention, and this may include feedback about the actions that the organisation has taken. Enacting organisations "construct their own environments. They gather information by trying new behaviours and seeing what happens. They experiment, test, and stimulate, and they ignore precedent, rules, and traditional expectations." (Daft & Weick, 1984: 288) Information use is focused on the actions that have been taken, and this information is used to reduce equivocality as well as to test existing rules and precedents.

An example of enacting would be a firm that introduces and markets a new product based on what it thinks it can sell, rather than waiting for research to assess market demand. Another example would be an organisation that actively influences and shapes the attitudes of its shareholders: it may try to 'manipulate shareholder perceptions towards itself, environmental issues, or political candidates by sending information to shareholders through various media.' (Daft & Weick, 1984: 290) In today's network economy, organisations with an internet presence have been using the World Wide Web as a channel for innovative ways of enacting their environment. For example, they have given away free products and services (browser software, open-source code, search engines) to test new products or increase market share; hosted online forums and communities to promote discussion and drum up support for issues; and created new websites to disseminate information as well as collect feedback on topics of interest.

During enacting, sense making is action-driven. The organisation intrudes actively into the environment to construct new features and to then concentrate sense making on these features. For example, an organisation may test-market a new product; organise a seminar or workshop; or produce a document for public comment. The information generated from these enactments then constitutes the new raw material for sense making. Thus, equivocality is reduced by testing and probing the environment. Tacit knowledge is important in enacting since the kind of enactments to be pursued depend on individual intuition and creativity (existing tacit knowledge), while the interpretation of enacted information depend on personal insight and instinct. New tacit knowledge may also be the outcome of enacting, as the organisation acquires new ways of seeing the environment while it reflects on data returned by their enactments. Daft and Weick (1984) suggest that decision making in enacting follows the process model described by Mintzberg et al. (1976): the organisation decides on a course of action, designs a custom solution, tries it, and recycles the process if the solution does not work. Decision-making processes tend to be phased and incremental, involving iterative cycles of design and trial-and-error (Mintzberg et al., 1976). In addition to the process model, we may also expect the decision process to resemble that of the anarchic mode presented earlier. Here, actions are not goal-driven but taken in order to discover goals. Decisions happen when solutions (enactments) appear to work and they become attached to problems.

Overall, the modus of learning in enacting is for the organisation to learn by doing – by trying out new actions in order to reveal new goals and methods.

Searching

Searching (labelled as Discovery in the original Daft and Weick paper) takes place when the organisation perceives the environment to be analysable and it actively intrudes into the environment to collect an accurate set of facts about the environment. Information needs are based on well-defined search goals that are broad, detailed, and open-ended. The organisation is prepared to be surprised by unexpected findings that reveal new information needs. Information seeking is for hard, formal, often quantitative data, typically from surveys, market research activities that are rigorous and objective. The organisation is likely to have its own scanning unit whose staff systematically analyses data to produce market forecasts, trend analysis, and intelligence reports. There are important differences between conditioned viewing and searching. Information seeking and use in conditioned viewing is restricted to a few issues; routinised; and based on received knowledge. On the other hand, searching is broad, open, and based on a willingness to revise or update existing knowledge. Decision making is based on logical, rational procedures, often including systems analysis and quantitative techniques.

An example of formalised searching would be Motorola's strategic intelligence system, one of the first to be established in corporate America in the 1980s. To develop the system, Motorola hired Jan Herring, a professional intelligence officer who later helped to found the Society for Competitive Intelligence Professionals. Herring designed the scanning system as follows. The corporate intelligence office maintained the central database, coordinated collection and served as the clearing house for strategic intelligence reporting, led the corporate-wide analysis projects, and supported operational divisions' intelligence activities. The operating divisions, on the other hand, ran their own operational or tactical intelligence collection, performed division-level analysis, and supported corporate collection and analysis efforts. A high-level policy committee, comprising all group vice-presidents and chiefs of headquarters' functions, assigns intelligence priorities to the unit. The staff of the corporate office are highly trained, some with both intelligence and business experience, and they analyse the information collected to arrive at and recommend alternative courses of action. Strong emphasis is placed on foreign intelligence. Motorola is one of the few US companies that systematically monitors technology developments in Japan, making large investments in obtaining technical literature, learning the language, and developing long-term relationships with Japanese researchers and organisations. (Sutton, 1988; Gilad, 1994; Penenberg & Barry, 2000)

During searching, sense making is based on formal, systematic scanning that is aimed at determining the objective facts of what is happening in the external environment. This systematic scanning can be both action-driven and belief-driven. Data gathering about the environment is relatively intense and may involve intrusive actions such as polls, surveys, focus groups, and so on. Following data collection, interpretation is likely to be belief-driven, where the organisation would extrapolate from past experience and construct meanings from current beliefs. Developing and working with explicit knowledge is the essence of searching. Measurement, modelling, forecasting, trends analysis, and other formal, quantitative methods are utilised to discover the true condition of the external environment.

The organisation believes that there is a stock of knowledge about the environment that it can draw upon for analysis and planning. Because the organisation is actively searching for information about an environment that it believes to be knowable, decision making is likely to follow the process mode described earlier. In this mode, the organisation takes the time and resources to look for or develop alternatives, and choosing a course of action is based on a diagnosis of the situation giving rise to the decision need. Decision making is based on logical, rational procedures, often including systems analysis and quantitative techniques.

Overall, the modus of learning in searching is for the organisation to invest resources in collecting information about and analysing the environment, and then to adjust its actions in the light of this new knowledge. The main difference between searching and conditioned viewing is that searching requires significant resources for entering the environment to create new features and/or to collect information. Another difference is that searching scans broadly and comprehensively in order to determine the true state of affairs, whereas conditioned viewing concentrates on selected areas or issues.

The different modes of scanning are compared in Figures 4 and 5. Research suggests that the model proposed by Daft and Weick is consistent with the empirical knowledge about organisational scanning (Choo, 2001). As indicated by the model, the amount of information seeking or scanning is related to the perceived analysability of the environment. Moreover, when the environment is perceived to be difficult to analyse, there is a tendency to use people sources more heavily in order to help reduce the higher levels of equivocality.

The concept of organisational intrusiveness underlines the relationship between the ability to manoeuvre actively in the environment and the gathering of useful information. This action-learning perspective is increasingly evident in the strategy literature that emphasises improvisation, discovery-based planning, and emergent strategy making. In summary, the scanning model appears as a viable framework for analysing the primary environmental and organisational contingencies that influence environmental scanning as cycles of information seeking and information use.

Implications for practice

The model presented in this paper is essentially a contingency framework that specifies two conditions influencing organisational scanning: environmental analysability and organisational intrusiveness. In today's highly volatile environment, organisations face a dilemma. On the one hand, the environment appears unanalysable because of its dense complexity and rapid rate of change. On the other hand, organisations recognise that they need to be proactive in scanning and shaping their environments. Some organisations believe that precisely because the environment is in flux, there is an opportunity (or a necessity in some cases) for them to intervene and influence developments to their advantage.

The model implies that for organisations wanting to encourage their members to scan more proactively, both the level of environmental analysability and the level of organisational intrusiveness need to be raised. To increase environmental analyzability, the organisation might keep in close touch with important actors in the environment; make information about customers, competitors, and the industry more widely available to employees; and encourage staff to be interested in and to discuss and collectively make sense of external developments. To increase organisational intrusiveness, the organisation might create channels to communicate with and influence stakeholders; encourage managers and employees to probe or test their environments by allocating resources or providing organisational slack; and be tolerant about innovative enactment experiments that do not succeed.

Implications for research

The model suggests a set of hypotheses that may be tested empirically. Although the model is consistent with the results of past studies, its specific predictions need to be investigated. As a metric

UNDIRECTED VIEWING		ENACTING	
Information Needs	General areas of interest	Information Needs	Specific Areas of exploration
Information Seeking	Informal	Information Seeking	Testing
Information Use	Noticing	information Use	Experimenting
CONDITIONED VIEWING		SEARCHING	
Information Needs	Sensitised areas of concerns	Information Needs	Detailed search goals
Information Seeking	Routinised	Information Seeking	Formal
Information Use	Watching	Information Use	Discovering

Assumptions about Environment — Unanalysable / Analysable

Passive — Active

Organisational Intrusiveness

Fig. 10.3   Environmental Scanning as Information Seeking

for assessing environmental analysability, we may look to the variable of perceived environmental uncertainty. Several scanning studies have operationalised perceived environmental uncertainty by measuring subjects' responses to questions about perceived complexity, rate of change, and importance of environmental sectors (e.g., Daft et al., 1988; Boyd & Fulk, 1996; Choo, 2001).

For organisational intrusiveness, possible metrics might include the amount of scanning, particularly the frequency and extent of use of external sources; or the size of the budget for acquiring external information (market research, database subscriptions, travel) and building information resources (library, information centre, records management). Other indicators might include the frequency and quality of communications and interactions with external stakeholders, and the use of enactments such as polls, surveys, and seminars. To identify modes of scanning predicted by the model, the characteristics of information seeking and use discussed in this paper could guide data collection and analysis. Studying the scanning modes in terms of sense making, knowledge creation, and decision making might call for a more narrative, ethnographic approach. This could involve, for example, analysing textual accounts of significant episodes of scanning and learning.

In summary, the model of environmental scanning presented here offers plausible explanations for the different levels and patterns of scanning that are observed in practice. We elaborated

UNDIRECTED VIEWING		ENACTING	
Sense Making	Waiting for important change	Sense Making	Create features in environment
Knowledge Creation	Little pre-existing knowledge	Knowledge Creation	Tacit knowledge: learn by doing
Decision Making	Coalition/Political mode	Decision Making	Anarchic/Process mode
CONDITIONED VIEWING		**SEARCHING**	
Sense Making	Driven by norms and beliefs	Sense Making	Determine objective reality
Knowledge Creation	Cultural knowledge: expectation, frames	Knowledge Creation	Explicit knowledge: hard data, formal models
Decision Making	Programmed/Rational mode	Decision Making	Process mode

(left axis: Environmental Analysability — Unanalysable / Analysable; bottom axis: Passive — Active — Organisational Intrusiveness)

Fig. 10.4   Environmental Scanning as Organisational Learning

environmental scanning as information seeking and organisational learning processes, discussed implications for managerial action, and stressed that much more could be learned by testing the model in field research.

Capacity Building and Environmental Scanning, and their relationship with KM

It is generally accepted that the concept of Learning Organisation (LO), championed by Peter Senge in the 1990s, was outdated. Though the concept of an organisation that continues to improve itself was appealing, few organisations were able to attain the LO title. The LO concept has since evolved, and many experts have proposed several concepts with the same premises as the LO–Capacity Building, Environmental Scanning, and Knowledge Management.

This article is meant for Knowledge Management (KM) practitioners, and thus I assume that the readers are familiar with the concept of Knowledge Management (KM). Organisations that practice KM, are supposed to manage their collective know-hows and experience, and share information. As such, KM activities may consist of:

- Transferring knowledge from the experienced staff to novices.
- Developing a common platform to share information and knowledge—Knowledge Portal.
- Facilitating knowledge creation through regular knowledge exchange sessions such as Dialogue, Communities of Practice.
- Connecting people with similar professional interests and creating awareness of who knows what.

Rather than explaining how the three terms are associated with the LO concept, I would provide an overview of Capacity Building and Environmental Scanning, and compare the two terms with Knowledge Management.

Capacity Building and Its similarities to KM

The United Nations Development Programme (UNDP) defines capacity building as the process by which individuals, organisations, institutions and societies develop abilities (individually and collectively) to perform functions, solve problems and set and achieve objectives. In similar mold, the World Customs Organisation (WCO) defines capacity building as activities which strengthen the knowledge, abilities, skills and behaviour of individuals and improve institutional structures and processes such that the organisation can effectively meet its mission and goals in a sustainable way.

However, capacity building is more than just analysing training needs and devising training programmes to meet those needs. Capacity building includes the following components:

1. Human resource development, the process of equipping individuals with the understanding, skills and access to information, knowledge and training that enables them to perform effectively.
2. Organisation development, the elaboration of management structures, processes and procedures, not only within organisations but also the management of relationships between different organisations and sectors (public, private and community).
3. Institutional and legal framework development, making legal and regulatory changes to enable organisations, institutions and agencies at all levels and in all sectors to enhance their capacities.

In summary, capacity building involves management interference where a group of people, either internal staff or external consultants, is tasked to examine key individual, work unit, or the organisation's current capacities, identifying what capacities they are lacking, and building the required capacities to meet the organisation's goals. Here the term capacity covers human resource, organisation development and legal aspect.

As mentioned above, Capacity Building could be from inside the organisation—the required capacity can be found in the organisation or outside the organisation—the required capacity lies outside the organisation. In this regard, Knowledge Management—managing what the organisation knows—is the internal capacity building since the organisation's capacities could be interpreted as the organisation's critical knowledge—knowledge that is crucial for the organisation's survival or knowledge that gives the organisation competitive advantage over its rival. The graph below illustrates this point.

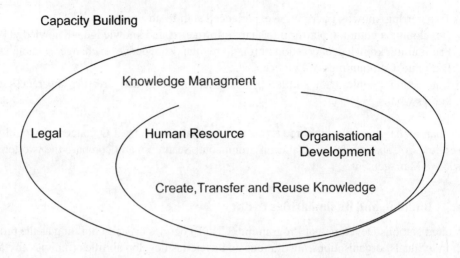

Capacity Building

Knowledge Managment

Legal

Human Resource

Organisational
Development

Create,Transfer and Reuse Knowledge

Fig. 10.5   Capacity Building and Knowledge Management

It is worth mentioning that the depth and breath of capacity building concept makes the word 'building' somewhat misleading, since it refers only to the creation of new organisation's capabilities. But, a closer look at the three components of capacity building makes it clear that the concept also implies development of infrastructure, management processes, relationships, organisation's structure and culture. Thus, a more appropriate term would be capacity development.

Environmental Scanning

Environmental scanning is the acquisition and use of information about events, trends, and relationships in an organisation's external environment, the knowledge of which would assist management in planning the organisation's future course of action (Aguilar, 1967; Choo & Auster, 1993). Organisations scan the environment in order to understand the external forces of change so that they may develop effective responses, which secure or improve their position in the future. They scan in order to avoid surprises, identify threats and opportunities, gain competitive advantage, and improve long-term and short-term planning (Sutton, 1988).

Thus, Environmental Scanning is very different from Capacity Building and Knowledge Management, although the earlier concept may evoke the latter two concepts. To make use of the Environmental Scanning output, an organisation may embark on Capacity Building /Knowledge Management activities. On the flip side, findings from Environmental Scanning can be used to justify Capacity Building / Knowledge Management activities.

Two questions were the focus of the present research: how developed was information acquisition in firms and why were there so few studies about it in the academic literature?

The results of our field study reinforced certain hypotheses on Environmental Scanning and competitive intelligence: firms are still underdeveloped, but higher sales, better information technology development, environmental uncertainty and an organisation turned outwards were correlated with a higher level of development.

Other hypotheses could not be retained. There was no significant improvement between 2001 and 2002 and size of firms measured in term of number of hierarchical levels or number of employees is not correlated with the development of environmental scanning systems.

And why are there so few empirical studies on Environmental Scanning? Probably because studies like this cover formal scanning activities only. The consciousness of employees to informal, ad hoc practices remains unknown and the question whether it is pertinent to formalise these activities remains unanswered. After all, we all scan our environment, we did it before the internet and computers and maybe long before Adam Smith. If the internet is only an additional tool, and it is used for ad hoc scans, there is no revolution in environmental scanning practices.

REMEMBER

- Not so long ago, when environments were relatively stable, organisations kept their eyes on internal operations.
- The definition of managerial work was decision making.
- Today, as environment becomes more and more volatile, organisations are turning their gaze to the horizon, watching and struggling with a confusion of signals.
- The core of managerial work now is to know what is going on in order to be able to decide what is to be done.
- Sensing and making sense of the environment is the new competency for organisational growth and survival.

SUMMING UP

Environmental Scanning is the seeking and use of information about events, trends and relationships in an organisation's external environment, the knowledge of which would assist management in planning the organisation's future course of action.

$$ES = CI + KM$$
$$ES = IS + OL$$

An organisation processes information to make sense of its environment, to create new knowledge, and to make decisions. Sense making is induced by changes in the environment that create discontinuity in the flow of experience, engaging the people and activities of an organisation. People enact or actively construct the environment that they attend to by bracketing experience, and by creating new features in the environment. Organisational sense making can be driven by beliefs or actions.

Knowledge consists of the beliefs an organisation holds to be true based on experience, observation, reflection about itself and its environment. Over time, an organisation develops shared beliefs about the nature of its main business, core capabilities, markets, competitors, and so on.

Organisations continuously create new knowledge by converting between the personal, tacit knowledge of individuals who develop creative insight, and the shared, explicit knowledge by which the organisation develops new products and innovations (Nonaka & Takeuchi, 1995).

CASE

Knowledge Management in Malaysia—Why Slow Adoption?

Knowledge Management in Malaysia is in infant stage. Very few Malaysian companies have initiated any KM programmes. A sharing culture is an essential key success factor of an effective Knowledge Management programme and has profound implications for KM practitioners in Malaysia, and perhaps throughout the developing world.

Generally, KM models are formulated in the context of a Western-centric framework in which freedom of expression and individualism are both accepted social norms. Within such a context, KM initiatives can automatically focus on determining a suitable framework to be implemented and procuring the correct infrastructure. By contrast, the same does not necessarily hold true in many local Malaysian corporations.

Indeed, right across the developing world, many corporations, large or important enough to implement KM, are probably still state-owned or have only recently been privatised. Consequently, many inherit a corporate culture that can sometimes still resemble a civil service in many ways, values such as deference of authority, seniority and hierarchy may still define social interactions. These values can potentially seriously inhibit the sort of exchange of ideas and information a KM strategy is designed to achieve.

Employees will always be conscious of the appropriateness of their contributions; superiors on the other hand would be cautious to ensure that their comments do not reveal their lack of familiarity with the subject. The result is a very sterilised and possibly superficial exchange that betrays the whole idea of knowledge sharing. Faced with such a situation, unsuspecting managements could easily fall into the trap of attempting to implement standard approaches of KM without paying sufficient regard to the social aspect of their organisations, only to meet with a lack of success, see millions of dollars wasted and contribute to demoralised cynical employees.

According to some researchers, Malaysian companies need to develop a strategic perspective when viewing knowledge. Companies should also analyse the corporate culture and focus on openness and sharing of knowledge without any fear of being penalised.

(Source: KM Malaysia—www.kmtalk.net,http://www.knowledgeboard.com/item/2643)

With the help of the above information, collect more information on why KM is slow in Malaysia and frame a case study with the help of your class Professor.

KEYWORDS

Environmental Scanning: It is the seeking and use of information about events, trends and relationships in an organisation's external environment, the knowledge of which would assist management in planning the organisation's future course of action.

Tacit Knowledge: It is the personal knowledge that is learned through extended periods of experience and doing a task, during which the individual develops a feel for and a capacity to make intuitive judgments about the successful execution of the activity.

Explicit Knowledge: It is knowledge that is expressed formally using a system of symbols, and may be object-based or rule-based.

INDIVIDUAL ASSIGNMENT

1. Do an environmental scanning of your area, where you are located and bring out the changes in environment during the last five years.
2. Read the following letter of communication from HR-Consultant to his HR-Manager and design a suitable training programme using Knowledge Management ideas.

Dear Sir,

You asked for training from our consultants for your staff on all corporate resources. We are the EXPERTS on this. We propose a one-day training, where we emphasise on Finance, Human, and Technical Resources. Our training will use overhead projector and our trainer has written a very successful book in 1999. You can really profit a lot from this course. Our price is at Rs.1000 for a one-day session.

Regards
Markus Mueller Sales
www.training-center.ch

GROUP ASSIGNMENT

Seekers

Seekers is a simple exercise, suitable for groups of 40 or 50 or more, and runs during the breaks or over lunch. It requires blank name badges, so either buy a supply of badges, or if you are in a badged event, ask people to turn their badges to the blank side. Ask them to write on the blank badge, in large clear letters, a question to which they would like an answer. It can be a work question, or a home-life question. Make sure it's a practical question! It should be "How do I plan a theme birthday party for my 5-year old" rather than "Does God exist" Do this in the morning, then during the break and lunch. If people see a question they can help answer, either giving good advice, or pointing people to a source of advice, then they go and introduce themselves and offer help. After the afternoon break, ask for a show of hands for "Who has got an answer?". You should see between a third and half the people raise their hands. You can then lead a discussion on motivation (What motivated people to help? What would motivate you to ask questions at work?), on the power of asking as a driver for knowledge transfer, on "How we can make our questions visible to others as part of our work", and on KM approaches such as community forums and peer assist.

INTERNET EXERCISE

Millionaire

This is a variation of the TV game "Who wants to be a Millionaire?", suitable for groups which number above 15. Buy the quiz book, and build yourself PowerPoint with two sets of questions. Get two volunteers (Role Playing)—Often look for one senior manager, and one very junior staff member. The senior manager has to answer the questions using his or her own knowledge. The junior staff member can "ask the audience" in every round. Guess who always wins! Then again, you have the same discussion on motivation (what motivated the audience to help), on how you could set up a system so people could "ask the audience" at work, on "who would the audience be" leading on to the topic of communities", on incentives and disincentives to asking, and so on.

QUESTIONS FOR DISCUSSION

Part-A

1. Explain the importance of Environmental Scanning in general.
2. What relevance does environmental scanning have with Knowledge Management?
3. How will you scan the environment?
4. Explain briefly the concept of information seeking and Organisational Learning.
5. Explain Nonaka's opinion on "Environmental Scanning & Organisational Learning".
6. Define Environmental Scanning.
7. State all the factors included in Macro and Micro Environmental Scanning of KM.
8. What is the difference between Business Intelligence and Competitive Intelligence?
9. What is Environment Scanning in Information Processing?

SUGGESTED READINGS

Aguilar, Francis J., Scanning the Business Environment, Macmillan Co., New York, 1967.

Aldrich, Howard E., Organisations Evolving, Thousand Oaks, CA: Sage Publications, 1999.

Allison, Graham T., & Zelikow, Philip, *Essence of Decision: Explaining the Cuban Missile Crisis*, 2nd ed. New York, NY: Addison-Wesley, 1999.

Boyd, Brian K., & Fulk, Janet, "Executive Scanning and Perceived Uncertainty: A Multidimensional Model." *Journal of Management*, 22 (1), 1–22, 1996.

Choo, Chun Wei, Information Management for the Intelligent Organisation: The Art of Scanning the Environment, 3rd ed. Medford, NJ: Information Today, Inc., 2001.

Choo, Chun Wei, The Knowing Organisation: How Organisations Use Information to Construct Meaning, Create Knowledge, and Make Decisions, New York: Oxford University Press, 1998.

Choo, Chun Wei, and Auster, Ethel, "Environmental Scanning: Acquisition and Use of Information by Managers", In *Annual Review of Information Science and Technology*, edited by M. E. Williams, Medford, NJ: Learned Information, Inc. For the American Society for Information Science, 1993.

Christensen, Clayton M., *The Innovator's Dilemma: When New Technologies Cause Great Firms to Fail*, Boston, MA, Harvard Business School Press, 1997.

Cohen, Michael D., March, James G. & Olsen, Johan P., "A Garbage can Model of Organisational Choice." Administrative Science Quarterly 17, 1–25, 1972.

Cyert, Richard Michael, & March, James G. A Behavioral Theory of the Firm. 2nd ed. Oxford, UK: Blackwell, 1992.

Daft, Richard L., & Weick, Karl E., "Toward a Model of Organisations as Interpretation Systems". Academy of Management Review 9 (2), 284–295.

WEBSITES

URL: http://www.infed.org/biblio/learning-organisation.htm [27th April, 2008]

International Learning Xchange (Undated). *ABN AMRO Achieve Effective Low Cost Development* URL: http://www.ilxgroup.com/desktop_abnamro.htm [29th April, 2008]

Knowledge Connections (Undated). *The Learning Organisation* URL: http://www.skyrme.com/insights/3lrnorg.htm [27th April, 2008]

Pedler M., T. Boydell & J. Burgoyne (1989). *Towards the Learning Company*

Pioneers of Change (Undated). *ABN AMRO Change Community* URL: http://pioneersofchange.net/ventures/abn/document_view [3rd May, 2008] Senge, Peter (2006). The Fifth Discipline

The BizTech Network (Undated). *Organisational Learning and Learning Organisations: AnOverview*URL: http://www.brint.com/papers/orglrng.htm [27th April, 2008]

http://www.nickmilton.com/2009/06/knowledge-management-exercises-and.html

http://www.changeup.org.uk/documents/regions/EastRegion-GuideToCapacityBuilding.pdf

http://www.iog.ca/Publications/policybrief6.pdf

http://en.wikipedia.org/wiki/Capacity_building

http://www.inwent.org/capacity_building/bei_inwent/index.php.en

http://www.recoftc.org/site/index.php?id=376

http://www.informationr.net/ir/7-1/paper112.html

http://www.informationr.net/ir/11-1/paper241.html

http://www.slideshare.net/mkconway/environmental-scanning-what-it-is-and-how-to-do-it

http://w3.atlcon.net/~mperla/cis8110/environmental_scanning.htm

CHAPTER 11

Technology & Knowledge Management

OBJECTIVE

At the end of this lesson, you would be able to understand:

- What is Technology?
- Recognise that human intervention is the common bond among technologies.
- Introduction to framework for thinking and action.
- Integration of technology and management.
- The relationships between technology and management.
- Key technologies used in KM.
- Different policy application.
- Benefits of technology in KM.

> *Bill Gates is a very rich man today...and do you want to know why?*
> *The answer is one word: versions.*
>
> —Dave Barry

INTRODUCTION

> *We tend to overestimate the short-term impact of a technology and*
> *underestimate the long-term impact.*
>
> — Dr. Francis Collins

The reach of know-how and experience possessed by individuals can be greatly extended once it is captured and explicated so that others can easily find it, an understand it and use it.

In ancient Greece, the philosopher, Plato, in his dialogues, captured and elaborated the thinking of his mentor Socrates, and so succeeding generations have been able to discover and share that thinking, and in turn reinterpret those thoughts and be stimulated to achieve fresh insights and creativity. In other cultures, the Analects of Confucius, The Art of War of Sun Tzu, or the pyramids of Egypt and Mexico, have served similar knowledge sharing functions.

In modern times, reports of activities, minutes of meetings, memoranda, proceedings of conferences, and document filing systems maintained by organisations are traditional and commonly-used devices for recording content in paper format so that it can be transferred to others.

More recently, electronic databases, audio and video recordings, interactive tools and multimedia presentations have become available to extend the techniques for capturing and disseminating content. Although these tools are not yet available everywhere in the developing world, they are spreading rapidly and present a unique opportunity for developing countries to benefit most from the technological revolution now unfolding: low-cost telecommunications systems can help countries to leapfrog ahead through distance education, distance health services, and much better access to markets and private sector partners abroad.

Nevertheless, even with modern tools, the process of knowledge transfer is inherently difficult, since those who have knowledge may not be conscious of what they know or how significant it is, or be able or willing to share it with others. Even when they are so willing, the readiness to accept the wisdom of others is often not obvious. Thus, know-how is "sticky" and tends to stay in people's heads.

The availability of the World Wide Web has been instrumental in catalysing the knowledge management movement. Information technology may, if well resourced and implemented, provide a comprehensive knowledge base that is speedily accessed, interactive, and of immediate value to the user. However, there are also many examples of systems that are neither quick, easy-to-use, problem free in operation, nor easy to maintain. The Web, for example, frequently creates information overload. The development of tools that support knowledge sharing in an appropriate and user-friendly way, particularly in organisation-wide knowledge sharing programmes, is not a trivial task.

> *Do you realise if it weren't for Edison we'd be watching TV by candlelight?*
> —Al Boliska

Most of the technological tools now available tend to help in the dissemination of know-how, but offer less assistance for knowledge use.

John Spencer rightly said, "The research rate of the future allows experimentation without manipulation of the real world. This is the cutting edge of modelling technology".

Tools that assist in knowledge creation are even less well developed, although collaborative workspaces offer promising opportunities, by enabling participation, across time and distance, in project design or knowledge-base development, so that those most knowledgeable about development problems—the people living them on a day-to-day basis—can actively contribute to their solution. Some of the more user-friendly technologies are the traditional ones—face-to-face discussions, the telephone, electronic mail, and paper-based tools such as flip charts. Among the issues that need to be considered in providing information technology for knowledge sharing programmes are:

- Responsiveness to user needs: continuous efforts must be made to ensure that the information technology in use meets the varied and changing needs of users.
- Content structure: in large systems, classification and cataloguing becomes important so that items can be easily found and quickly retrieved.
- Content quality requirements: standards for admitting new content into the system needs to be established and met to ensure operational relevance and high value.
- Integration with existing systems: since most knowledge sharing programmes aim at embedding knowledge sharing in the work of staff as seamlessly as possible, it is key to integrate knowledge-related technology with pre-existing technology choices.
- Scalability: solutions that seem to work well in small groups (e.g., HTML websites) may not be appropriate for extrapolation organisation-wide or on a global basis.
- Hardware-software compatibility is important to ensure that choices are made that are compatible with the bandwidth and computing capacity available to users.

Synchronisation of technology with the capabilities of users is important so as to take full advantage of the potential of the tools, particularly where the technology skills of users differ widely. Knowledge sharing programmes that focus on the simultaneous improvement of the whole system, both technology tools and human practices, are likely to be more successful than programmes that focus on one or the other.

> *Humanity is acquiring all the right technology for all the wrong reasons.*
> —R. Buckminster Fuller

One of the major risks in Knowledge Management programmes is the tendency for organisations to confuse Knowledge Management with some form of technology, whether it be Lotus Notes, the World Wide Web, or one of the off-the-shelf technology tools that are now proliferating. In the process, the essentially ecological concept of Knowledge Management becomes degraded into a simple information system that can be engineered without affecting the way the work is done. It is not that information systems are bad. Rather, it is important to recognise that knowledge management is a different and better way of working which affects people, and requires social arrangements like communities to enable it to happen on any consistent and sustained basis.

In the words of Lewis Mumford, "Western society has accepted as unquestionable a technological imperative that is quite as arbitrary as the most primitive taboo: not merely the duty to foster invention and constantly to create technological novelties, but equally the duty to surrender to these novelties unconditionally, just because they are offered, without respect to their human consequences".

The sad reality is that human beings tend to resist taking on new knowledge, if it contradicts their existing views and beliefs. The phenomenon, which psychologists call the confirmation bias, was noted by Francis Bacon almost 400 years ago: "The human understanding when it has once adopted an opinion…draws all things else to support and agree with it. And though there be a greater number and weight of instances to be found on the other side, yet these it either neglects and despises, or else by some distinction sets aside and rejects, in order that by this great and pernicious predetermination, the authority of its former conclusions may remain inviolate."

TECHNOLOGY AND FUTURE

If you want to turn an activity into a good habit you have to keep it up for a longer period (at least 21 days). After that your brain and body get used to it and it will be easier to keep up. The Web is a well established good habit. It is here and has conquered a place in our lives and in our society.

Let's take a look at some short-term developments in 2010. As expected the world didn't suddenly and drastically change this year. But a few issues are worth following:

Google

For a long time Google has been the darling of the tech industry. They were geeky, displayed good karma, offered great technology (for free!) and could 'do no evil' even if they tried.

It is clear that this is in longer the case. Google is now unavoidable, an effective monopoly, and the only choice for many services. With all the benefits that one choice brings, customers aren't revolting, not yet.

But customers like choice. The hippest bar in town is hip until everybody knows it and then the hipsters move along to the next hip thing. With Google, there is no alternative.

With Google getting more aggressive in competing with other giants (in search, browsing, publishing and every other area they are expanding in) even more changes were brought in customer perspective in 2010 wherein Google might become more like Microsoft (even though mostly in customer perception) than they could have ever dreamt of.

Microsoft

The original monopoly has gone from the stock market favourite and innovator to the butt of every one's jokes in less than 10 years. With the lawsuits, the exit of Bill Gates and Steve Ballmers, many public performances they gave journalists, bloggers and the general audience, there is enough fuel for laughter and complaints to last a decade. The following 10 years will be instrumental.

Will the company adapt to a new world where the desktop is no longer the centre of computing? Will Bing turn into a serious competitor to Google? Will Windows Vista be a dud or the operating system that will lead the way to the future?

All these matters won't be decided in the coming 12 months, but this year will mark either the return of Microsoft or the beginning of a death spiral. And yes, I'm well aware that Windows is still the dominant operation system. But who really cares about Operating Systems in the age of the Web?

Facebook

December marked the first month that Facebook generated more traffic in the US than Google did. It might have been just an end of the year peak in traffic but it is revolutionary nonetheless. So far, traffic has been flowing from, through and around Search Engines. The fact that we still need search engines seems to suggest we are internally lost and searching for places to go. With facebook now taking so much time from us it seems we have found somewhere to be for the first time.

It could very well mark the beginning of a trend of the Web becoming a place where you actually 'do' stuff instead of just 'browse' around. The 'browsing' paradigm fit the 'old' Web very well. We browsed from homepage to homepage and from blogpost to blogpost, never stopping to actually use, read or enjoy an individual site.

Maybe, after 21 years, we are comfortable enough with the medium to just stick around somewhere.

Twitter

Twitter, like the World Wide Web, has arrived. It is here, and has taken a permanent place in our society. And growing very rapidly.

Certainly Twitter will grow even more this year. But how much? Will they double? Triple? Maybe even grow tenfold and be the first company to reach a billion users?

Whatever happens this year will be defining Twitter's future. Somewhere in the 2nd quarter they will launch revenue making services. That will have a huge impact on its perceived value. If they manage to generate a lot of revenue the future will look bright. But if user growth slows down and revenue doesn't look as promising as hoped, 2010 might as well mark the beginning of the end of its unchallenged growth.

All in all 2010 will be the most exciting and defining year for Twitter's future.

Apple

The tablet. What will it be, how will it look and what will it do? And more importantly; how awesome, amazing and world-changing will it be?

Without a doubt Apple has shown that it can transform industries and build game changing products. Will this Apple Tablet be the launch of a new way of computing? Will it be nothing more than a bigger iPhone or a better Kindle?

Whatever it will be a launch as important as the launch of the first iPod and iPhone. Year 2010 will be the beginning, or end, of tablet computing and Apple will define it.

You

Last year Time Magazine's most important person of the year was consumer. The consumer was at the centre of the Web and the world turned around personalisation, user generated content and consumer empowerment. Meanwhile computers, and the Web, are still notoriously hard to use and are still not making our lives any easier.

Richer, Yes. Easier? No.

Since 1984 not much has changed in the way we interact with our PCs. Even today 90% of what we do is type text. The first Macintosh could accept text 20 times faster than the fastest typist in the world could type.

So here we are, 36 years later, with iPhones that still don't 'get' what I write when I want to write and desktop PCs that, after thousands or repeat entries, still don't 'understand' that I am again writing my full name.

Our keyboards are still based on the QWERTY layout. A layout that was introduced to make us type slower so the keys on our mechanical typewriters wouldn't get tangled up. I can (almost) live with the fact that we still don't have flying cars. But the advances in human to computer interfacing are disappointing, to say the least.

- Smart phones account for 35% of North American cellphone sales now, up from zero before the iPhone came out a couple of years ago.
- There is an accelerated and compressed innovation cycle in mobile data. Network operator CAPEX has increased, even during the recent recession, to handle the big boom in mobile data traffic.

- Wireless is a very personal technology, especially when it is location enabled. Mobile advertising is and will take advantage of personal user preferences and locations to deliver more targeted ads.
- But there are limitations (or impediments to growth): small screen size, difficulty inputting data (via keyboard or touchscreen), ROI economics of wireless are very different from fixed broadband wireless access, network capacity and aggregate bandwidth limitations have been important issues for mobile network operators (especially for AT&T's 3G network).

The key wireless trends, according to Mr. Lowenstein are the following:

- Growth of app stores to sell applications developed by small, embrionic software start-ups.
- Finding better ways of discovering (presence and location) of mobile data users.
- Voice will play a key role in mobility (presumably referring to Google voice and Skype over VZW).
- How will "Always on" devices be distributed and priced?
- Mobile commerce and advertising offer huge opportunities. How will this evolve?

In its first two years of existence, the mobile internet has grown eight times faster than the wireline internet during its comparable first two years (no source was given for this statistic). For Google, "mobile has become the primary internet access device." Mobile device search generates five times more search queries than fixed access PCs. And smart phone searches are 30 to 50 times more than searches initiated from feature phones.

A very interesting statistic was that for Android enabled smart phones, 30% of searches have been through voice queries (rather than touch screen or keyboard entries). Another is that there are more than 50M active users of Google Maps, most of them from mobile devices. 65K Android phones are sold every day by Google and partners (e.g., network operators offering Android phones from Motorola and HTC). Mario ticked off the following key issues for the mobile industry:

- Availability and adoption of 3G and soon 4G mobile data networks.
- Smart browsers and OSs (e.g., Chrome OS) to make internet access simpler and faster.
- Making phones "smarter".
- Powerful application development platform (e.g., Android).
- Simple data plans.

An example for electronic novel is e-book. So what is an e-book?. The box 11.1 explains what an e-book is.

Box 11.1   Example of Electronic Novel

An e-book is an electronic book, one that you read digitally on your computer, laptop screen or on devices called e-book readers. You will find them in various formats and until the industry has a standard format accessible from all devices, these various formats will exist. PDF format is a popular format for e-books. All platforms are able to gain access to and read PDF formatting. So, regardless of whether you have a PC or Mac, you are in business! PDF requires the Acrobat Reader but this software comes on many new computers and if not included, it's a free downloaded from Adobe http://www.adobe.com. There are still many who prefer printing out the pages of an e-book to read and PDF files have always been good for this purpose. Visit the IRS online and you will see every tax form they have available on PDF to print, fill out and send.

FRAMEWORKS FOR THINKING AND ACTION

> *Soon silence will have passed into legend. Man has turned his back on silence.*
> *Day after day he invents machines and devices that increase noise and distract*
> *humanity from the essence of life, contemplation, meditation.*
>
> —Jean Arp

From the perspective of a knowledge architect, frameworks provide a convenient way of thinking about the role of ICT in supporting knowledge processes. Most frameworks map different ICT tools according to their function and whether they are used individually or by teams. One such framework is shown in Table 11.1.

From an analysis of a wide range of tools and classifications, Jan Wyllie of Trend Monitor International has developed the functional schema shown below:

A framework that most managers can easily relate to is that which maps various ICT tools according to the knowledge processes they enhance. Having learnt about Business Process Reengineering,

Table 11.1   Knowledge Transfer Mechanisms

	Passive (information)	**Active (knowledge)**
Person to Person	Computer Conferencing Expert Networks	Meeting Support Videoconferencing
Person to Computer	Document Management Info Retrieval Knowledge Bases	Expert Systems Decision Support
Computer-Computer	Data Mining	Neural Networks Intelligent Agents

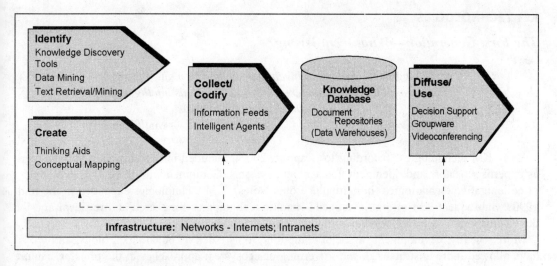

Fig. 11.1 Representative Information Systems Solutions Mapped Against the Knowledge Processes They Augment

A. MIND: Assimilation and Interpretation
   a) Mapping   b) Summarisation   c) Significant Pattern Discovery   d) Decision Support

B. COLLABORATION: Network and Communication
   a) Conversing   b) Workflow   c) Information Sharing   d) Resource Sharing
   e) Groupware

C. CONTENT: Gathering and Retrieval
   a) Preparation   b) Classifying   c) Searching   d) Filtering   e) Indexing

D. MEDIA: Storage and Form
   a) Numeric Databases   b) Text Bases   c) Image Bases   d) Multimedia

Fig. 11.2 Schematic Knowledge Process

many are now well oriented to the process view of the firm. Figure 11.2 shows Schematic Knowledge Processes (similar to a value chain), whose left hand categories distinguish the two strands of Knowledge Management—identifying existing knowledge and creating new knowledge. A representative selection of ICT tools are mapped into different knowledge processes.

Any follower of Knowledge Management will know that one of the things that change most frequently is KM technology. Ten years ago, Lotus Notes was probably the most cited knowledge sharing technology among KM leaders, while products like content management suites or expertise profilers barely existed.

KEY TECHNOLOGIES

The First Generation—What Went Wrong?

> *All of the biggest technological inventions created by man—the airplane,*
> *the automobile, the computer—says little about his intelligence,*
> *but speaks volumes about his laziness.*
> —Mark Kennedy

Early KM technologies, according to (Capozzi 2007), included online corporate yellow pages as expertise locators and document management systems. Combined with the early development of collaborative technologies (in particular Lotus Notes), KM technologies expanded in the mid-1990s. Subsequent KM efforts leveraged semantic technologies for search and retrieval and the development of e-learning tools for communities of practice.

More recently, development of social computing tools (such as bookmarks, blogs, and wikis) have allowed more unstructured, self-governing or ecosystem approaches to the transfer, capture and creation of knowledge, including the development of new forms of communities, networks, or matrixed organisations. However, (Andrus, 2005), feels that such tools for the most part are still based on text and code, and thus represent explicit knowledge transfer. These tools face challenges in distilling meaningful reusable knowledge and ensuring that their content is transmissible through diverse channels.

Software tools in Knowledge Management are a collection of technologies and are not necessarily acquired as a single software solution. Furthermore, these Knowledge Management software tools have the advantage of using the organisation's existing information technology infrastructure. Organisations and business decision makers spend a great deal of resources and make significant investments in the latest technology, systems and infrastructure to support Knowledge Management. It is imperative that these investments are validated properly, made wisely and that the most appropriate technologies and software tools are selected or combined to facilitate Knowledge Management.

Knowledge Management has also become a cornerstone in emerging business strategies such as Service Life cycle Management (SLM) with companies increasingly turning to software vendors to enhance their efficiency in industries including, but not limited to, the aviation industry.

Computer support of knowledge activities is far from new. In the 1970s there was a proliferation of 'expert systems', and heightened interest in artificial intelligence. It was suggested that they might radically transform knowledge activities within firms. The reality, as we know in hindsight, is that they fell far short of expectations. They could handle only a narrow range of problems, they required extensive knowledge elicitation, and they failed to grasp the fundamental nature of human thought processes. This era is best characterised as the one where we tried to make computers think, rather than using computers to help humans think.

Today, after years of steady progress, artificial intelligence has evolved new techniques, such as neural networks and intelligent agents, and is being widely applied in a growing number of applications. Our research also found that it is used, to some degree, in a significant proportion of world-class knowledge management programmes that we investigated.

What is ICT? Information and Communication Technologies in education deal with the use of Information and Communication Technologies (ICTs) within educational technology. ICT (Information and Communications Technology) is an umbrella term that includes any communication device or application, encompassing radio, television, cellular phones, computer and network hardware and software, satellite systems, and so on, as well as the various services and applications associated with them, such as videoconferencing and distance learning. ICTs are often spoken of in a particular context, such as ICTs in education, health care, or libraries. The main hurdle affecting all applications of ICT to Knowledge Management is coping with the fundamental difference between explicit and tacit knowledge (Figure 11.1).

Was AI going to be the pervading knowledge technology in 1970s? Things did not happen that way because AI lends itself only to specific types of problems it struggles in dealing with "common sense". However, developments in areas like natural language processing, neural networks, genetic algorithms (even ant algorithms) mean that it is holding a definite niche in knowledge discovery, such that insurers can more accurately assess risk, or retailers identify clusters of products that are bought together.

Whereas explicit knowledge is that which can be codified into documents, databases and other tangible forms, tacit knowledge is that which is in the heads of individuals.

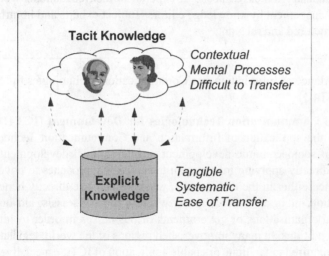

Ask someone to describe explicitly how to ride a bicycle and one cannot, yet one knows how to. This distinction and the processes by which tacit knowledge is converted into explicit knowledge and vice versa, is one of the central planks of Nonaka and Takeuchi (1995).

Our research found it one of the most widely cited concepts by Knowledge Management practitioners, yet one that is often ignored by information systems professionals. There seems to be a Western tendency to capture knowledge by "getting it into a database". Yet some of the most successful applications of ICT in Knowledge Management include those that help human-human communications, most notably groupware, and especially Lotus Notes. There is another important development in Information Technology. It is called Information and Communication Technologies for Development (ICT4D). Read Box11.2 for reference of (ICT4D).

The impact of each technology varies enormously from situation to situation. Several technologies recur in many Knowledge Management programme, partly because they are generic and pervade many core activities and processes. The main ones are now briefly reviewed.

Intranet, Internet

The ubiquitous internet protocols make it easy for users to access "any information, anywhere, at anytime". Further, browsers and client software can act as front-ends to information in many formats and many of the other knowledge tools such as document management or decision support. Remember too, that the basic functions of e-mail, discussion lists and private newsgroups often have the biggest short-term impact.

Intranet is the generic term for a collection of private computer networks within an organisation. An intranet uses network technologies as a tool to facilitate communication between people or workgroups to improve the data sharing capability and overall knowledge base of an organisation's employees.

Intranets utilise standard network hardware and software technologies like Ethernet, WiFi, TCP/IP, Web browsers and Web servers. An organisation's intranet typically includes internet access but is firewalled so that its computers cannot be reached directly from the outside.

Booz Allen & Hamilton's Knowledge Online is an Intranet that provides a wealth of information (e.g., best practice, industry trends, database of experts) to their consultants worldwide. Through active information management by knowledge editors (subject experts and librarians) the information remains well structured and relevant.

Box 11.2 Importance of Information and Communication Technologies for Development (ICT4D)

Information and Communication Technologies for Development (ICT4D) is a general term referring to the application of Information and Communication Technologies (ICTs) within the field of socioeconomic development or international development. ICT4D concerns itself with directly applying information technology approaches to poverty reduction. ICTs can be applied either in the direct sense, wherein their use directly benefits the disadvantaged population, or in an indirect sense, wherein the ICTs assist aid organisations or non-governmental organisations or governments or businesses in order to improve general socioeconomic conditions. In many impoverished regions of the world, legislative and political measures are required to facilitate or enable application of ICTs, especially with respect to monopolistic communication structures and censorship laws.

The concept of ICT4D can be interpreted as dealing with disadvantaged population anywhere in the world, but is more typically associated with applications in developing countries. The field is becoming recognised as an interdisciplinary research area as can be noted by the growing number of conferences, workshops and publications. Such researches have been spurred on, in part, by the need for scientifically validated benchmarks and results, which can be used to measure the efficacy of current projects. Many international development agencies recognise the importance of ICT4D. For example, the World Bank's GICT section has a dedicated team of some 200 staff working on these issues.

A good example of the impact of ICTs on development are farmers getting better market price information and thus boosting their income. Another example includes mobile telecommunications and radio broadcasting fighting political corruption in Burundi.

GROUPWARE—LOTUS NOTES

What groupware products like Lotus Notes add over and above Intranets are discussion databases. Users such as Thomas Miller, a London based manager of insurance mutuals, access their 'organisational memory', as well as current newsfeeds in areas of interest, through one of Lotus's key features, its multiple 'views'. When writing new insurance proposals, existing explicit knowledge can be assembled from the archive, guided by an expert system's front-end, while tacit knowledge is added through discussion databases.

Intelligent Agents

The reverse initials of AI, but using AI techniques, typically to scour the Web and find relevant information and to alert users of updates. Many solutions that started as search engines (e.g., Verity and Autonomy) are now broader in scope and have intelligent agents that assess what a user is working on and alert the user with links to the relevant content, a forerunner of truly adaptive systems that infer what a user is working on and offers appropriate assistance.

The problem of information overload is becoming acute for many professionals. Intelligent agents can be trained to roam networks to select and alert users of new relevant information. Additionally they can be used to filter out less relevant information from information feeds. However, in practice it seems that at a well run knowledge centre, such as that at Price Waterhouse, the best intelligent agent is still a human being!

A related technology is that of text summarising, which British Telecom has found can summarise large documents, retaining over 90% of the relevant meaning with less than a quarter of the original text.

Mapping Tools

There are an increasing number of tools, such as COPE and IDONS, that help individuals and teams develop cognitive maps or 'shared mental models'. These have been used by companies such as Shell to develop future scenarios and resolve conflicting stakeholder requirements. In addition, other mapping tools, such as those found in Knowledge X, can represent conceptual linkages between different source documents.

Document Management

Documents, and especially structured documents, are the form in which much explicit knowledge is shared. With annotation and redlining facilities, they can become active knowledge repositories, where the latest version and thinking is readily shared amongst project teams.

By using a document management system for the construction of the Thelma North Sea oil platform, AGIP reduced construction time by 9 months and reduced document handling costs by 60%. Suppliers like Dataware are repositioning their products as knowledge management products and are also adding 'knowledge enriching' functionality.

Knowledge Enriched Solutions

With a burgeoning and lucrative market for Knowledge Management solutions, many companies are simply relabelling their products and approaches, e.g., information management as Knowledge Management, databases as knowledge bases, data warehouses as knowledge repositories. True Knowledge Management solutions are not simply new labels, but add knowledge-enriching features. These include:

- Adding contextual information to data—where was this information used? What factors need to be considered when using it?
- Using multimedia, e.g., adding video clips or voice to databases of best practice or problem solution databases.
- Providing annotation—adding informal notes to individual data items; using MAPI enabled software, where a document or file can be sent with a forwarding note by e-mail.
- Qualifying information—giving details of originator, users adding comments about the quality of information.
- Providing links to experts—a 'click' button to contact an expert (either by e-mail or phone). GIGA, for example, lets its client access global experts through its website (http://www.gigaweb.com).
- These all help the transfer of tacit knowledge, and any tool should increasingly provide hooks that add new levels of interaction, not just person-to-computer but person-to-person.

Knowledge Collaboration Architecture

Over time, the boundaries of individual tools blur (c.f. groupware and internet, document management and information retrieval), and effective usage requires seamless interoperability and fluidity of information and knowledge flow.

Therefore, organisations using ICT to support knowledge activities need to think about an overall architecture. Some companies, such as Glaxo Wellcome are recognising that Knowledge Management requires changes in established technical architectures. Our analysis of several companies who have developed architectures that support Knowledge Management indicates that tools and supporting processes are needed at several levels (Figure 11.3).

At the base level is the requirement that people should be able to connect into knowledge whenever and wherever they are (in the office, at remote sites, on the move, etc.). At higher levels, there must be mechanisms for threaded conversations and structured collaborative work.

As you move up through each architectural layer (each of which depends on the one below), more of the challenges are people and organisation related, rather than being technology related. In our experience, most large organisations, taking their overall position, are still between the bottom two levels.

Database Management Systems

A database is a collection of data or information. Database Management System (DBMS) is a program that manages data in a database. It is a computerised record-keeping system that stores, maintains, and provides access to information. A database could be as simple as a phonebook or

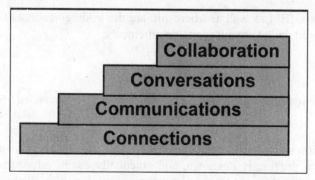

Fig. 11. 3   Levels of an IT Knowledge Infrastructure

stock tables, or as sophisticated as a biological repository with terabytes of data. Relational DBMS are those that follow the relational data model described by E.D. Codd. Object Oriented Database Management System (OODBMS) refers to those that store objects directly, or use mapping technology to store objects instead of simple data entities. A database system involves four major components:

- Data
- Hardware
- Software
- Users

The primary purpose of a DBMS is to allow a user to store, update, and retrieve data in abstract terms and thus, make it easy to maintain and retrieve information from a database. A DBMS relieves the user from having to know about the exact physical representations of data and having to specify detailed algorithms for storing, updating and retrieving data. A DBMS is usually a very large software package that carries out many different tasks including the provisions of facilities to enable the user to access and modify information in the database. The database is an intermediate link between the physical database, the computer and the operating system, and on the other hand, the users. To provide various facilities to different types of users, a DBMS normally provides one or more specialised programming languages often called database languages. Different specialised programming languages often called database languages. Different DBMSs are provide different database languages. However, structured query language (SQL) is the *de facto* standard. Database languages come in different forms. A language is needed to describe the database to the DBMS as well as provide facilities for changing the database and for defining and changing physical data structure. Another language is needed for manipulating and retrieving data stored in the DBMS. These languages are called Data Definition Language (DDL) and Data Manipulation Language (DML) respectively.

The latest development in the field of Database Management Systems relate to the development of Object Oriented Relational Databases or OORDBMS. This is based on the generally established concept of Object Oriented Analysis and Design or OOAD and provides for simplification of data storage, access, and retrieval as well as effective manipulation.

Oracle Corporations, IBM as well as Microsoft, are the leading vendors of DBMS and have a range of products to suit varied organisational requirements.

Data Mining

It has become appallingly obvious that our technology has exceeded our humanity.
—Albert Einstein

Data mining or knowledge discovery in databases (KDD), as it is also known, in the non-trivial extraction of implicit, previously unknown, and potentially useful information from data. This encompasses a number of different technical approaches, such as clustering, data summarisation, learning classification rules, finding dependency networks, analysing changes, and detecting anomalies. Data mining is concerned with the analysis of data and the deployment of software techniques for uncovering patterns and regularities in sets of data. The idea is that it is possible to discover patterns and relationships in unexpected places as the data mining software extracts patterns not previously discernible or so obvious.

Data Mining is the search for relationships and global patterns that exist in large databases but are hidden among vast amounts of data, such as a relationship between the temperature of a room and the productivity of an employee. These relationships represent valuable knowledge abut the database and the objects in the database relating to an organisation or the internal or external environment. The following figure (Figure 11.4) shows Data Mining as a step in an iterative knowledge discovery process.

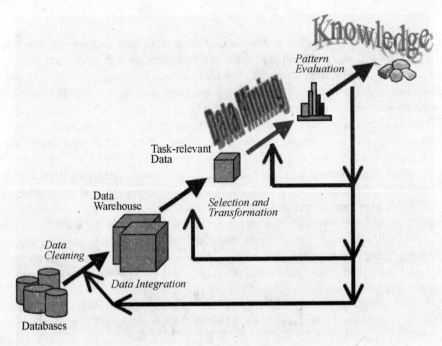

Fig. 11.4   Data Mining is the Core of Knowledge Discovery Process

Data Mining Analysis tends to work upwards from the available data and the best techniques are those developed with an orientation towards large volumes of data, making use of as much of the collected data as possible to arrive at reliable conclusions and decisions. The analysis process starts with a set of data, uses a methodology to develop an optimal representation of the assumption that the larger data set has a structure similar to the sample data. Again this is analogous to a mining operation where large amounts of low grade materials are shifted through in order to find something of value. The mining process begins with the raw data and gets terminated with the extracted knowledge.

Knowledge analysis

The past two decades have seen a dramatic increase in the amount of information or data being stored in electronic format. This accumulation of data has taken place at an explosive rate. It has been estimated that the amount of information in the world doubles every 20 months and the size and number of databases are increasing even faster. The increase in the use of electronic data gathering devices such as point-of-sale or remote sensing devices has contributed to this explosion of available data. There was also the introduction of new machine learning methods for knowledge representation based on logic programming, etc. in addition to traditional statistical analysis of data. The new methods tend to be computationally intensive, hence, a demand for more processing power.

It was recognised that information is at the heart of business operations and that decision makers could make use of the data stored to gain valuable insight into the business. DBMSs provide access to the data stored but this was only a small part of what could be gained from the data. Traditional online transaction processing systems are good at inserting data into databases quickly, safely and efficiently but are not good at delivering meaningful analysis in return. Analysing data can provide further knowledge about a business by going beyond the data explicitly stored to derive knowledge about the business. Data Mining or knowledge discovery in databases provides an organisation with highly benefits in the area of analysis.

ACHIEVING THE BENEFITS

> *Modern technology, owes ecology, an apology.*
> —Alan M. Eddison

As any manager of change or implementer of ICT infrastructure knows, it is the human, organisational and cultural factors that are the ultimate determinants of success. ICT solutions for Knowledge Management are, in essence, social computing, and therefore need such an approach. Implementations that are successful are typically found to share the following characteristics:

- Clear vision and leadership—a solid appreciation of the contribution of knowledge to business success and how IT can help.
- Multidisciplinary teams—including information managers (librarians), facilitators, business experts as well as technologists.

- User and business-centric. Users are actively engaged in developing solutions that enhance knowledge activities.
- Well designed processes that engage humans where they are best, and allow them to interact with computers where computers perform best. A business process that does not consider applying best knowledge (and updating it) is an incomplete process.
- Active learning and experimentation. There is no such thing as a finished requirement specification. Solutions evolve and adapt.
- A knowledge sharing culture. People want to share information and their experience and are rewarded for doing so.

REMEMBER

Information and communications technologies are an important ingredient of virtually every successful Knowledge Management programme. An ever wider range of highly effective solutions are coming to market, including a new generation of artificial intelligence solutions, new flavours of document management systems and various collaborative technologies such as the internet.

Successful implementation depends, as always, on giving appropriate focus to the non-technical factors such as human factors, organisational processes and culture, the multidisciplinary skills of hybrid teams and managers, and the already existing knowledge repository of prior learning—providing, of course, that it is well structured, accessible and gives you access to critical expertise!

SUMMING UP

In modern times, reports of activities, minutes of meetings, memoranda, proceedings of conferences, and document filing systems maintained by organisations are traditional and commonly used devices for recording content in paper format so that it can be transferred to others.

More recently, electronic databases, audio and video recordings, interactive tools and multimedia presentations have become available to extend the techniques for capturing and disseminating content. Nevertheless, even with modern tools, the process of knowledge transfer is inherently difficult, since those who have knowledge may not be conscious of what they know or how significant it is, or be able or willing to share it with others. Even when they are so willing, the readiness to accept the wisdom of others is often not obvious.

Technologies used in Knowledge Management are mainly internet, intranet, Lotus, document management, mapping tools, intelligent management, etc.

Information and communications technologies are an important ingredient of virtually every successful Knowledge Management programme. An ever wider range of highly effective solutions are coming to market, including a new generation of artificial intelligence solutions, new flavours of document management systems and various collaborative technologies such as the internet.

Successful implementation depends, as always, on giving appropriate focus to the non-technical factors such as human factors, organisational processes and culture, the multidisciplinary skills of hybrid teams and managers, and the already existing knowledge repository of prior learning—providing, of course, that it is well structured, accessible and gives you access to critical expertise!

CASE

The following is a case on Programme Evaluation including focus on the programme's process, technology outcomes and facilitation. The case here conveys a holistic depiction of the experience gathered by the CEO of RK Communication Systems.

Bhaskar is the chief executive of RK Communication Systems with a small budget and staff. Bhaskar's overall goal in his circle was to communicate with other executives about projects and challenges they face with respect to technology, including brainstorming solutions together. He mentioned numerous challenges that he faced in running his organisation, some of which needed specific and technical information to address.

In the first meeting, he mentioned issues related to Human Resource like redefining employee roles and the benefits attached with updated technology. In comparison to other members in his circle, he had the most issues. He also wanted help managing his technology and time more effectively and he wanted to improve the effectiveness of his board by introducing SAP. He stated, "They don't even know what we're about. They just sit there when we meet." And he wanted to improve his understanding of his role as a chief executive. He asked, "How do I know what I can ask the board to do?" "What is my role with them?" In another area, he said he wanted some ideas about how to expand his organisation's revenue.

In the first meeting, members asked him many questions, mostly to obtain additional information about his issues. Bhaskar responded that his most pressing project was technology management. Another member responded, "I'd challenge you on that," and asked Bhaskar if he would have upgraded technology, will he get more support from his board? Bhaskar laughed and answered, "I suppose so." Other group members concurred. From his first meeting, he took actions including listing and ranking his issues, scheduling a technology management course, and identifying a course that would provide an overview of the chief executive's role. One member asked him to also list and rank his issues for the next meeting.

In the second meeting, Bhaskar produced the following list: improving his understanding of the chief executive and board roles, developing/energising the board, and conducting strategic planning with the board that would include expanding the revenue in his organisation with the help of the latest technology. Other group members agreed with Bhaskar's list.

During the discussion in the second meeting, Bhaskar acknowledged that he was doing more than a chief executive's job and role. He also realised that he was overloaded because he got little or no support from his board. He indicated that he did not feel confident, though, approaching his board members for more support. As a result of other circle members' support and coaching, he resolved to approach the board—and a month later, he had. He and the board members committed to complete board training. He arranged training to include a strong focus on strategic planning, which included expanding revenue. To further build rapport, he elected to have lunch with one board member a month, including giving them a tour of the organisation.

Bhaskar noted on his evaluation questionnaire: "The meeting regarding technology management had the right amount of structure. The conversation is pretty free-flowing, but there's enough attention paid to time so that everyone gets a fair chance." His top reported outcomes were in the categories of access to a network, professional development, and effectiveness. The tech meet provided an opportunity to meet other chief executives and hear about projects that they faced and how they handled those projects." He stated, "The programme has restored some order to my job," and "A lot has happened with my job."

Source: http://managementhelp.org

From a Case written by Carter McNamara, MBA, Ph.D, Authenticity Consulting, LLC.

LESSON & ACTIVITY

When it comes to Knowledge Management, many people "are comfortable in the belief that they're doing enough simply because they have computers, access to the internet and some databases." Comment.

KEYWORDS

Groupware—Lotus Notes: What groupware products like Lotus Notes add over and above Intranets are discussion databases. Users such as Thomas Miller, a London based manager of insurance mutuals, access their 'organisational memory', as well as current newsfeeds in areas of interest, through one of Lotus's key features, its multiple 'views'. When writing new insurance proposals, existing explicit knowledge can be assembled from the archive, guided by an expert system's front-end, while tacit knowledge is added through discussion databases.

Intelligent Agents: The problem of information overload is becoming acute for many professionals. Intelligent agents can be trained to roam networks to select and alert users of new relevant information. Additionally, they can be used to filter out less relevant information from information feeds. However, in practice it seems that at a well run knowledge centre, such as that at Price Waterhouse, the best intelligent agent is still a human being!

Mapping Tools: There are an increasing number of tools, such as COPE and IDONS, that help individuals and teams develop cognitive maps or 'shared mental models'. These have been used by companies such as Shell to develop future scenarios and resolve conflicting stakeholder requirements. In addition, other mapping tools, such as those found in Knowledge X, can represent conceptual linkages between different source documents.

Document Management: Documents, and especially structured documents, are the form in which much explicit knowledge is shared. With annotation and redlining facilities, they can become active knowledge repositories, where the latest version and thinking is readily shared amongst project teams.

Knowledge Enriched Solutions: With a burgeoning and lucrative market for Knowledge Management solutions, many companies are simply relabelling their products and approaches, e.g., information management as Knowledge Management, databases as knowledge bases, data warehouses as knowledge repositories. True Knowledge Management solutions are not simply new labels, but add knowledge-enriching features.

QUESTIONS FOR DISCUSSION

1. Explain the relationship between technology & management.
2. Briefly explain the features of mail technological application in Knowledge Management.

3. Explain the benefits of application of technology and Knowledge Management.
4. Write short notes on: (i) Lotus Notes (ii) Internet & Intranet (iii) Intelligent Agent (iv) Mapping Tools (v) Document Management (vi) Knowledge Enriched Solutions.

SUGGESTED READINGS

Amidon, Debra M., *Innovation Strategy for the Knowledge Economy—The Ken Awakening*, Butterworth Heinemann, 1997.

Chase, Rory L., The Knowledge-Based Organisation—An International Survey, *Journal of Knowledge Management*, pp. 38-49, September, 1997.

Drucker, Peter F., *Post-Capitalist Society*, Butterworth-Heinemann, 1993.

Murray, Peter and Myers, Andrew, The Facts about Knowledge, *Information Strategy*, September, 1997.

Nonaka, I. and Takeuchi, H., *The Knowledge Creating Company*, Oxford University Press, 1995.

Quinn, James B., *Intelligent Enterprise—A Knowledge and Service Based Paradigm for Industry*, Free Press, 1992.

Skyrme, David J. and Amidon, Debra M., *Creating the Knowledge-based Business*, Business Intelligence, 1997.

Stewart, Thomas A., *Intellectual Capital—The New Wealth of Organisations*, Nicholas Brealey, 1997.

Wiig, Karl, *Knowledge Management—The Central Focus for Intelligent Acting Organisations*, Schema Press, 1994.

WEBSITES

http://www.hoffmanmarcom.com/marketing-communications/case-studies.php
http://www.cfsd.org.uk/smart-know-net/links/casestudies.htm
http://viodi.com/2010/05/19/tiecon-2010-report-wireless-market-status-trends-and-future-direc tions/

CHAPTER 12

Knowledge Mapping—A Strategic Entry Point to KM

OBJECTIVE

At the end of this lesson, you would be able to understand:

- The concept of knowledge mapping.
- Principles of knowledge mapping.
- Methods of knowledge mapping.
- Benefits.
- Reason for knowledge mapping.
- Focus on mapping.
- Types of Map.
- Why one should bother about Knowledge Map?
- Knowledge mapping tools.

> *"If confusion is the first step to knowledge, I must be a genius."*
> —Larry Leissner

INTRODUCTION

Each of the past centuries has been dominated by single technology. The 18th century was the time of the great mechanical systems accompanying the Industrial Revolution. The 19th century was the age of steam engine. After these, the key technology has been information gathering, processing and distribution. Among the other developments, the installation of worldwide telephone networks, the invention of radio and television, the birth and unprecedented growth of the computer industry and the launching of communication satellites are significant. Now people started thinking that only information was not enough, what mattered was 'knowledge'. So there has been seen a shift from Information to Knowledge.

A bit of information without context and interpretation is data such as numbers, symbols.

Information is a set of data with context and interpretation. Information is the basis for knowledge.

Knowledge is a set of data and information, to which is added the expert opinion and experience, to result in a valuable asset which can be used or applied to aid decision making. Knowledge may be explicit and/or tacit, individual and/or collective.

> *True knowledge exists in knowing that you know nothing.*
> *And in knowing that you know nothing, that*
> *makes you the smartest of all.*
> —Socrates

The term, Knowledge Mapping, seems to be relatively new, but it is not. We have been practising this in our everyday life, just what we are not doing is that we are not documenting it, and we are not doing it in a systematic way. Knowledge Mapping is all about keeping a record of information and knowledge you need such as where you can get it from, who holds it, whose expertise is it, and so on. Say, you need to find something at your home or in your room; you can find it in no time because you have almost all the information/knowledge about what is where and who knows what at your home. It is a sort of map set in your mind about your home. But, to set such a map about your organisation and organisational knowledge in your mind is almost impossible.

This is where K-map becomes handy and shows details of every bit of knowledge that exists within the organisation including location, quality, and accessibility; and knowledge required to run the organisation smoothly—hence making you capable of finding your required knowledge easily and efficiently.

A knowledge map is the intellectual infrastructure for KM initiatives. Knowledge map is an important and effective instrument of corporate Knowledge Management. A great number of unordered knowledge resources in the enterprises bring about difficulties to the knowledge map construction. The basis for it consists of multiple taxonomies for content repositories, dynamic categorisation of people, their expertise, and the communities they belong to, and finally a set of taxonomies for the variety of tasks that are performed within and by the company communities.

The taxonomies of content, people, and tasks then have to be mapped across the three components in order to provide a foundation for the integration of such KM enterprise projects as knowledge retrieval, for both document based knowledge and the tacit knowledge located within the minds of the companies' experts. It is also the foundation for collaboration, both for capturing the knowledge that is generated in those collaborative communities, and for providing the framework within which knowledge facilitators or knowledge managers will operate as they provide services for those collaborative communities.

DEFINITION

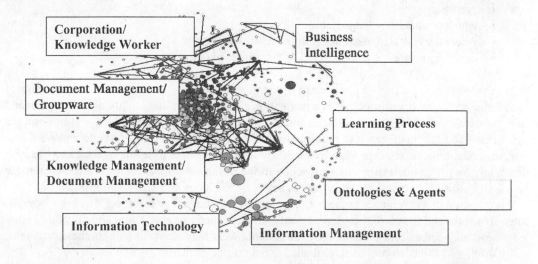

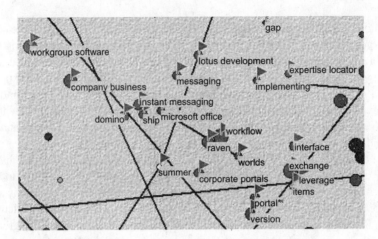

Fig. 12.1   Knowledge Map of KM Tools

Figure 12.1 depicts the structuring of keywords based on their co-occurency in documents. Knowledge mapping externalises networks of cognitive relationships and renders them in graphic form. This pictorial approach to individual or group knowledge assists in the formation and maintenance of shared mental models and streamlines collaboration. Knowledge maps are commonly referred to as mind maps, semantic networks, and concept maps, Jonassen and Carr (2000) and Novak (1998).

- A knowledge map describes what knowledge is used in a process, and how it flows around the process.
- It is the basis of determining knowledge commonality, or areas where similar knowledge is used across multiple processes…
- It describes:
  - who has what knowledge (tacit),
  - where the knowledge resides (infrastructure), and
  - how the knowledge is transferred or disseminated (social)

A knowledge map portrays a perspective of the players, sources, flows, constraints and sinks of knowledge within an organisation. It is a navigation aid to both explicit (codified) information and tacit knowledge, showing the importance and the relationships between knowledge stores and the dynamics. The final 'map' can take multiple forms, from a pictorial display to yellow pages directory, to linked topic or concept map, to inventory lists or a matrix of assets against key business processes. As per characteristics of knowledge usage in the enterprise, the enterprise knowledge map is defined as a domain-centred system to display knowledge and their relationships.

It is common that enterprises possess a large number of knowledge resources involving complicated structures and the employees have to unfortunately spend so much time and effort on knowledge searching and selection before they can find out what they want. To address these problems, many solutions have been proposed. Knowledge map is one of them.

Knowledge map is an effective Knowledge Management tool (Davenport and Prusak, 1998; Vail, 1999; Mertens et al., 2003). For the convenience of knowledge navigating and searching, it specifies the captured knowledge and their relationships and displays them in friendly forms. Currently, the enabling technologies of knowledge map are mainly intranet-based software solutions which combine powerful visualisation techniques with Database Management System (Eppler, 2001). Yet, while the technological implementation can lead to a useful knowledge map artefact, the process of mapping is even more challenging. Essentially, the knowledge mapping process is the process of knowledge organisation and classification. Many approaches have been suggested to organise knowledge in organisations that basically fall into two groups. On the one hand, AI methods are suggested to support knowledge modelling and classification, especially for some kinds of Web contents. On the other hand, business processes' models are used as a starting point to identify the most critical business knowledge in organisations (Studer et al., 1998). However, in the organisations so far mostly pragmatic approaches are applied. In most of the cases, knowledge classification is determined by a committee in a workshop without much methodical support (Maier, 2004). No matter how the knowledge map is constructed, it has to be characterised with the following factors:

- it can effectively map a large number of knowledge items that are represented in a variety of media into some reasonable categories,
- the taxonomy in the enterprise knowledge map has to reflect the characteristics of business process and be comprehensive to knowledge workers.

According to the above requirement, the existing methods are more or less unsuitable for enterprise knowledge map construction. Knowledge mapping is always such a complicated process that we intend to discuss the issue from a systematic perspective. Systems science has been considered the basis for information systems. A wealth of research in information systems in the framework of systems science has produced an astonishing array of theoretical results and empirical insights, and a large suite of tools and methods (Xu, 2000; Warfield, 2007, 2008).

Systems science also promises to be an important foundation of Knowledge Management. Besides information technologies, human beings are the indispensable component in enterprise Knowledge Management. They are involved in knowledge creation, sharing and usage activities. At the same time they interact with each other and learn from each other. It is necessary to put more emphasis on an individual's cognition on knowledge map construction. So here, social classification is introduced to assist the knowledge organisation at the individual level. Upon that, domain level and inter-domain level will be constructed to show how individual knowledge structure will affect the organisational knowledge structure.

KNOWLEDGE MAP

Many definitions of knowledge maps that we have found in the academic papers are similar, but less specific. Generally, a knowledge map is the display of acquired knowledge and relationships (Davenport and Prusak, 1998; Vail, 1999). The knowledge in knowledge map may involve various shared contents, such as text, graphics, videos, models and data. The relationships among them are determined by linking concepts or topics discovered from these shared contents. Knowledge mapping is defined as the process of associating items of information or knowledge in such a way that the mapping itself also creates additional knowledge (Vail, 1999).

Knowledge mapping is an important practice consisting of survey, audit, and synthesis. It aims to track the acquisition and loss of information and knowledge. It explores personal and group competencies and proficiencies. It illustrates or "maps" how knowledge flows throughout an organisation. Knowledge mapping helps an organisation to appreciate how the loss of staff influences intellectual capital, to assist with the selection of teams, and to match technology to knowledge needs and processes.—Denham Grey

Knowledge mapping is about making knowledge that is available within an organisation transparent, and is about providing the insights into its quality.—Willem-Olaf Huijsen, Samuel J. Driessen, Jan W. M. Jacobs

Knowledge mapping is a process through which organisations can identify and categorise knowledge assets within their organisation—people, processes, content, and technology. It allows an organisation to fully leverage the existing expertise resident in the organisation, as well as identify barriers and constraints to fulfilling strategic goals and objectives. It is constructing a roadmap to locate the information needed to make the best use of resourses, independent of source or form.—W Vestal, APQC, 2002

Knowledge map describes what knowledge is used in a process, and how it flows around the process. It is the basis for determining knowledge commonality, or areas where similar knowledge is used across multiple processes. Fundamentally, a process knowledge map contains information about the organisation's knowledge. It describes who has what knowledge (tacit), where the knowledge resides (infrastructure), and how the knowledge is transferred or disseminated (social).—IBM Global Services

A knowledge map is the intellectual infrastructure for KM initiatives. The basis for it consists of multiple taxonomies for content repositories, dynamic categorisation of people, their expertise, and the communities they belong to, and finally a set of taxonomies for the variety of tasks that are performed within and by the company communities.

The taxonomies of content, people, and tasks then have to be mapped across the three components in order to provide a foundation for the integration of such KM enterprise projects as knowledge retrieval, for both document based knowledge and the tacit knowledge located within the minds of the companies' experts. It is also the foundation for collaboration, both for capturing the knowledge that is generated in those collaborative communities, and for providing the framework within which knowledge facilitators or knowledge managers will operate as they provide services for those collaborative communities. Some of the examples of knowledge maps are exhibited in Box 12.1

HOW ARE THE KNOWLEDGE MAPS CREATED?

> *As we acquire more knowledge, things do not become*
> *more comprehensible, but more mysterious.*
> —Albert Schweitzer

Knowledge maps are created by transferring tacit and explicit knowledge into graphical formats that are easy to understand and interpret by the end users, who may be managers, experts, system developers, or anybody.

Box 12.1   Knowledge Map Addresses

National Missile Defence Map

<www.macrovu.com/nmd.html>
<www.stanford.edu/~rhorn/nmd.html>

Multnomah Mental Health Task Force Cross-Boundary Dynamics Map

<www.stanford.edu/~rhorn/portlandmap.html>

Alameda County Long Term Care Task Force Map

<www.macrovu.com/alamedamap.html>
<www.stanford.edu/~rhorn/alamedamap.html>

New Scientist Genetically Modified food prototype maps

<www.macrovu.com/gmtest.html>

Consciousness Maps

<www.macrovu.com/cns.html>

Unknown territory map -- What we don't know about genetically modified food and crops

<www.macrovu.com/GMUnknownterritory.html>

Knowledge is not static. What is innovative knowledge today will become the core knowledge of tomorrow. The key lies in staying consistently ahead of the competition. The knowledge map that is created (above box) provides a snapshot of where that company is at any given time (such as today) relative to its competitors.

Here's how it works. Categorise each market player, including yourself, as an innovative leader, capable competitor, straggler or risky player. Next, identify your own business strengths and weaknesses on various facets of knowledge to see where you lag behind or lead your competitors. Use that information accordingly to reposition either your knowledge or strategic business focus.

For example, if you are analysing customer support knowledge in a competing company and realise that your competitor is an innovator and your own company is only a capable competitor, you can choose either to invest in catching or simply to compete in a different market segment.

A popular knowledge map used in human resources is a skills planner in which employees are matched to jobs. Steps to build the map:

- A structure of the knowledge requirements should be developed.
- Knowledge required of specific jobs must be defined.

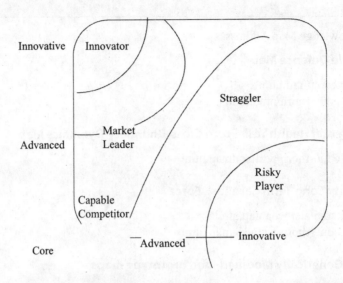

Fig. 12.2   Creating a Knowledge Map to Evaluate Corporate Knowledge

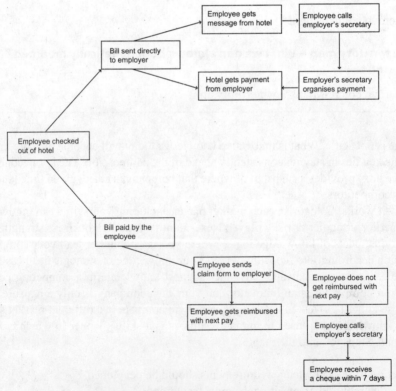

Fig. 12.3   Construction of Knowledge Map

- You should rate employee performance by knowledge competency.
- You should link the knowledge map to some training programme for career development and job advancement.

BACKGROUND

> *Knowledge increases in proportion to its use—that is,*
> *the more we teach the more we learn.*
> —H. P. Blavatsky

The term, Knowledge Mapping, seems to be relatively new, but it is not. We have been practicing this in our everyday life, just what we are not doing is that we are not documenting it, and we are not doing it in a systematic way. Knowledge Mapping is all about keeping a record of information and knowledge you need such as where you can get it from, who holds it, whose expertise is it, and so on. Say, you need to find something at your home or in your room, you can find it in no time because you have almost all the information/knowledge about what is where and who knows what at your home.

It is a sort of map set in your mind about your home. But, to set such a map about your organisation and organisational knowledge in your mind is almost impossible. This is where K map becomes handy and shows details of every bit of knowledge that exists within the organisation, including location, quality, and accessibility; and knowledge required to run the organisation smoothly—hence making you able to find out your required knowledge easily and efficiently.

Knowledge map is a visual representation of a successfully solved problem, including solving process (Stanford, 2000). The solving process should contain at least four steps of the Simon's problem decomposition, i.e., intelligence activity, design activity, choice activity, and review activity (Simon, 1960). Gordon (2002) also shows that knowledge maps may be referred to as maps of the way of acquiring knowledge. The knowledge maps are important as building knowledge tools as well as thinking tools (Rogers, 2000). There are various definitions of the terms 'knowledge map' and 'knowledge mapping'. Stanford (2001) defines it as follows: ''Knowledge mapping quite simply is any visualisation of knowledge beyond textual for the purpose of eliciting, codifying, sharing, using and expanding knowledge.'' Graphic symbols play a key role in each knowledge map; their positions and spatial relationships are mostly expressed with the use of arcs or edges. The knowledge map must show a progression of ideas with relationships beyond their being just spatial. Knowledge maps include conceptual relationships, such as chronological, hierarchical, associative, causal, logical and evaluative (Stanford, 2001). Each knowledge map, as a special type of reality model, for instance, a reality image, simplifies the visualisation of reality.

Similar to the typology of models based on the model form, knowledge maps could be divided into two main groups: analogical maps and iconic maps where the analogy between real objects and symbols, plus their spatial relationships and behaviour are crucial for map understanding.

- Symbolic maps emphasising the meaning of symbols, usually mathematical or verbal. There kind of maps generally don't insist on the symbol position. Elements of these maps are rather abstract (terms, expressions) and relations between them are expressed using mathematical formulas or verbal sentences or phrases.
- Another typology of knowledge maps is based on the character of judgment or solution of the (successfully) solved problem (Baron, 2004).

- Descriptive maps (weak and strong), describing and simulating the real situation as precisely as possible.
- Normative maps, relating to a typical standard or norm, to optimal solution, or to the best decision.

Knowledge Map Construction

> *The saddest aspect of life right now is that science gathers*
> *knowledge faster than society gathers wisdom.*
> —Isaac Asimov

The development of an organisational knowledge map begins with the development of a conceptual framework in conjunction with a working dictionary of the major organisational structure being considered. These structures can be construed as 'spaces', wherein, the knowledge map is organised and formalised. A general organisational map is constructed of four interconnected representational 'spaces' as mentioned below:

Dialogue space: The dialogue space represents an area for free exploration, notation and diagramming that helps the organisational knowledge mapper to question and clarify intents, identify justifications, categorise the key constructs and explore the possible relationship between constructs. This space is analogous to whiteboards, brainstorming sessions or similar techniques employed for effective problem solving.

Construct-relation space: This space represents the area where each of the constructs developed in the dialogue space is formally defined, described and whose key characteristics are listed based on the described relationship. This includes information about the author of a construct (references, pedigree, date, etc.), its inheritance (level of dependence), what other constructs and relationships it is dependent on or what other constructs are defined or organised by it. It is a complete record of the definitions of the domains, constructs and relationships, and the symbols (legends) used to represent them.

Operational space: The place where the constructs defined above are represented, located, combined, classified, categorised and interrelated resulting in the generation of further structures and emerging domains (combinations of key constructs and relationships). It is where the operational evaluation of the approach to the solution is carried out to observe whether the stated intents are achieved. It is the space that shows the evolving map of the overall organisation.

Interpretive space: The additional knowledge that may be required by a user to understand the map created in the operational space is introduced or the additional knowledge creates navigational constructs and relations necessary to guide the user through specific pathways in the process of solving a problem. It is where one can explain how the effects of different judgments, values, constraints and priorities influence bias or limit navigation through the association space.

PURPOSE

The basic purpose of knowledge maps is to enable both:

- *knowledge definition, and*
- *knowledge sharing.*

FOCUS OF MAPPING

Knowledge mapping has broadly two areas of focus; namely, strategic level and tactical level. Under the strategic level there are two sub-levels; enterprise level and cross-functional level. Tactical level mainly deals with working group/process. The different levels are depicted in Figures 12.4 and 12.5.

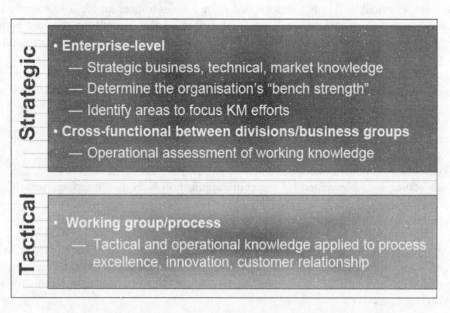

Fig. 12.4   Levels of Knowledge Mapping

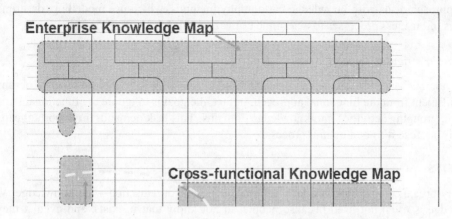

Fig. 12.5   Cross-functional Levels of Knowledge Mapping
(*Source:* http://knowledge.usaid.gov/KfD_Seminar_2.pdf)

ABOUT KNOWLEDGE MAPPING METHODS

Most decision making and goal setting is done without full knowledge, input, and motivation of the entire group. Consensus is said to be achieved but when examined it is usually group thinking set by leaders, enforcers, and followers; the outsider who has mission critical information is usually the one who is forced to the position of stating "I can live with it" (the decision)–yet it is the outsider's views that are so valuable. All that was needed to be known to prevent the 9/11 tragedy and the Columbia Mission failure was known – the problem being that knowledge was not connected. Knowledge maps can pool the knowledge into one place and as (anonymous) facilitation tools ensured, we can see the entire "big" picture.

In the traditional approach of knowledge mapping, information gathering was about people, and several other sources. For example, to collect some information people used to look into the following ways:

- Personal Address book
- Corporate User/Departments directory
- Contact Management System
- Each source is implemented by a specific application with own interface, search, naming conventions
- What can be used to collect, analyse, synthesise information about people?

Knowledge cartography is a process that helps to discover the location, value and use of organisational knowledge in the sense of (Tshuchiya, 1993). It is a new research field in Knowledge Management and there are few academic papers. Knowledge mapping methods can be categorised into two approaches:

A "Process" oriented approach

This approach deals with knowledge cartography methods, which use modelling, description and analysis of business processes to determine critical knowledge.

A "Domain" oriented approach

In this approach, we try to make an analysis from a mass of information in order to organise it in logic different from the functional approach. In fact, the goal is to ignore the functional structure of the firm, grouping activities into knowledge domains. This task demands an important capacity of analysis because it's not a natural process.

BENEFITS

In many organisations there is a lack of transparency of organisation-wide knowledge. Valuable knowledge is often not used because people do not know that it exists, and even if they know that the knowledge exists, they may not know where. These issues lead to knowledge mapping. Following are some of the key reasons for doing knowledge mapping:

- to find key sources of knowledge creation
- to encourage, reuse and prevent reinvention

- to find critical information quickly
- to highlight islands of expertise
- to provide an inventory and evaluation of intellectual and intangible assets
- to improve decision making and problem solving by providing applicable information
- to provide insights into corporate knowledge

The map also serves as the continuously evolving organisational memory, capturing and integrating the key knowledge of an organisation. It enables employees learning through intuitive navigation and interrogation of the information in the map, and through the creation of new knowledge through the discovery of new relationships. Simply speaking, K-map gives employees not only -know what-, but also -know how-.

KEY PRINCIPLES OF KNOWLEDGE MAPPING

Knowledge mapping is a very effective tool for integrating the key knowledge in an organisation. The following key principles must be kept in mind in the process:

- Because of their power, scope, and impact, the creation of organisational level knowledge map requires senior management support as well as careful planning
- Share your knowledge about identifying, finding, and tracking knowledge in all forms
- Recognise and locate knowledge in a wide variety of forms: tacit, explicit, formal, informal, codified, personalised, internal, external, and permanent
- Knowledge is found in processes, relationships, policies, people, documents, conversations, links and context, and even with partners
- It should be up-to-date and accurate

A TYPICAL KNOWLEDGE MAP

> *To be conscious that you are ignorant is a great step to knowledge.*
> —Benjamin Disraeli

The following are the steps to understand 'how to create a knowledge map?'
First of all, identify:

- Business functions
- Main entity types
- Main resource types
- Properties and associations for entities, resources and functions
- Map and integrate existing data sources
- Find and fill the gaps
- Finally, use topic maps to implement enterprise knowledge map!

A typical knowledge map looks very complex. Given ahead is a knowledge map on the subject of "arithmetic". If you look at it, you can easily understand how it is constructed.

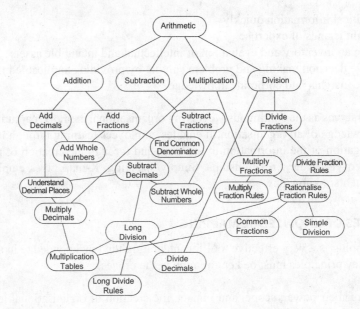

Fig. 12.6 Rationale, or Why Should I Bother to Map Knowledge?

Mentioned below are the few reasons why we should bother to map knowledge:

■ To find key sources, opportunities and constraints to knowledge creation and flows.
■ To encourage reuse and prevent reinvention, saving search time and acquisition costs.
■ To highlight islands of expertise and suggest ways to build bridges to increase knowledge sharing and exchange.
■ To discover effective and emergent communities of practice where informal learning is happening.
■ To provide baseline data for measuring progress with KM projects and justifying expenditures.
■ To reduce the burden on experts by helping staff to find critical solutions & information quickly.
■ To improve customer response, decision making and problem solving by providing access to applicable information, internal and external experts.
■ To highlight opportunities for learning and leverage of knowledge by distinguishing the unique meaning of 'knowledge' within that organisation.
■ To provide an inventory and evaluation of intellectual and intangible assets and assess competitive advantage.
■ To supply research for designing knowledge architecture, making key strategic choices, selecting suitable software or building corporate memory.
■ To garner support for new knowledge initiatives designed to improve the knowledge assets.

OK then what do I need to map?

- Location, ownership, validity, timeliness, domain, sensitivity, access rights, storage medium, use statistics, media and channels used.
- Documents, files, systems, policies, directories, competencies, relationships, authorities.
- Boundary objects, knowledge artifacts, stories, heuristics, patterns, events, practices, activities and flows.
- Explicit and tacit knowledge which is closely linked to strategic drivers, core competencies and market intelligence.
- Portray both the codified and the informal stuff, highlight constraints, assumptions, policies, culture, bottlenecks, brokers, repositories and boundary spanners.

It can be very difficult sometimes to quickly identify important knowledge assets because people forget about what they know until they need to know it. Consequently, it can be useful to collect stories of how people work to remind others of the knowledge they rely on. This story base provides evidence which helps the knowledge mapper know where to look and what to include in the map.

KNOWLEDGE MAPPING TOOLS

> *It is the supreme art of the teacher to awaken*
> *joy in creative expression and knowledge.*
> —Albert Einstein

Visual concept: It is a visual thinking software; providing a medium for all kinds of creative and systems thinking. It enables ideas to be developed as a basis of planning, designing, authoring, organising, relating, mapping, scenario building and countless other activities, it enables one to easily structure ideas and print them out, communicate them, transfer them and relate them to other visual maps with links to ideas expressed in any Windows environment. It also helps one capture large amounts of information and create knowledge maps either as ideas occur or as they are extracted from audits, meetings, lectures or texts. The software acts as an outliner to automatically develop clearly structured stories, essays and reports. By mapping interrelationships, one can greatly increase the organisational capacity to understand complex issues. On a corporate network, visual concept comes to the fore as a medium for sharing and developing ideas.

Concept mapping: Concept maps are tools for organising and representing knowledge. The fundamental idea promulgated by David Ausubel, an expert on learning psychology is that, learning takes place by the assimilation of new concepts and propositions into existing concept propositional frameworks held by the learner. The basic idea is similar to that of a knowledge map. They include concepts, usually enclosed in circles or boxes of some type and relationships between concepts or propositions, indicated by a connecting line between the two concepts. Words on the line specify the relationship between the two concepts.

BENEFITS OF KNOWLEDGE MAPPING

Knowledge maps have been used to do the following: Aid learning, e.g., recall and retention (embed knowledge); transform information into knowledge; facilitate understanding, communicate meaning; make implicit knowledge explicit and explicit knowledge implicit; settle conflict and move forward; brainstorm for creativity; capture knowledge; elicit knowledge; share knowledge; transfer knowledge; use knowledge; improve communication; define knowledge cultures; determine the mission; complete the mission; plan strategy; discover what you know versus what you don't know; uncover needs; link sources to needs; show barriers and benefits; show strengths, skills and areas for growth; assist decision making; examine the present and the past; point the way to the future (prophesying or visioning); prevent corporate amnesia.

SUMMING UP

A knowledge map is the intellectual infrastructure for KM initiatives. The basis for it consists of multiple taxonomies for content repositories, dynamic categorisation of people, their expertise, and the communities they belong to, and finally a set of taxonomies for the variety of tasks that are performed within and by the company communities.

A knowledge map portrays a perspective of the players, sources, flows, constraints and sinks of knowledge within an organisation. It is a navigation aid to both explicit (codified) information and tacit knowledge, showing the importance and the relationships between knowledge stores and the dynamics. The final 'map' can take multiple forms, from a pictorial display to yellow pages directory, to linked topic or concept map, to inventory lists or a matrix of assets against key business processes.

Knowledge maps are created by transferring tacit and explicit knowledge into graphical formats that are easy to understand and interpret by the end users, who may be managers, experts, system developers, or anybody.

The map also serves as the continuously evolving organisational memory, capturing and integrating the key knowledge of an organisation. It enables employees' learning through intuitive navigation and interrogation of the information in the map, and the creation of new knowledge through the discovery of new relationships. Simply speaking, K-map gives employees not only -know what-, but also -know how-.

INDIVIDUAL ACTIVITY

1. Allen and Hamilton have suggested that—amazingly—up to 84% of all knowledge management programmes fail. What do you make of this statement, and what can organisations do to increase the likelihood of success?
2. Develop an effective executive support system (ESS) for the vice president of logistics for a retail chain. Use the knowledge mapping system to describe the features of ESS. Develop a set of reasons using knowledge mapping construction process.
3. Imagine you have hired to develop a recruitment programme for a small-sized company. Frame the knowledge mapping technology.

KEYWORDS

Knowledge Map: A knowledge map portrays a perspective of the players, sources, flows, constraints and sinks of knowledge within an organisation. It is a navigation aid to both explicit (codified) information and tacit knowledge, showing the importance and the relationships between knowledge stores and the dynamics. The final 'map' can take multiple forms, from a pictorial display to yellow pages directory, to linked topic or concept map, to inventory lists or a matrix of assets against key business processes.

"Process" oriented approach: This approach deals with knowledge cartography methods, which use modelling, description and analysis of business processes to determine critical knowledge.

"Domain" oriented approach: In this approach, we try to make an analysis from a mass of information in order to organise it in logic different from the functional approach. In fact, the goal is to ignore the functional structure of the firm, grouping activities into knowledge domains. This task demands an important capacity of analysis because it's not a natural process.

QUESTIONS FOR DISCUSSION

1. What do you understand by knowledge mapping?
2. Explain the importance of knowledge mapping.
3. Describe the different methods of knowledge mapping.
4. Narrate the benefits of knowledge mapping. Draw a typical knowledge mapping diagram.
5. Why we should bother about knowledge map?
6. What is the purpose and benefits of knowledge map?

SUGGESTED READINGS

Bartlett, Christopher A., The Knowledge-Based Organisation, In *The Knowledge Advantage* (Ruggles), 1999. Frappaoli, Carl, *Knowledge Management*, Wiley, 2006.

Bergeron, Bryan, *Essentials of Knowledge Management*. Wiley, 2003.

Boughzala, Imed, Trends in Enterprise Knowledge Management, 2008.

Jonassen, D. H., & Carr, C. S., Mindtools: Affording Multiple Representations for Learning, In S. P. Lajoie (ed.), *Computers as Cognitive Tools: No More Walls*, vol. 2 (pp. 165-196), Mahwah, NJ: Lawrence Erlbaum Associates, 2000.

Nonaka, Ikujiro; von Krogh, Georg, "Tacit Knowledge and Knowledge Conversion: Controversy and Advancement in Organisational Knowledge Creation Theory". *Organisation Science*, 20 (3): 635–652, 2009.

Novak, J. D., *Learning, Creating, and Using Knowledge: Concept Maps and Facilitative Tools in Schools and Corporations*, Mahwah, NJ: Lawrence Erlbaum Associates, 1998.

Savage, Charles M., *5th Generation Management*. Digital Press, 1990.

Sensky, Tom, "Knowledge Management", In *Advances in Psychiatric Treatment*, 8 (5): 387–395, 2002.

Serenko, Alexander; Bontis, Nick, "Meta-Review of Knowledge Management and Intellectual Capital Literature: Citation Impact and Research Productivity Rankings". *Knowledge and Process Management* 11 (3): 185–198, 2004. doi:10.1002/kpm.203. http://www.business.mc-master.ca/mktg/nbontis//ic/publications/KPMSerenkoBontis.pdf.

Serenko, Alexander; Bontis, Nick; Booker, Lorne; Sadeddin, Khaled; Hardie, Timothy, "A Scientometric Analysis of Knowledge Management and Intellectual Capital Academic Literature (1994-2008)", *Journal of Knowledge Management*, 14 (1): 13–23, 2010.

Snowden, Dave, "Complex Acts of Knowing—Paradox and Descriptive Self Awareness". *Journal of Knowledge Management,* Special Issue 6 (2): 100–111, 2002. doi:10.1108/13673270210 424639. http://www.cognitive-edge.com/articledetails.php?articleid=13.

Spender, J. C.; Scherer, Andreas Georg, "The Philosophical Foundations of Knowledge Management: Editors' Introduction". *Organisation* 14 (1): 5–28, 2007. http://ssrn.com/abstract=958768.

Thomas, J. C., Kellogg, W. A., & Erickson, T., The Knowledge Management Puzzle : Human and Social Factors in Knowledge Management [Electronic Version]. *IBM Systems Journal,* 40(4), 863–884, 2010.

Thompson, Mark P.A.; Walsham, Geoff, "Placing Knowledge Management in Context". *Journal of Management Studies,* 41 (5): 725–747, 2004.

Tissen, René, Andriessen, Daniel & Deprez Frank Lekanne, *The Knowledge Dividend: Creating High-Performance Companies Through Value-Based Knowledge Management.* London: *Financial Times,* Prentice Hall, 2000.

Tsoukas, Hardimos & Vladimirou, Efi., What is Organisational Knowledge? *Journal of Management Studies,* 38 (7), 973–993, 2001.

Wenger, E., *Communities of Practice,* Cambridge: Cambridge University Press, 1998.

Wenger, Etienne; McDermott, Richard; Synder, Richard, *Cultivating Communities of Practice: A Guide to Managing Knowledge—Seven Principles for Cultivating Communities of Practice.* Boston: Harvard Business School Press, pp. 107–136, 2002.

Wilson, T.D., "The Nonsense of 'Knowledge Management'", *Information Research,* 8 (1), 2002.

Wright, Kirby, "Personal Knowledge Management: Supporting Individual Knowledge Worker Performance", *Knowledge Management Research and Practice,* 3 (3): 156–165, 2005.

WEBSITES

http://papers.ssrn.com/sol3/papers.cfm?abstract_id=559300.
http://apt.rcpsych.org/cgi/content/full/8/5/387.
http://hbswk.hbs.edu/archive/2855.html.
http://informationr.net/ir/8-1/paper144.html.
http://www.systems-thinking.org/dikw/dikw.htm
http://www.media-access.com/whatis.html
http://findarticles.com/p/articles/mi_7349/is_2_26/ai_n32164187/

CHAPTER 13

Futuristic Knowledge Management

OBJECTIVE

At the end of this lesson, you would be able to understand:

- Understand what knowledge engineering is.
- Theory of Computation.
- Data Structure.
- The Human Factor and Social Factor of Knowledge Management.
- Future KM.

INTRODUCTION

> *Knowledge rests not upon truth alone, but upon error also.*
> —Carl Jung

Knowledge engineering is a field within artificial intelligence that develops knowledge-based systems. Such systems are computer programs that contain large amounts of knowledge, rules and reasoning mechanisms to provide solutions to real-world problems.

A major form of knowledge-based system is an expert system, one designed to emulate the reasoning processes of an expert practitioner (i.e., one having performed in a professional role for very many years). Typical examples of expert systems include diagnosis of bacterial infections, advice on mineral exploration and assessment of electronic circuit designs.

Knowledge engineering process of eliciting, structuring, formalising, operationalising information and knowledge involved in a knowledge-intensive problem domain, in order to construct a program that can perform a difficult task adequately.

History of Knowledge Systems

> *Sharing knowledge is not about giving people something, or getting*
> *something from them. That is only valid for information sharing.*
> *Sharing knowledge occurs when people are genuinely interested*
> *in helping one another develop new capacities for action;*
> *it is about creating learning processes.*
> —Peter Senge

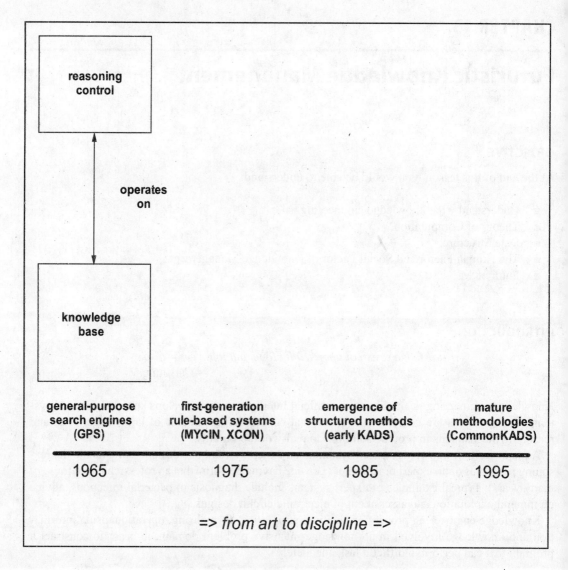

Fig. 13.1   First Generation "Expert" Systems

DEFINITION

In 1983, Edward Feigenbaum and Pamela McCorduck defines knowledge engineering as:

"A discipline that involves integration of knowledge into computer system in order to solve complex problems normally requiring a high level of human expertise. It refers to the building, maintaining and development of knowledge-based systems".

Problems in knowledge engineering are that they have:

- complex information and knowledge is difficult to observe
- experts and other sources differ
- multiple representations of information found in:
  - textbooks
  - graphical representations
  - heuristics
  - skills

There are many concepts which are common in software engineering, computer science and artificial science including databases expert system, decision support system (DSS) and geographic, information systems.

The various activities of knowledge engineering are as follows:

1. Assessment of the problem
2. Development of a knowledge-based system structure
3. Acquisition and structuring of related information, knowledge and specific preferences
4. Implementation of the structures' knowledge into knowledge basis
5. Testing and validation of the inserted knowledge
6. Integration and maintenance of the system
7. Revision and evaluation of the system

Knowledge engineering is still in its infant stage because of the field being art rather than being science. The phases having been overlapped, the process might be iterative and there are lot of opportunities open for the knowledge engineer.

PRINCIPLES OF KNOWLEDGE ENGINEERING

In today's environment, hoarding knowledge ultimately erodes your power. If you know something very important, the way to get power is by actually sharing it.
—Joseph Badaracco

Knowledge engineers have developed a number of principles, methods and tools to improve knowledge acquisition and ordering during the mid-1980s. Some of the major principles are as follows:

- Knowledge engineers acknowledge that there are different types of knowledge, and that the right approach and technique should be used for the knowledge required.
- Knowledge engineers acknowledge that there are different types of experts and expertise, such that methods should be chosen appropriately.
- Knowledge engineers recognise that there are different ways of representing knowledge, which can aid the acquisition, validation and reuse of knowledge.
- Knowledge engineers recognise that there are different ways of using knowledge, so that the acquisition process can be guided by the project aims.
- Knowledge engineers use structured methods to increase the efficiency of the acquisition process.

There are two main views to knowledge engineering:

- Transfer View—This is the traditional view. In this view, the assumption is to apply conventional knowledge engineering techniques to transfer human knowledge into artificial intelligence systems.
- Modelling View—This is the alternative view. In this view, the knowledge engineer attempts to model the knowledge and problem-solving techniques of the domain expert into the artificial intelligence system.

KNOWLEDGE ENGINEERING TRENDS

Human knowledge is required to solve the problem and this knowledge is transferred and implemented into the knowledge base. The basic principle of KE assumes that concrete knowledge is already present in humans to solve the problem. This concrete knowledge could either be explicit knowledge or tacit knowledge. The transfer in view disregards the tacit knowledge an individual acquires in order to solve a problem. This is the latest trend in KE. It may be regarded as a paradigm shifts towards modelling view. This shift is compared to that of a first generation expert system to second generation expert system. The latest trend of modelling view is closer to approximate of reality and perceives problem solving as dynamic, cyclic, incessant process dependent on the knowledge acquired. It also depends on the interpretation made by the system. This is similar to how an expert solves the problem in real life.

KNOWLEDGE ENGINEERING METHODOLOGIES

Epistemics is involved in three methodologies to support the development of knowledge systems:

> *"A successful species not only has to be adapted to the environment,*
> *it also has to be adapted to adapting to the environment".*
> *The Blind Watchmaker*—by Richard Dawkins.

1. Common KADS
2. The SPEDE methodology
3. MOKA

1. Common KADS is the methodology that is most commonly followed at Epistemics when developing knowledge engineering systems. Common KADS is a complete methodological framework for the development of a knowledge-based system (KBS). It supports most aspects of a KBS development project, such as:

- Project management
- Organisational analysis (including problem/opportunity identification)
- Knowledge acquisition (including initial project scoping)
- Knowledge analysis and modelling

- Capture of user requirements
- Analysis of system integration issues
- Knowledge system design

Perspectives

Common KADS describes KBS development from two perspectives:

- Result perspective: A set of models, of different aspects of the KBS and its environment, that are continuously improved during a project life cycle.
- Project management perspective: A risk-driven generic spiral life cycle model that can be configured into a process adapted to the particular project.

2. SPEDE

The SPEDE methodology is a combination of principles, techniques and tools taken from knowledge engineering and adapted for use in Knowledge Management. It provides an effective means to capture, validate and communicate vital knowledge to provide business benefit.

The SPEDE methodology was developed under the guidance of Rolls Royce plc and involved staff from Epistemics acting as consultants.

Structure and Deliverables

SPEDE has been specifically developed to act as a training course for novice knowledge engineers or those seconded to a Knowledge Management activity. SPEDE projects typically involve a week of intensive training followed by 2–3 months of scoping, knowledge acquisition and delivery phases.

The main deliverable of most SPEDE projects is an intranet website. However, previous projects have delivered quality procedures, process improvement information and expert systems.

Projects using the SPEDE methodology follow a set of procedures coordinated by experienced staff. All projects have a coach who manages the activities of one or more knowledge engineers on a daily basis.

Gates

All SPEDE projects must pass through a series of gates. These are meetings held at various stages throughout the project to act as a "go/no go" into the next phase of the project. Each gate comprises various criteria to ensure the project is on track to meet the objectives and identify any problems, hazards and actions. There are 5 gates: project launch review, scoping review, technical review, delivery review and post-delivery review.

3. Methodology and tools Oriented to Knowledge-Based Engineering Applications (MOKA)

MOKA is a methodology for developing Knowledge-Based Engineering Applications, i.e., systems that support design engineers. It is particularly aimed at capturing and applying knowledge within aeronautical and automotive industries of the design of complex mechanical products.

Whilst huge benefits can be gained by the use of Knowledge-Based Engineering (KBE) technology, the lack of a recognised methodology has resulted in a significant risk when developing and maintaining KBE applications. MOKA aims to provide such a methodology, that:

- Reduces the lead times and associated costs of developing KBE applications by 20–25%.
- Provides a consistent way of developing and maintaining KBE applications.
- Will form the basis of an international standard.
- Makes use of a software tool to support the use of the methodology.

Need for MOKA

Companies have to manage and reuse engineering knowledge to improve business processes, to reduce time to find new solutions, to make *correct first time* and to retain best practices. The aim of MOKA is to provide a methodology to capture and formalise engineering knowledge to reuse it, for example, within KBE applications. Development and maintenance of knowledge intensive software applications is a complex and potentially expensive activity. The number of Knowledge-Based Engineering (KBE) systems used in the aeronautical and automotive industries have increased in recent years. Experience has shown that long-term risk can be reduced by employing a systematic methodology that covers the development and maintenance of such systems. The ESPRIT-IV funded project called MOKA (No. 25418) is intended to satisfy this need by providing both a methodology and a supporting software tool, both of which are independent of any KBE platform.

MOKA Analysis and Modelling

MOKA identifies two models to be used in the KBE application development life cycle:

- Informal Model: A structured, natural language representation of engineering knowledge using predefined forms.
- Formal Model: A graphical, object-oriented representation of engineering knowledge at one level of abstraction above application code.

Within each of these models, various knowledge representations are used to help capture, analyse and structure the knowledge required for KBE applications.

Within the informal model, the main knowledge objects are:

- **Entities**
  - **Structural Entities** (the components of the product being designed)
  - **Functional Entities** (the functions of the product and its sub-components)
- **Constraints** (the design requirements of the product and its sub-components)
- **Activities** (the tasks performed during the design process)
- **Rules** (decision points in the design process that affect what tasks to perform)
- **Illustrations** (examples that illustrate aspects of the product and design)

MOKA tool supports the capture, analysis, modelling and publishing of design knowledge using a MOKA framework.

THEORY OF COMPUTATION

The theory of computation or computer theory is the branch of computer science and mathematics. It deals with how efficiently problems can be solved by using an algorithm. This particular field is divided into two major branches.

1. Computability theory
2. Complexity theory.

Both the branches deal with formal models of computation. Computer scientist works with the mathematical abstraction of computers, which is called the model of computation. But, there are other several models which are used that could be examined by Turing machine. This Turing machine is simple to formulate, analyse and use to prove results as it represents many powerful models of computation. Turing machine generally requires only a finite amount of memory. Therefore, any problem that can be solved by Turing machine can also be solved by the computer within the bounded amount of memory.

The theory of computation can be considered a creation of models of all types in the field of computer science. In the theory of computation, mathematics and logic are used. Computability theory deals primarily with the question of the extent to which a problem is solvable by a computer. Turing machine gives the best results in computability theory. Computability theory is based and built on solving a concrete problem and halting the problem for result. Computability theory uses Rice's theorem which states that on non-trivial properties of partial functions, it is undesirable to state whether Turing machine computes a partial function with that property. Computability theory is closely related to the branch of mathematical logic called recursion theory, which removes the restriction of studying only those models of computation which are reducible to the Turing model.

Data Structure

> *The fact that I can plant a seed and it becomes a flower, share a bit of*
> *knowledge and it becomes another's, smile at someone and receive a*
> *smile in return, are to me continual spiritual exercises.*
> —Leo F Buscaqlia

Data structure is the process of storing and organising data in a computer that can be used efficiently. Different kinds of applications

> *"For attractive lips, speak words of kindness. For lovely eyes, seek*
> *out the good in people. For a slim figure, share your food with the hungry.*
> *For beautiful hair, let a child run his fingers through it once a day.*
> *For poise, walk with the knowledge you'll never walk alone"*
> —Sam Levenson

Modern Knowledge Management Applications

Who should lead KM efforts?

Since KM is not a technology-based concept but a business practice, enterprisewide KM efforts should not be lead by the CIO. (The CIO is a suitable choice to lead KM efforts within the IT department, however.) Some companies have dedicated KM staff headed by a chief knowledge officer or some other high-profile executive. Other companies rely on an executive sponsor in the functional area where KM is implemented.

What constitutes intellectual or knowledge-based assets?

Not all information is valuable. Therefore, it's up to individual companies to determine what information qualifies as intellectual and knowledge-based assets. In general, however, intellectual and knowledge-based assets fall into one of the two categories: explicit or tacit. Included among the former are assets such as patents, trademarks, business plans, marketing research and customer lists. As a general rule of thumb, explicit knowledge consists of anything that can be documented, archived and codified, often with the help of IT.

Much harder to grasp is the concept of tacit knowledge, or the know-how contained in people's heads. The challenge inherent with tacit knowledge is figuring out how to recognise, generate, share and manage it. While IT in the form of e-mail, groupware, instant messaging and related technologies can help facilitate the dissemination of tacit knowledge, identifying tacit knowledge in the first place is a major hurdle for most organisations.

KM Requires Ongoing Maintenance

As with many physical assets, the value of knowledge can erode over time. Since knowledge can get stale fast, the content in a KM programme should be constantly updated, amended and deleted. What's more, the relevance of knowledge at any given time changes, as do the skills of employees. Therefore, there is no endpoint to a KM programme. Like product development, marketing and R&D, KM is a constantly evolving business practice.

Getting Employees on Board

The major problems that occur in KM usually result because companies ignore the people and cultural issues. In an environment where an individual's knowledge is valued and rewarded, establishing a culture that recognises tacit knowledge and encourages employees to share it is critical. The need to sell the KM concept to employees shouldn't be underestimated; after all, in many cases employees are being asked to surrender their knowledge and experience—the very traits that make them valuable as individuals.

What technologies can support KM?

KM is not a technology-based concept. Don't be duped by software vendors touting their all-inclusive KM solutions. Companies that implement a centralised database system, electronic message board, Web portal or any other collaborative tool in the hope that they've established a KM programme are wasting both their time and money.

That being said, KM tools run the gamut from standard, off-the-shelf e-mail packages to sophisticated collaboration tools designed specifically to support community building and identity. Generally, tools fall into one or more of the following categories: knowledge repositories, expertise access tools, e-learning applications, discussion and chat technologies, synchronous interaction tools, and search and data mining tools.

The Knowledge Management Puzzle: Human and Social Factors in Knowledge Management

Why focus on the human factor?

> *"What has tended to happen in development is that organisations*
> *have generally leaned towards linear and technocentric interpretations*
> *of KM, more in line with the descriptive early traditions of knowledge*
> *management and organisational development or 'institution building.'"*
> —(Hovland, 2003)

"Careful attention is needed in the processes by which values and purpose are defined and articulated so as to create an enabling environment for Knowledge Management to succeed. Without these processes, organisational learning and Knowledge Management merely become toolkits and methodologies in a vacuum" (Pasteur et al., 2006). There is also a need to better understand how knowledge and learning may practically address and deal with issues of personality, culture, language, religion, and so on (Ramalingam, 2005).

Dealing with human factors and managing change in Knowledge Management:

As Davenport and Prusak (1998) put it: *"Effective knowledge management cannot take place without extensive behavioural, cultural and organisational change (…) Technology alone won't make a person with expertise share with others. Technology alone won't get an employee who is uninterested in seeking knowledge to hop onto a keyboard and searching or browsing."*

Knowledge Management is first and foremost a people issue. Does the culture of your organisation support ongoing learning and knowledge sharing? Are people motivated and rewarded for creating, sharing and using knowledge? Is there a culture of openness and mutual respect and support? Or is your organisation very hierarchical where 'knowledge is power' and so people are reluctant to share? Are people under constant pressure to act with no time for knowledge-seeking or reflection? Do they feel inspired to innovate and learn from mistakes, or is there a strong 'blame and shame' culture?

These questions are essential to ask and to solve. There is a need to further understand the reasons why people engage in knowledge sharing behaviour.

Ten human factors affect the implementation of knowledge management initiatives, including fear, cultural change, capturing of tacit knowledge, ease of use, stakeholder involvement, and benefits realisation. To deal with these factors, a phased change management approach is given below for better understanding of human contribution in KM that would consist of an assessment, strategic planning, organisation development, systems design, orientation and training, team building, and continuous evaluation and improvement.

Career analyst Dan Pink examines the puzzle of motivation, starting with a fact that social scientists know but most managers don't: Traditional rewards aren't always as effective as we think.

Being a social scientist myself I completely agree with the things he's saying. Making the monetary rewards parallel with Knowledge Management will not do the trick of stimulating effective knowledge sharing and adoption on the long run. Even worse: they might turn out to damage the organisation if people post just to get "participation points" and keep on appearances of sharing to receive certain monetary rewards. Besides it'll lead to a more narrow focus described by Dan Pink: not very useful in our extremely complex international situations where thinking out of the box and innovations on a local scale are key for succes.

The Theory of Planned Behaviour from Ajzen (1991) is one of the most researched and validated models in social psychology that explain the factors that influence our behaviour. In this case I focused on 'knowledge behaviour'. In general, it says that the motivation to perform a certain behavior is positively correlated with the frequency of actually doing it.

This motivation is in its turn caused by a combination of three variables:

- The attitude one has towards the behaviour in question
- The perceived control one has over actually performing this behaviour
- And the perceived social norm the individual feels to perform the behaviour in question

An attitude is formed by the other elements of the model, but also by an evaluation of costs and outcomes. What outcomes does a person want from his jobs?...What outcomes does a person want from performing knowledge behaviour?...Questions that organisations should ask themselves in order to influence motivation.

The attitude of a person can be altered by a process of continuously stressing the importance of a certain behaviour, sharing positive results, positive feedback and appraisal mechanisms. There should be constant reminders on the benefits of what effective knowledge management can achieve, not only for the organisation, but also personal, saving his/her valuable time and needless effort. Rewarding mechanisms influence the attitude of a person in a positive way as well, but keep in mind the difference between formal and informal rewards. Informal rewards proved to be much more useful in this case. This is validated by an extensive body of research in social science.

For communication among the workforce, the following Box 13.1 gives you a successful story.

Having "lack of time" is nothing unusual - it's what we all have if we have to fulfil our cause and daily routines...What do you do if you see that time is not an unlimited resource? You focus on the things which are important for you, of course. What's important for the target audience?

Is the system you want to put in place important for them, what could be their benefit from using / contributing? Do you know the answer or do you guess based on assumptions / info you got from a third party?

Another issue directly related to this: "Incentives" are something one artificially invents for extrinsic motivation, which is nice to have. The essence is simply to find out what is important for the people and to provide solutions which are helping them to do what's important for them; to do better without more effort or reach the same result with less effort.

For doing so stakeholder interviews might be a good instrument. Just find out "what do you need me for" and create trust in people. Who you are really interested in? Otherwise, your risk is just spending much time in convincing people of using km methods and promising a benefit they might

Box 13.1   A Success Story

Nearly six years ago, Misys Healthcare's (now part of new Allscripts) Homecare business unit, a provider of healthcare information systems serving 600 providers of home healthcare, hospice, and private-duty services, installed SharePoint as a platform for improving communication between Allscripts and SoftServe, and between different departments within Allscripts' Homecare Product Development. Because Allscripts Health System Group designs installs and supports software for the automatic billing, scheduling, and clinical functions of its healthcare clients in the US it is imperative that their clients-agency directors, finance directors, management information officers, and private duty organisations receive accurate, up-to-date information for their business needs.

"It's important to share information not only across the world, but also with our vendor SoftServe, as well as with the people across the hall," says David Staudenmaier, product development manager, Allscripts Health Systems Group. "It's inefficient to have to repeat information or constantly tell the people you work with where the information is stored," he adds. "It's also important for all the new employees who are working here to know that vital information is always in SharePoint." SharePoint's hierarchical structure defines the levels of user access across the company and the rules for how to access information and establishes a project management system. SharePoint has improved communication between Allscripts Homecare and SoftServe as well as between different departments within the company. SharePoint has also improved productivity through continuity of business information, which is of significant value to both companies. SharePoint has enhanced Allscripts Homecare's relationship with SoftServe by eliminating redundant tasks, e-mails, and questions between the two companies. Now both companies know where to find the vital information they need when they need it.

SharePoint has made sure that everyone has the latest versions of the product and that no one is working on the wrong software enhancement due to a lack of clear communication. If this had occurred in the past, SoftServe would have been required to stop, go back, and redo part of the software. SharePoint has enabled a working environment where business can be conducted efficiently and timely so that both companies are able to meet their goals. For example, it is no longer necessary for a developer to talk to Staudenmaier or a manager in order to get the information that is needed to work on a project. Everyone is on the same team and collaboration takes place between the two companies according to what the market requires.

In the end, Allscripts Homecare's software allows its clients to run their businesses more efficiently due to the software products created by SoftServe and Allscripts. And employees no longer must remember where critical business information is located or who owns it. Most important, Allscripts Homecare's customers are getting accurate, up-to-date, and consistent information, regardless of who they are speaking with, which ultimately leads to higher satisfaction levels.

SoftServe and Allscripts work together closely to complement each other in three important ways:

- SoftServe is a committed and reliable partner in product development

- SoftServe has shown the same passion for quality as Allscripts
- There is a highly skilled team integrated with the Allscripts Homecare's team at a person-to-person level

All this is made possible because SharePoint provides a common platform and online collaboration solution for the communication and organisation of business intelligence between the two organisations, ensuring that the right people are working on the right features at the right time. Staudenmaier concludes, "Together, we deliver great value for our customers on time and within budget.".

About Allscripts

Allscripts is a provider of software, services, information and connectivity solutions that empower physicians and other healthcare providers to deliver best-in-class patient safety, clinical outcomes and financial results. www.allscripts.com

About SoftServe, Inc.

SoftServe, Inc. is an independent multinational software development and consulting company. www.softserve.com

not wish to have. And then of course the resistance to change our own style of work for something you don't see as important for you is very strong and sustainable.

In terms of organisational culture two things are critically important:

1. Incentives: Incentives are put in place to encourage and reward collaboration and recognise contribution. These can be both informal (visible recognition of contributions, finding ways for peers to give positive feedback to one another, etc.) and more formal such as including this in job descriptions, performance assessments, office performance indicators, etc.

2. Role modelling: Senior leaders in the organisation not only speak about the importance of collaboration but also behave in a way which demonstrates that it is really important (by their own actions or how they recognise and reward others).

Getting Work Done: The Human Side of Project Management Project Management is defined as the art and science of getting work done with the active cooperation of individuals and organisations that are directly or indirectly involved with the project. This includes senior management, project sponsors(s), customers, end-users, stakeholders, team members, sub-contractors, vendors and consultants. Given the reality of minimal authority and total responsibility for the outcome of the project, the Project Manager's biggest challenge consists of "Getting Work Done."

One may mention that 'not having the time' to use Knowledge Management system shouldn't be an answer for why people don't use it. However, some phone interviews with practitioners were conducted to get a sense of what they would want in a system and how they would use it, or not.

When asking if they would or would not use the system, for those who said that they wouldn't actually commented that they just wouldn't have the time. Of course the idea is to persuade people that they do in fact have the time so long as the product has quality, however, it's a bit of a psychological hurdle. Let's face it, people are busy and even if good information is out there a lot of people don't want to take the time to 'explore'. If they knew where to go and information could be found easily than the time obstacle gets cut down to some degree, but still remains. So I would just caution on dismissing the rationality of 'not having enough time'. It is, in fact, a major issue to contend with.

FUTURE OF KNOWLEDGE MANAGEMENT

Over the past decade, KM solutions have become effective at managing content, automating business processes and analysing data, but information was not always easily shared across different applications and functional areas. The result was that valuable insights were lost and decision making lacked empirical support.

Now, however, organisations are closing the loop on knowledge sharing. In some cases, the connections are coming from application integration (see "tighter integration"), and in others, from rethinking underlying processes. Either way, the enhanced information flow is supporting better decision-making and promoting continuous improvement.

Although emerging technologies such as social networking are contributing substantially to greater exchange of information, much of the progress can be credited to mature KM solutions that are being used more effectively. Organisations are taking significant steps in gathering and synthesising information to ensure that it ends up where it will do the most good.

Over the past decade a number of powerful drivers have transformed the environment in which most organisations operate. Probably the most dynamic is the factor that emerges out of the conjunction of innovations in ICT and new value network dynamics. This is a shift in the way value is created to "advantage through knowledge".

Although many commentators agree that the western economies have shifted from industrial to intangible forms of wealth creation, the fact is that many older organisations have emerged into this new landscape with much of their legacy intact. There are many k-based organisations operating in a k-advantage environment that retain traditional management approaches. There are also organisations that have accurately made sense of these emergent realities. They have successfully innovated and experimented to create k-advantage. The positive impact of adopting more appropriate management approaches are many and varied; from smarter sensing, responding and adapting, to faster speed of execution and increased flexibility, attracting the best talent, mobilizing innovation and creating and delivering value.

We term organisations that maintain traditional approaches to management, yet operate in dominantly k-advantage environments K-T, where K stands for k-advantage environment and T represents the negative impact of traditional legacy management. We believe that this is a very real issue for many large, old and complex organisations in Europe. The term K+ is used for organisations that are successfully creating knowledge advantage. This means that there is a good fit between the organisation and its knowledge-advantage environment.

So, if the above description of current realities is correct, how are K-T organisations going to catch up with the K+ organisations? In our experience many organisations have not formally undertaken a holistic transformation process in response to the new set of environmental drivers. Instead managers may be unsure of how and where the organisation needs to change, or may be unaware of the imperative to transform at all.

The assumption is that K-T organisations are going to operate suboptimally in a number of areas. These include the strategic, process, operational and functional dimensions. In knowledge-based organisations people are often the critical value-adding component. Many of the sub-optimal forces in K-T organisations centre on how people are managed, organised, motivated, directed, supported and developed.

In the words of Dave Pollard (2003),
The evidence is everywhere:

The following box 13.2 gives us a picture of how an Enterprise Finder Works.

Box 13.2   Enterprise Finder Works

You are the CFO of Company Y, depicted in the lower right corner of this chart Fig. 13.2. You need to find out about a proposed change in the tax code for R&D Tax Credits. Before Social Network Enablement (SNE) software, you would have typed the term into the intranet search engine, checked the public CCRA/IRS website or some purchased tax service your company buys, or just picked up the phone and called Jan, your accountant who works for Company X. Alas, Jan just left for a three-week vacation. Since you've implemented SNE software, however, it's easy. You key the term into your Expertise Finder and up pops the picture below. As you expected, Jan appears as one of the experts.

This Expertise Network diagram in Figure 13.2 shows all and only the experts and connections related specifically to the subject of R&D Tax Credits. It tells you that the R&D department of your company has some information on tax credits on their team blog, which they've posted to the R&D Community of Practice intranet site. It also tells you that Jan has access to this intranet site, and that this intranet site subscribes to Jan's Tax Credit blog category. It also identifies two other people at the accounting firm that have expertise on this topic, since Jan is unavailable, and a customer of both your company and your accountant, who outsources his R&D to your company and qualifies for a 'flow-through' of the Research Tax Credit and hence is very knowledgeable about how these credits work. And a supplier who sells a Tax Credit Analyser to your accountants, and a tax credit expert advisor to your accountants who, it turns out, went to high school with you and might cough up the knowledge you want for free, are also identified.

So you have lots of alternatives. In Jan's absence you can phone or e-mail or IM any of the six other identified experts, or subscribe to their blogs, or buy the Tax Credit Analyser yourself (knowing your accountants thought it good enough to buy), or tap into the R&D group's CoP tool or the accountants' extranet. Problem solved.

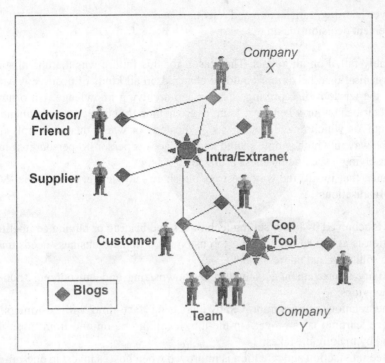

Fig. 13.2   Expertise Network Diagram

- Budgets for KM have been slashed everywhere, and whole KM departments eliminated
- Many companies are now trying to outsource KM, no longer viewing it as a core competency
- Where at one time six of the top 10 bestsellers at Books for Business were about KM, now very few KM titles even crack the list
- Writers who are starting to predict 'the death of KM' lament 'where KM went wrong' and even decry 'the autism of KM'
- There are now fewer Chief Knowledge Officers in Fortune 500 companies than there were five years ago
- Half of the KM conferences scheduled in the past year in Toronto were cancelled for lack of interest

There is no question that most organisations, especially large ones, do a poor job at managing their intellectual capital, and that this capital provides an increasingly important part of the organisations' value. Desktops and laptops have become ubiquitous in business, but the return on this investment generally ranges from unmeasurable to dissatisfactory. The expectations were that KM would be able to improve:

- Growth and innovation in organisations
- Productivity and efficiency (reflected in absolute cost savings)
- Customer relationships

- Employee learning, satisfaction and retention, and
- Management decision-making.

It has arguably failed on all counts. The reason for this failure was the unrealistic expectation that human organisational behaviour could be changed, in all kinds of positive ways, by persuading people of the wisdom of capturing, sharing and archiving knowledge. Unfortunately, people only change their behaviour when there is an overwhelmingly compelling argument to do so (not the 'leap of faith' on which much of KM was predicated), or where there is simply no alternative. Before KM, the way in which people shared knowledge was person-to-person, just-in-time, and in the context of solving a specific business problem.

A decade later, that is still the way most people share knowledge, even in the 'Most Admired Knowledge Organisations':

- growth is achieved by better selling techniques and beating or buying competitors;
- Innovation is achieved by listening to customers articulate business needs and developing creative solutions that address them;
- Productivity improvement is achieved by downsizing and outsourcing 'non-core-competency' activities;
- Customer relationships are improved by increasing 'face-time' with customers.
- Employee learning is improved on-the-job, learning one-on-one from those doing the job now, and by making mistakes;
- Employee satisfaction and retention is improved when bosses invest in one-on-one face-time with employees and offer them interesting assignments, responsibility and promising career opportunities; and
- Decision-making is improved when management and front-line people know their business, know their customers, know the business environment, and apply this knowledge intelligently.

The value proposition for KM, lies in Peter Drucker's assertion that the *greatest challenge to business management in the 21st century is, and will be, improving the personal productivity and effectiveness of front-line workers doing increasingly complex and unique jobs.* Unlike the work world of the last two centuries, most employees today either come into their jobs knowing more than their boss about how to do it, or quickly acquire such superior knowledge from their peers and from personal experience on-the-job. Every job today, every process, is unique, and therefore the expectation that KM systems could capture 'best practices' and 'success stories' and 'lessons learned' that could be reapplied by others again and again was unrealistic.

For most organisations that have invested heavily in KM, this would represent a radical change. Table 13.1 contrasts the current and future KM functions.

Table 13.1   Current and Future KM Functions

Function	Current State	Future State	Note on Roles
Research & Analysis	May be part of KM business unit or split among other business units.	Researchers will provide personalised training on how to do research and analysis yourself; and will do less research themselves.	
Intranet & Extranet Architecture Development & Management	Centrally-managed tools and repositories and publishing and permissioning environment.	Personal weblog-based 'world of ends' architecture; anyone can publish, anyone can subscribe, peer-to-peer browsing, expertise finders, knowledge mining and other 'social software'; Centrally-managed expert systems where processes are prescriptive; Extranet is an extension of the Intranet, with different permissioning protocols.	Conversion of existing Intranet & Extranet to new Weblog-based architecture will be a major one-time project; development of social software applications and expert systems will be ongoing.
Community of Practice (CoP) Management	Usually centrally-managed support function.	Self-managing communities and self-managed community tools and spaces (another 'social software' category).	CoP facilitator will be part of the CoP itself rather than a central function.
Database Purchasing & Subscriptions	May be part of the KM business unit or split among other business units; fixed price site licences negotiated in advance plus pay-as-you-go services.	External databases and resources are subscribed to and accessible individually the same way internal weblogs are, with automatic tracking for volume rebate purposes.	Gradually diminished need as external vendors move to automatic RSS subscription basis.
Knowledge Training, Communication & Content Management	Centrally-developed curricula, web-based learning tools, e-newsletters & content management architecture; users are trained in taxonomy, database layout and access.	Personal, one-on-one scheduled training; each front-line worker selects their own taxonomy, organisation and access (permissioning).	Big shift from development and running of courses and communications to one-on-one personal, scheduled training.

Source: Dave Pollard (2003)

To conclude, in creating a knowledge future the main challenge is to engage all individuals in the discussion about Information Management and Knowledge Management, and help them to understand what the benefits will be for them. They are the ones who may have to change business practices (like ceasing to maintain a separate, but duplicate and now out-of-date version of a database) when there is to be one trusted source of that particular data.

Organisations are encouraged to take a long-term view of Information Management and Knowledge Management and to identify the major information and knowledge obstacles faced by staff now, and to plan for the elimination of these over time. If there are 'low hanging fruit' that will deliver quick wins once Information Management and Knowledge Management strategies are adopted, then these should be tackled immediately.

An audit of all the information and knowledge systems in an organisation may be an action that can help identify the urgent need for Information Management and Knowledge Management strategies (identifying the multiplicity of data sources held in filing cabinets, insecure laptops, hard disks that are not regularly backed-up, in the heads of key staff approaching retirement, etc). The audit can also be a tool for identifying priorities for attention in the Information Management and Knowledge Management strategies.

SUMMING UP

A project management approach enabled the company to meet their production needs for the future, while at the same time not disrupting their current production to fulfil client demand. There was never a glitch in the production line while new processes were being tested and evaluated. Continuous communication ensured that everyone was in the loop on changes to processes and actually had the benefit of increasing participation from employees on how to improve processes to better meet client needs. Additionally, continuous review and adjustments to the risk management plan ensured that the end result was well thought out and tested and ensured that any glitches in proposed changes were caught immediately and could be addressed.

Adhering to a standard project management methodology enabled this company to implement a very high risk project efficiently, on budget and within reasonable time to meet long-term strategic goals.

CASE

Process Changes for a Manufacturing Company

This is an overview of a case study of a manufacturing company that saw the value in taking a project management approach to a process change initiative.

Overview

Company XYZ has been aware that its production of widgets will not continue to satisfy clients' demands. They have seen an increase of 10% year after year for widgets over the last 5 years with no end in sight for the increase in demand. The CEO had asked an internal team to review the current manufacturing processes and propose changes in the processes, along with upgrades in equipment to meet the demand for the future. When the team's proposal was submitted to the CEO, it recommended upgrading the manufacturing equipment and redesigning the production line with no solid metrics relating to the number of anticipated increases. Also missing (and critical to the outcome) was an analysis of what would happen in procurement, delivery, as well as warehousing, if these changes were made to the manufacturing process, and whether these departments would be able to manage those changes. After seeing such deficiencies in the team's plan, and with past experiences in such projects at another company, the CEO chose to engage a project management consulting company, ABC Projects, to outline a project plan for this initiative. ABC Projects specialised in process improvement initiatives. The CEO knew that these efforts were more likely to be successfully implemented when run as a well-managed project.

The Project Plan

ABC Projects outlined a project plan with tentative timelines and cost ranges until discovery was completed. The project plan included the discovery and identification of needs for increased production, as well as identification of the affected departments and/or processes if the increase in production was to be carried out.

ABC Projects knew from experience that other areas besides the manufacturing line would be affected. For example, procurement had a set budget for purchases. The expenditure necessary for materials that were not ready to be used in manufacturing would wreck havoc on cash flow and require consideration on how to store materials until they were ready to be used for manufacturing. Further, additional vendors from whom to purchase the materials would need to be identified, should the current vendors be unable to meet procurement's increased demands. Alternative vendors needed to be in place before any supply issues arose. It was evident that the processes for procurement must be very closely integrated with the manufacturing processes to maintain an ongoing flow of materials for production.

The project team developed a detailed plan for identifying the stakeholders and how they would proceed to gather the data necessary to accurately document the manufacturing processes. The plan included a detailed list of questions to ask each stakeholder to ensure that all interviewers asked the same questions and gathered the same data. The project team knew from experience that documenting processes required a thorough understanding of the business, because, when being interviewed, individuals often unintentionally skipped relevant details. Thus, experienced people were required to extract information needed for an accurate and detailed documentation of processes.

The project team also developed a plan for potential risks and strategies for managing them should they come to fruition. They wanted to be sure that once they determined the options for making changes to the manufacturing processes, they could accommodate potential changes to other processes. They knew that changing one process would likely have a domino effect throughout the company. For example, during one of the scenario planning sessions, the project team found that if procurement was unable to fulfil the material needs of manufacturing from one vendor, without a back up vendor in place, there would potentially be a shortage of materials which would cause a delay in production or costs would increase by at least 30%. This would be unacceptable and would ultimately cause customer dissatisfaction which could lead to a loss of business to competitors.

The team also put together a change management plan; because a major component of the project would be communicating changes company-wide and ensuring the appropriate people were onboard and prepared to work with the new processes. Additionally, the project team needed the individuals involved on the production line to be willing to test new processes as well as new equipment with no interruption in meeting current client demand. Without support from these individuals, this would be an impossible task and one that had a high potential of risk associated with it.

Additionally, the project team sent out a company-wide communication so that employees knew what was happening and why, and they asked for suggestions from employees. By getting the input of the individuals who were doing the job day in and day out, they increased the likelihood of success on the project.

The Work Breakdown Structure included several milestones to allow the company to move forward with working with new processes and upgrades to equipment without interrupting the current production schedule. At each milestone, there were several tasks for measuring progress and comparing it to the expected results and baselines. Assessments were completed regularly to ensure the current plan held true to the objectives. At any point during the project, if the assessments showed deficiencies from the objectives, then an evaluation of the process design and, if necessary, a correction occurred. The Work Breakdown Structure included training time to get individuals up to speed on new equipment.

The Risk Management Plan included contingencies should current employees be incapable of learning to use the new equipment and performing their role in a timely fashion. Part of the contingency plan was to use employees who adapted quickly to the new equipment on the new production line and maintain the old production line with employees who learned less quickly, until they were able to get up to the speed. An integrated team concept, including mentoring, was put in place to assist people in getting up to speed on new equipment.

Regular status meetings were scheduled with manufacturing, procurement, delivery and other departments to maintain lines of communication and general awareness of the project status. These meetings also served to ensure that employees were comfortable with change and were able to participate in decisions that would affect how they perform their job.

Project Results

Prior to undertaking the project, Company XYZ was producing 250 widgets per day. At the time of the undertaking of the process improvement initiative, client demand had just reached 250, and demand had increased by 10% annually over the last five years and it appeared that the increase would continue for the foreseeable future.

The directive from the executives was to improve manufacturing processes through changes in processes as well as upgrading equipment, towards a goal of producing up to 400 widgets per day. Based on current projections, the company would experience a five year timeline before having to undertake another increase in production to satisfy growing client demand. At that point, if client demand continued to increase, the company would be in a better position to invest in another manufacturing site in order to meet demands after the five year mark.

Additionally, in the current production line there was, on an average, a 3.6% defect rate in widgets produced. One of the directives specific to this project was to attempt to reduce this defect rate by at least half within the next two years.

The following were discovered during the project:

■ Capacity for procurement was limited due to cash flow and budgetary issues, as well as storage. Any new process needed to take this into consideration once production increased and would have to allow for a smooth flow between procurement and manufacturing.

■ It became apparent that once the number of widgets manufactured increased, demands on warehousing and delivery would increase accordingly. A plan was put in place to change warehousing and delivery processes to reduce the strain on these functions.

The project had run slightly over the projected timeline, but did remain within budget. The increase in the timeline resulted from an underestimate of the space required to store manufactured widgets prior to delivery. This occurred to a great extent because the decrease in the defect rate was .06%, significantly exceeding the goal of 1.8%, thus causing an increase in the number of widget units to be stored. Although this was not anticipated in a contingency plan it did not cause the executives any unhappiness. It was a good problem.

Source: By Gina Abudi http://www.projectsmart.co.uk/project-management-approach-for-business-process-improvement.html

QUESTIONS FOR DISCUSSION

1. Define Knowledge Engineering.
2. Explain the principles of knowledge engineering.
3. Write short notes on: (i) SPEDE (ii) MOKA.
4. Write briefly about the future of Knowledge Management.
5. What do you understand by organisation culture? Write briefly.
6. How do technologies support the KM System?
7. Write short notes on: (i) Theory of computation (ii) Data Structure

SUGGESTED READINGS

A. Th. Schreiber, J. Akkermans, A. Anjewierden, R. De Hoog, N. Shadbolt, W. Van De Velde & B. Wielinga, Knowledge Engineering and Management: The Common KADS Methodology, MIT Press 2000, ISBN 0-262-19300-0.

Alberthal, Les, Remarks to the Financial Executives Institute, Dallas, TX October 23, 1995.

Bateson, Gregory, *Mind and Nature: A Necessary Unity*, Bantam, 1988.

Bellinger, Gene, Systems Thinking: An Operational Perspective of the Universe.

Bellinger, Gene, The Effective Organisation.

Bellinger, Gene, The Knowledge Centred Organisation.

Csikszentmihalyi, Miahly, *The Evolving-Self: A Psychology for the Third Millennium*, Harperperennial Library, 1994.

Davidson, Mike, *The Transformation of Management*, Butterworth-Heinemann, 1996.

Fleming, Neil, *Coping with a Revolution: Will the Internet Change Learning?*, Lincoln University, Canterbury, New Zealand

Senge, Peter, *The Fifth Discipline: The Art & Practice of the Learning Organisation*, Doubleday-Currency, 1990.

WEBSITES

www.asme.org.
http://books.google.co.in/books?id=zbWNI8IPh6kC&pg=PA8&lpg=PA8&dq=history+
of+knowledge+engineering&source=bl&ots=tabSsygY-M&sig=g_sB3YD7RP0py7u4SOQ6shFA
JIQ&hl=en&ei=NE32S6uxB4rGrAf_hPC3Cg&sa=X&oi=book_result&ct=result&resnum=5&ve
d=0CCAQ6AEwBA#v=onepage&q=history%20of%20knowledge%20engineering&f=false
http://www.km4dev.org/group/thehumanfactorinkm4dev?groupUrl=thehumanfactorinkm4dev&id
=2672907%3AGroup%3A2986&page=3#comments
http://www.knowledgeboard.com/item/990

CHAPTER 14

Knowledge Audit and Analysis

OBJECTIVE

At the end of this lesson, you would be able to understand:

- What is Knowledge audit?
- Measurement of Knowledge Growth.
- Implementing, documenting and analysing Knowledge audit.
- Audit methods.

> *The greater our knowledge increases the more our ignorance unfolds.*
> —John F. Kennedy

INTRODUCTION

Knowledge audit is the formal process to determination and evaluation of how and where information knowledge is used within the organisation. The audit examines policies, forms, procedures, storage and any other ways that knowledge is collected, stored, and catalogued.

In the compilation work of Naguib Chowdhury 'Knowledge audit is a systematic examination and evaluation of organisational knowledge health, which examines organisation's knowledge needs, existing knowledge assets/resources, knowledge flows, future knowledge needs, knowledge gap analysis as well as the behaviour of people in sharing and creating knowledge. In one way, a knowledge audit can reveal an organisation's knowledge strengths, weaknesses, opportunities, threats and risks'. A knowledge audit should also include an examination of the organisation's strategy, leadership, collaborative, learning culture, technology infrastructure in its various knowledge processes.

In order to transform an organisation into a learning organisation and ensure an effective knowledge management strategy, a knowledge audit should be conducted, which will provide a current state of knowledge capability of the organisation and a direction of where and how to improve that capability in order to be competitive in this fast changing knowledge era.

Objectives of Knowledge Audit

1. K-audit helps an organisation to clearly identify what knowledge is needed to support overall organisational goals and individual and team activities.
2. It gives tangible evidence of the extent to which knowledge is being effectively managed and indicates where improvements are needed.
3. It explains how knowledge moves around in, and is used by, that organisation.

4. It provides a map of what knowledge exists in the organisation and where it exists, revealing both gaps and duplication.
5. It provides an inventory of knowledge assets, allowing them to become more visible and therefore more measurable and accountable.
6. It provides vital information for the development of effective knowledge management programmes and initiatives that are directly relevant to the organisation's specific knowledge needs and current situation.
7. It helps in leveraging customer knowledge.

According to Ann Hylton, (2002), 'Knowledge audit should be the first step in any Knowledge Management initiative. Properly done, it would provide accurate identification, quantification, measurement and assessment of the sum total of tacit and explicit knowledge in the organisation'. Wiig, (1993), identified knowledge audit as comprising the following:

1. Information glut or scarcity
2. Lack of awareness of information elsewhere in the organisation
3. Inability to keep abreast with relevant information
4. Significant 'reinventing' of the wheel
5. Common use of out of date information
6. Not knowing where to go for expertise in a specific area

Liebowitz (2000), feels that knowledge audit assesses what knowledge assets are possessed by a specific organisation. By knowing what knowledge is possessed, it is possible to find the most effective method of storage and dissemination.

DEFINITION

A knowledge audit (an assessment of the way knowledge processes meet an organisation's knowledge goals) is to understand the processes that constitute the activities of a knowledge worker, and see how well they address the "knowledge goals" of the organisation (Lauer and Tanniru, 2001). Liebowitz defines knowledge audit as a tool that assesses potential stores of knowledge. It is the first part of any KM strategy. By discovering that knowledge is possessed, it is then possible to find the most effective method of storage and dissemination. It can then be used as the basis for evaluating the extent to which change needs to be introduced to enterprise. Part of the knowledge audit is capturing "tacit" knowledge (Liebowitz et al., 2000).

In brief, knowledge audit is the process to identify every knowledge produced by an organisation, that produces and uses it, how frequently the knowledge is used, and where the knowledge is stored.

Components of a Knowledge Audit

A Knowledge audit can have the following components:

A. Knowledge need analysis
B. Knowledge inventory analysis
C. Knowledge flow analysis
D. Knowledge mapping

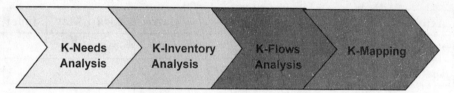

Fig. 14.1 K-Audit Components

Knowledge Need Analysis (K-Needs Analysis)

The major goal of this task is to identify precisely what knowledge the organisation, its people and team currently possess and what knowledge they would require in the future in order to meet their objectives and goals.

Knowledge need analysis can help any organisation to develop its future strategy. Amrit Tiwana suggested Figure 14.2 to explain the Knowledge-Strategy Link.

The K-need analysis can also measure the staff skills and competency enhancement needs and opportunities for training and development, corporate knowledge culture practices such as knowledge sharing attitude, collaboration, team spirit, rewards and recognitions & staff relationship with their superiors, peers and subordinates.

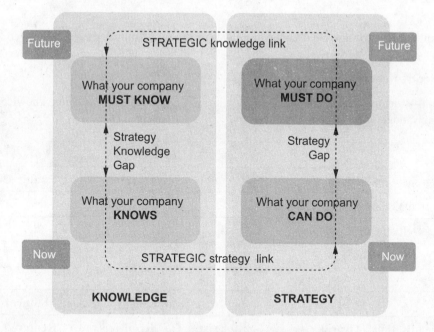

STRATEGIC K GAP ANALYSIS

Framework as depicted in Amrit Tiwana," The KM Toolkit", Prentice-Hall, 2000

Fig. 14.2 Knowledge-Strategy Link

No.	Activities	March	April	May	June	July
1	Study of Orgn's major goal & objectives					
2	Draft an initial K-need/K-flow matrics					
3	Organise team to work on the analysis—internal					
4	Data Collection					
	Finalize the questionnaire					
	Conduct survey					
	Focus group interviews					
	Interview with the HODs					
5	Data Analysis					
6	Data Evaluation					
7	Reporting					

An example of Knowledge need/K-flow analysis in the questionnaire format is given below:

1. Knowledge Needs/K-flow Analysis

Major goal—Identify the current and the future knowledge needs as well as how knowledge flows in an organisation

	Current		Future
Organisation—Division	Exists	Required	Required
Functions			
Key Deliverables			
Core competencies			

	Current		Future
Organisation—Overall	Exists	Required	Required
Functions			
Key Deliverables			
Core competencies			

Organisation Division—Individual Level	Current		Future
	Exists	Required	Required
Types of Knowledge			
Sources of Knowledge			
Frequency of usage			
Key stakeholders			
Key K-processes			
K-deliverables			
K-resources sharing partners			
Time spent in searching for knowledge			

Perception on Knowledge Sharing

No.	Area: The overall environment of my dept.	Strongly agree	Agree	Neutral	Disagree	Strongly disagree
1	Facilitates knowledge creation					
2	Facilitates knowledge storage/retrieval					
3	Facilitates knowledge transfer					
4	Enables me to accomplish tasks more quickly					
5	Improves my job performance					
6	Is useful in my job overall					
7	Enables the organisation to react more quickly to changes in the marketplace					
8	Speeds decision making					
	Perception about Knowledge in the organisation	**Strongly agree**	**Agree**	**Neutral**	**Disagree**	**Strongly disagree**
9	The specific knowledge that I need resides with the experts rather than being stored in the portal because the knowledge is typically difficult to clearly articulate					
10	The knowledge stored in the portal cannot be directly applied without extensive modifications because of the fast-paced, dynamic environment in which my department operates.					

	Perception about knowledge in the organisation	Strongly agree	Agree	Neutral	Disagree	Strongly disagree
11	As the tasks of my department change frequently, I am always having to seek new knowledge that is not directly available in the K-portal or databases					
12	I am able to extensively reuse knowledge from the K-portal after making few, if any, changes to adapt the retrieved knowledge to the current situation					
13	The knowledge that I find in the K-portal can be directly applied to current situations with little or no need to seek out or create new knowledge					
	Do you think the members of your department are:	Strongly agree	Agree	Neutral	Disagree	Strongly disagree
14	Satisfied by the degree of collaboration					
15	Supportive for knowledge sharing & creation					
	There is a willingness to:	Strongly agree	Agree	Neutral	Disagree	Strongly disagree
16	Collaborate across organisational units within our organisation					
17	Accept responsibility for failure					
	I always find the:	Strongly agree	Agree	Neutral	Disagree	Strongly disagree
18	Precise knowledge I need					
19	Sufficient knowledge to enable me to do my tasks					
20	Knowledge that is available in my dept. to use					
	There should be reward system for	Strongly agree	Agree	Neutral	Disagree	Strongly disagree
21	Creating reusable knowledge resources					
22	Reusing existing knowledge resources					
23	Contributing to a library of reusable knowledge resources					

CONDUCTING A KNOWLEDGE AUDIT

A knowledge audit is a systematic method of determining the status of critical knowledge in your organisation/group, a way of 'knowing what you know.' It is essential to the development of a KM strategy. In general, the knowledge audit involves the following steps:

1. Categorise your critical knowledge items. After doing your task analysis (*Step 4, Guide on Developing a KM Strategy*), you will have an idea about what knowledge items are critical to the tasks your group/organisation has to perform.

    You may find that these are essentially of three types *(Brooking, 1999):*

    *   Knowledge about the users of your outputs, products and services, or assets that give your organisation power in the marketplace—market knowledge;
    *   Knowledge about the collective expertise, creativity, leadership and managerial skills of people in the organisation—human-centred knowledge;
    *   Knowledge about the way the organisation works: processes and standards, leadership and management, culture and values involved in its operations—infrastructure knowledge.
    *   Knowledge about products of mental processes in an organisation that legally belong to it, e.g., its name, logo, brands, product designs, trade secrets—knowledge of intellectual property.

    You may want to use some or all of these categories to classify your critical knowledge items, although as a development organisation you should not be concerned if you find no items to classify under the fourth. You may choose to organise your critical knowledge using a different set of categories that you think are more appropriate. What's important is that you classify your items for efficiency in data-gathering and subsequent analysis.

2. For each category of critical knowledge items, select a method of gathering data. Your method should be able to capture the data or information you require to determine the status (relative strength/weakness) of each critical knowledge item, to help you develop an effective strategy.
3. Formulate the appropriate instruments for gathering the data and information you need. Formulate a guide for analysis of your data or information; you need these to make sense, interpret, and utilise your data in developing your KM strategy subsequently. Samples of instruments and guides for analyses are given here for your reference. Feel free to modify them to suit your needs.
4. Plan how you will do your knowledge audit. This includes to answer all the following questions.
    *   How will you administer your instruments?
    *   Will you be taking notes, voice-taping, or video-taping the proceedings?
    *   Who will you ask to participate in your knowledge audit?
    *   Should you include everyone, or just a sample?
    *   When will you conduct your audit?
    *   How will you present your results?

5. Conduct your knowledge audit as planned. Be sure to explain the purpose and the process involved to your participants. Collect data and information accurately, efficiently, and with utmost respect for your participants.

6. Organise your data and information for subsequent analysis and presentation. Use tables, matrices and lists.

7. Analyse and interpret your data and information. What do they mean? Then make your conclusions on the status of your organisation's critical knowledge (*Refer to Step 5, Guide on Developing a KM Strategy*).

An example of audit of market knowledge in a Development Organisation Knowledge Audit Methods: Interview, Documents Analysis from the Knowledge Management Course, AIJC and written and compiled by Madz Quiamco is produced here.

AUDIT OF MARKET KNOWLEDGE INSTRUCTION

Please answer the following questions as completely as possible.

A. One of the audit methods that is to be followed is the Interview method which is given as an example below:

INTERVIEW SCHEDULE

1. How do people think about your organisation? Is it what your organisation really is?

2. What are the development goals and objectives of your organisation; that is, what is it trying to achieve in terms of developing the full potential of people in the community?

3. What do you think your organisation has accomplished for your community? What indicators of these accomplishments do people see?

4. Who are the prominent people/organisations who have acknowledged and supported activities of your organisation towards these development goals and objectives?

5. Who are the individuals/organisations who advocate, promote, and implement activities towards these goals/objectives? What capacities and resources do they bring into these activities? What will they get out of achieving these goals and objectives?

6. What benefits will the attainment of these goals bring to different sectors of the community? Are these benefits well known to the people?

7. Who are participating in the community's activities that you know of? How often and for how long have they been participating?

8. Do you know some donors and sponsors of the community? What activities have they supported?

9. What organisations and groups are collaborating with your organisation in implementing development projects? In how many projects are they collaborating?

10. Do you know how people can participate in the development activities of your organisation —who to approach, what to do? Do people know this?

Audit of Market Knowledge

B. Method: Documents analysis

List of Project Data/Information for Analysis

- **Projects**
  - Numbers—total, current, changes
  - Activity areas—past, current, potential
  - Trends
  - Project development history
  - Proportion of unsubscribed projects
  - Collaboration, local support received
  - Implementation problems
  - Percentage of goals accomplishments
- **Beneficiaries/Participants**
  - Groups benefiting/participating
  - Demographics
  - Frequencies of participation
  - Percentage of beneficiaries/participants to actual qualified population
- **Sponsors (Current and Potential)**
  - Demographics
  - Special requirements
  - Reasons for sponsorship
  - Proportion of repeat sponsorships
  - Percentage of actual sponsors to total prospective sponsors
- **Collaborators/Partners (Current and Potential)**
  - Demographics
  - Special requirements
  - Goals and objectives parallel with that of your community
  - Number/Duration/Value of collaboration with your community
  - Resources available for collaborative activities

An example of Audit of Knowledge on Human-centred Assets is given in Box 14.1.

Box 14.1 Audit of Knowledge on Human-centred Assets

Knowledge Audit Method: Self-assessment of Competence and Proficiency

INSTRUCTION: Please answer the following questions as completely as possible.
1. What is my present position?
I am a _____ _____
How many years have I been in this position?
_____ years

---

2. What formal education have I attained?
Educational Level Major Degree-granting
Institution
Year in which Obtained

3. What professional training or capacity building programmes have I participated in?
Training/Capacity
Building Programme
Subject Matter/Area Implementing
Institution
Date

4. What are my competencies* related to my position? How proficient am I in each?
Competency related to current job Proficiency level**

5. Besides the ones I listed in No. 4 above, what other competencies do I have?
How proficient am I in each?
Other Competencies Proficiency level*

6. What three adjectives do my colleagues use to describe me at work? Why?
Adjective Reason/s
(1)
(2)
(3)

Competencies—knowledge and skills needed for a person to adequately perform a function or set of functions associated with a position.

**Proficiency levels:*
- *Beginner*
- *Advanced beginner*
- *Competent performer*
- *Proficient performer*
- *Expert*
- *Master*
- *Grandmaster*

Knowledge Inventory Analysis (K-inventory Analysis)

Knowledge inventory is a knowledge stock taking to identify and locate knowledge assets and resources throughout the entire organisation. This process involves counting, indexing, and categorising of corporate tacit and explicit knowledge.

Knowledge inventory analysis comprises two entities: Physical (Explicit) Knowledge inventory and Corporate Experts (sources of tacit knowledge) inventory.

i.   *Physical (Explicit) Knowledge inventory of an organisation:*
- Numbers, types and categories of documents, databases, libraries, intranet websites, links and subscriptions to external resources.

- Knowledge locations in the organisation, and in its various systems.
- The organisation and access of the knowledge (how knowledge resources are organised and how easy it is for people to find and access them).
- Purpose, relevance and quality of knowledge (why do these resources exist, and how relevant and appropriate they are for that purpose, are they of good quality—up-to-date, reliable, evidence based, make sense, relevant to the organisation?)
- Usage of the knowledge (are they actually being used? If yes, by whom, when, what for and how often?)

ii. *Corporate Experts (sources of tacit knowledge) inventory:*
- Staff directory and their academic and professional qualifications, skills & core competency levels and experience.
- Training and learning opportunities.
- Future potentials leadership.

The K-inventory analysis may involve a series of surveys and interviews in order to get relevant answers to the above questions on both tacit and explicit knowledge that an organisation may hold and have.

By making comparison between knowledge inventory and the earlier analysis of knowledge needs, an organisation will be able to identify gaps in their organisation's knowledge as well as areas of unnecessary duplication.

No.	Activities	March	April	May	June	July
1	Study of Org. K-portal and other databases	▓				
2	Draft an initial K-inventory matrics	▓				
3	Organise small team to work on the listing	▓				
4	Data Collection	▓				
	Start listing of the files	▓				
	Conduct survey	▓				
	Interview with the HODs	▓				
5	Data Analysis		▓			
6	Data Evaluation		▓			
7	Develop Taxonomies		▓	▓		
8	Reporting & Expert Directory			▓	▓	

An example of Knowledge Inventory Analysis Physical Knowledge is given in Box 14.2.

Box 14.2   Knowledge Inventory Analysis (Physical Knowledge)
Major goal: To identify and locate knowledge assets and resources throughout the entire organisation.

Organisation Division	Current		Future
	Exists	Required	Required
No. of databases			
No. of files in the system			
ERP			
Primary storage			
Decision Support System			
Filing system			
Groupware			
File sharing with other departments			
Physical file/report storage			
Archiving			

General audit
Categories of knowledge available

1. Total no. of files
2. No. of new knoweldge created by the staff
3. No. of new knoweldge collected from external sources

Box 14.3   Knowledge Inventory Analysis (Human Capital)
Major goal: To identify and locate internal experts within the organisation.

Organisation Division	Current		Future
	Exists	Required	Required
Staff and their expert areas			
Expert Databases			
Staff development plans			
Succession Planning			
HRM system			
List of ex-staff			
Database of External Experts			

General audit

1. Expert categories
2. Comparative analysis of staff placement to their expertise
3. Analysis of Expert database—existing vs. future development
4. Sucession planning in the organisation
5. Knowledge capture of leaving experts—any procedures exist? Plans?
6. Development of external industry experts—any databases?
7. Plans for expert knowledge sharing on regular basis
8. Development of best practices using experts

The knowledge flow analysis looks at people, processes and systems:

i. Analysis of people: examine their attitude towards, habits and behaviours concerning, and skills in knowledge sharing, use and dissemination.
ii. Analysis of process: examine how people go about their daily work activities and how knowledge seeking, sharing, use and dissemination forms parts of those activities, existence of policies and practices concerning flow, sharing and usage of information and knowledge, for example, are there any existing policies such as on information handling, management of records, web publishing, etc. Or are there other policies that exist that may directly or indirectly affect or relate to knowledge management, which may act as enablers or barriers to a good knowledge practice?
iii. Analysis of system: examine technical infrastructure, for example, information technology systems, portals, content management, accessibility and ease of use, and current level of usage. To what extent do those existing systems facilitate knowledge sharing and flow, and help to connect people within the organisation.

An analysis of knowledge flows will allow an organisation to further identify gaps in their organisation's knowledge and areas of duplication; it will also highlight examples of good practice that can be built on, as well as blockages and barriers to knowledge flows and effective use. It will show where an organisation needs to focus attention in their knowledge management initiatives in order to get knowledge moving from where it is to where it is needed.

No.	Activities	March	April	May	June	July
1	Study of organisation's major goal & objectives					
2	Draft an initial K-need/K-flow matrics					
3	Organise team to work on the analysis—internal					
4	Data Collection					
	Finalise the questionnaire					
	Conduct survey					
	Focus group interviews					
	Interview with the HODs					

5	Data Analysis			▨		
6	Data Evaluation			▨		
7	Reporting				▨	

Knowledge Mapping (K-Mapping)

The knowledge map is a navigation aid to explicit (codified) information and tacit knowledge, showing the importance and the relationships between knowledge stores and dynamics. The knowledge map, an outcome of synthesis, portrays the sources, flows, constraints and sinks (losses or stopping points) of knowledge within an organisation. There are two main approaches to knowledge mapping:

1. Mapping knowledge assets and resources—the map shows what knowledge exists in the organisation and where it can be found (holders of the knowledge - knowledge creator, collector, connector, users and knowledge critics, data repositories)
2. Mapping knowledge flows—the map shows how knowledge moves around the organisation from where it is to where it is needed.

No.	Activities	March	April	May	June	July
1	Study K-need/K-flow matrics reports					▨
2	Draft an initial K-map					▨
3	Team analysis K-map					▨
4	Knowledge Map Reporting					▨

Deliverables of a knowledge audit

Common approaches and tools that can be applied to conduct a knowledge audit are: Site observation, questionnaire-based surveys, face-to-face interviews, focus group discussion, forums. A knowledge audit could be divided into four parts: background study, data collection, data analysis and data evaluation. So the deliverables of a knowledge audit could be:

- A list of knowledge items (K-needs & current K-assets) in the form of spreadsheets.
- A knowledge network map which shows the flow of knowledge items.
- A social network map that reveals the interaction among staff on knowledge sharing.

These deliverables will help an organisation in identifying the gap between "what is" at present and "what should be" in the future from a KM perspective.

SUMMING UP

A knowledge audit (an assessment of the way knowledge processes meet an organisation's knowledge goals) is to understand the processes that constitute the activities of a knowledge worker, and see how well they address the "knowledge goals" of the organisation. In brief, knowledge audit is the process to identify every knowledge produced by an organisation, who produces and uses it, how frequent is the knowledge used, and where it is stored.

A knowledge audit is a systematic method of determining the status of critical knowledge in your organisation/group, a way of 'knowing what you know.'

Knowledge inventory is a knowledge stock taking to identify and locate knowledge assets and resources throughout the organisation. This process involves counting, indexing, and categorising of corporate tacit and explicit knowledge.

The K-inventory analysis may involve a series of surveys and interviews in order to get relevant answers to the above questions on both tacit and explicit knowledge that an organisation may hold and have.

By making comparison between knowledge inventory and the earlier analysis of knowledge needs, an organisation will be able to identify gaps in their organisation's knowledge as well as areas of unnecessary duplication.

Knowledge flow analysis looks at knowledge resources moving around the organisation, from where it is to where it is needed. In other words, it is to determine how people in an organisation find the knowledge they need, and how they share the knowledge they have.

The knowledge map is a navigation aid to explicit (codified) information and tacit knowledge, showing the importance and the relationships between knowledge stores and dynamics. The knowledge map, an outcome of synthesis, portrays the sources, flows, constraints and sinks (losses or stopping points) of knowledge within an organisation.

INDIVIDUAL EXERCISE

The following is a knowledge need analysis: Individually do this exercise in the classroom and discuss with your teacher the components of knowledge audit, taking an example of a medium-sized company.

Rate the answers from 1 to 5 (5 being the most important)

1. Did any dept./people ask your help for their knowledge needs? Of the questions that you were asked by others in the organisation, what knowledge was requested that you consider to be
   a) essential for business performance   _____
   b) essential for the company's competitive advantages   _____
   c) important for leading to innovation and creative work   _____
   d) outdated and no longer useful for the business   _____

2. How did you acquire most of the skills/expertise that you have been using in your job over the past 6 months?
   a) in this organisation   _____
   b) through self-learning   _____
   c) through formal training   _____
   d) at my last job or elsewhere _____

3. Where is most of the information, that you need to do your work, located or stored?
   a) In paper-based documents _____
   b) In our team/dept.'s members' heads _____
   c) In our central information system _____
   d) On my personal workstation
   e) computer/hard drive _____
4. Knowledge that I acquire in my present job/organisation, belongs first and foremost to
   a) Me alone _____
   b) The company alone _____
   c) Depends on how much I had put into it _____
   d) Both myself and the company _____
5. How often do you make use of documented procedures to do your work when you are stuck
   a) Constantly _____
   b) Very often _____
   c) Quite often _____
   d) Not often/rarely _____
6. Which of the following is the biggest barrier to your being able to store information you receive more efficiently and effectively
   a) Lack of time/too busy _____
   b) Poor tools/technology _____
   c) Organisation policy/directives _____
   d) Poor information systems/processes _____
7. How often do you share information with other departments in a formal way
   a) Constantly _____
   b) Very often _____
   c) Quite often _____
   d) Not often/rarely _____
8. What are the challenges in sharing information with people from other departments
   a) Don't perceive there is an urgent need to share _____
   b) Lack of open-minded sharing environment _____
   c) Lack of trust of other people's knowledge _____
   d) No proper organisational guidelines on sharing _____
   e) Bureaucratic procedures involved in sharing info/knowledge _____
   f) Task doesn't require cross-dept. info sharing _____
   g) No proper IT platform to share _____
   h) Do not know about the other person's knowledge needs _____

QUESTIONS FOR DISCUSSIONS

1. What is knowledge audit?
2. Explain the objectives of knowledge audit.
3. What are the components of knowledge audit? Explain briefly.
4. Write short notes on "Knowledge mapping".
5. What is K-flow analysis? Explain.
6. Write short notes on K-inventory analysis.

SUGGESTED READINGS

Chong, Y.Y. D., Rethinking Knowledge Audit: Its Values and Limitations in the Evaluation of Organisational and Cultural Asset, The Hong Kong Polytechnic University, Kowloon, Hong Kong, 2004.

KeKma-Audit, *KeKma-Audit, Knowledge audit & KM,* from http://www.kekma-audit.com/index.htm

Liebowitz, J., Rubenstein-Montano, B. et al. (Jan/Mar 2000), The Knowledge Audit, *Knowledge and Process Management*, VII,1, 3.

National Electronic Library for Health, *Conducting a Knowledge Audit,* from http://www.nelh.nhs.uk/knowledge_management/km2/audit_toolkit.asp.

Tiwana, A., *The Knowledge Management Toolkit: Orchestrating IT, Strategy and Knowledge Platforms*, Prentice Hall, New Jersey, 2002.

WEBSITE

http://www.kmtalk.net/article.php?story=20060905001530455

INDEX